Trailblazers

Trailblazers

THE TRAGIC LIVES OF GRAM PARSONS NICK DRAKE & JEFF BUCKLEY

DAVID BRET

This book is for Michel Bidault, *Les Enfants de Novembre,* and for Barbara, the greatest *auteur-compositeur-interprete* who ever lived.

N'oublie pas...
La vie sans amis c'est comme
un jardin sans fleurs

First published in Great Britain in 2009 by
JR Books, 10 Greenland Street, London NW1 0ND
www.jrbooks.com

A catalogue record for this book is available from the British Library.

ISBN 978-1-906779-32-0

Plate section: page 7 (top) Corbis; all others Getty Images.

1 3 5 7 9 10 8 6 4 2

Printed by MPG Books, Bodmin, Cornwall

Contents

Acknowledgements

Writing this book would not have been possible had it not been for the inspiration, criticisms and love of that select group of individuals who, whether they be in this world or the next, I will always regard as my true family and *autre* coeur: Barbara, Irene Bevan, Marlene Dietrich, René Chevalier, Axel Dotti, Dorothy Squires and Roger Normand, *que vous dormez en paix*. Lucette Chevalier, Maria da Fé, Jacqueline Danno, Doris Day, Héléne Delavault, Tony Griffin, Betty and Gérard Garmain, Annick Roux, John and Anne Taylor, Terry Sanderson, Charley Marouani, David & Sally Bolt. Also a very special mention for Amália Rodrigues, Joey Stefano, those *hiboux, fadistas* and *amis de foutre* who happened along the way, and *mes enfants perdus*.

On behalf of Nick, my heart goes out to Michel, one of the few people on this Earth who genuinely made him happy – and to M_ – for making Jeff's heart flutter that little bit faster. Thanks also to Mary, Brenda, Marianne, and to Emmylou for being there for Gram. To Joe Hayes and Jack Rhodes for the magnificent epitaph, 'Satisfied Mind'.

Thanks too to Mikey Blatin, Theo Morgan, and the late Bruno Coqautrix.

And where would I be without Jeremy Robson and the munificent team at JR Books? Likewise my agent Guy Rose and his lovely wife, Alex? Also to my wife, Jeanne, for putting up with my bad moods and for still being the keeper of my soul.

And finally a *grand chapeau bas* to Gram, Nick and Jeff for having lived.

David Bret

Introduction

Working on each of these three young men was akin to embarking on a personal crusade, or on a trio of discreet but ultimately doomed love affairs. Three young men: handsome, temperamental, sublimely gifted – sent before their time, their lodestars burning all too briefly before being extinguished in mysterious but distressing circumstances. Three young men with much more in common than an early demise.

It is only in death that Gram Parsons, Nick Drake and Jeff Buckley have realised their true and full potential. Their strongest achievement, besides the beautiful music they made, is that posthumously they have influenced a whole host of so-called 'stars' who now crowd the charts on both sides of the Atlantic – not one of which possesses a smidgeon of their innate talent and charisma. Yet we must be grateful for these latter day five-minute wonders for drawing a new generation of adherents to the Parsons-Drake-Buckley banners – in Gram's and Nick's case, fans who were not even born when they died.

So, what else does this gifted trio have in common? Two were Francophiles, citing Piaf and Rimbaud as amongst their greatest influences. Two came from broken homes and were raised to look upon paranoia as a way of life. All three put their careers before personal relationships, frequently using the men and women in their lives as stepping-stones or disposable chattels – inasmuch as those purporting to be acting in their interests were more interested in feathering their own nests than they were in trying to nurture and understand these precocious icons in the making.

Gram Parsons was raised in a privileged but unstable environment within which alcoholism, domestic drama and even suicide were recognised as the norm. A true child of the Deep South, he despised racial prejudice and was influenced by the great black artists of the day, developing the unique style of country-blues-rock which became synonymous with his name. He called it Cosmic American Music. Outrageous, outspoken but impeccably polite, Gram never knew how to hide his light under a bushel, yet beneath the veneer of bravado there lurked a fragile soul unable to cope with the hard living he so enjoyed. His death not, as previously believed, the result of his excesses but from the after-effects of a road accident, hit the headlines when two friends with whom he had allegedly made a pact stole his corpse and carried out his last wishes – al fresco cremation in the Joshua Tree National Park.

Of the trio of talents detailed in this book, Nick Drake remains the most elusive. Because of the way he died – alone, depressed, surrounded by a wealthy but negative family who never took the time to get to know him – biographers have invariably searched for the equally negative, maudlin aspects of his life. A whole generation after his death, friends and acquaintances who had assigned him to some darkened corner of their past have leapt, sheep-like, on to the '15 minutes of fame' bandwagon to recall some kind of serial *maladive* who appears to have spent his entire life just waiting to die. Similarly, ersatz music experts have trawled through his lyrics in search of clues towards his supposed obsession with impending doom. In doing so, they have missed the point entirely. Nick Drake was not a 'moon-rhymes-with-June' merchant but a realist who, like those who influenced him, was adept at observing every aspect of the human condition – nothing more, nothing less.

Jeff Buckley was the son of ill-fated, self-destructive experimental vocalist Tim, whom he never knew. Diminutive but far from fragile, his vocal range spanned an astonishing four octaves. He could sing any style from Piaf to Gershwin, from scat to Oum Kalthoum, besides his own superb realist compositions. As such, his repertoire was far more extensive than any of his contemporaries, an achievement which remains unrivalled to this day. This chirpy little sparrow with absolutely no airs and graces was on the verge of mega-stardom – having been awarded the prestigious *Grand Prix du Disque* following the critical acclaim of his debut album, *Grace* – when he lost his life in the Mississippi River.

With every passing year, the legends of these three musical geniuses grow. They left behind an unusually rich and varied legacy of unreleased material, a wealth of fond memories, and an assurance that we shall never see their likes again.

This is their story . . .

Gram Parsons:
A Song For You

'When Gram was together, there was nothing like his presence on stage. He had this extraordinary command, this amazing charisma. You just knew that everything was going to be all right.'

Emmylou Harris

Chapter One
The Waycross Waif

He was arguably the only singer of his genre who, though blatantly heterosexual, got away with overtly displaying his feminine side – the unmistakable sob in the voice, the highly charged and emotive content of his work. Yet despite his arresting physical presence, charisma and tremendous good looks, not to mention his seemingly limitless talent, during his tragically brief lifetime Gram Parsons remained largely uncommercial. Even so, his style – described by him as 'Cosmic American Music' – provided the template for country rock, which was a term he despised. It was a style that was perceived by him as all-embracing, as he explained to Jan Donkers, a Dutch reporter, in November 1972, one year before his death:

> *I don't know if I'm playing with fire, or if I'm doing the right thing or not – I think I am – when I say that long-hairs, short-hairs, people with overalls and people with their velvet gear on can all be in the same place at the same time, for the same reason. And that turns me on!*

Gram listed among his influences The Louvin Brothers, which was in itself ironic: Ira Louvin's only way of handling fame had been an increasing dependency on alcohol – one of his concert showpieces had been 'Kneeling Drunkard's Plea' – and he too had died young, the victim of a car crash. The Louvins had started out at around the time of Gram's birth as gospel harmonists, but progressed towards bluegrass and hillbilly. Gram Parsons' repertoire included such material, and more, save that when he covered another artist's song, he would unintentionally make this song his personal property. Does anyone really care who first performed 'Cash on the Barrelhead' and 'Love Hurts?' The Eagles, U2, Elvis Costello, Tom Petty and even the Rolling Stones were all influenced by him and more than frequently emulated him, and owe him an enormous debt of gratitude. Of these acts, only the Stones will achieve the lasting posthumous glory and respect that he enjoys now, three decades after his death.

It is the manner of Gram's death, and its grisly aftermath, that for a time provided more interest to many than the quality of his music. This was fuelled by the persistent anecdotes recounted by his road manager, Phil Kaufman, who appears to glean almost sardonic pleasure from it each time he is interviewed on the subject. For many, it was easier to visualise the events of that grim day at Cap Rock than it was to conjure up a single song title. Though what happened that day can never be far from the back of one's mind while one listens to his work, with every fresh retrospective of his legacy what becomes important *is* the legacy of this lodestar, which all too quickly burned itself out. On the negative side, Gram's was an enigma who seemed hell-bent on self-destruction from the day he picked up his first guitar – a trait that for years superseded his phenomenal talent. Yet, as will be seen, little of this was his own fault, unless one holds him responsible for his weakness in trusting others and taking them at face value instead of being more critical. In this respect, he had much in common with Judy Garland, Billie Holiday and Elvis Presley. His entire adult life was blighted by the actions of so-called friends, peers and producers, who let him down, time and time again.

To better understand the son, one must first attempt to unravel the complexities of the parents, and the Parsons were like a pair of grotesques plucked directly from a Pirandello melodrama – with more than a liberal dash of Tennessee Williams tossed into the mix for good measure. His father was Ingram Cecil Connor Jr, born in 1917 in Columbia, Tennessee. Affectionately known as 'Coon Dog' – on account of his sad expression and protruding ears – he came from a wealthy family, and had been progressing well at university when he dropped out to enlist with the US Army Air Force. During World War II, Coon Dog acquired hero status, serving at a base near Pearl Harbor and, while under the command of General MacArthur, flew over 50 sorties against the Japanese over the Timor Sea, for which he was awarded a presidential citation. Early in 1943, Coon Dog fell ill with malaria and begun suffering recurring bouts of shell shock. Flown back to the United States, he took an officer training post at an Army Air Force base in Jacksonville, Florida, where he formed a close friendship with a man named John Snively.

The Snivelys were one of the wealthiest families in the state, owning most of the citrus orchards in Orange County at a time when there was a nationwide advertising campaign to encourage the population to eat more fruit following the wartime shortages. In 1945, when the war ended, they were reputed to be worth in excess of $200 million. They lived in a mansion at Winter Haven, overlooking Lake Eloise, where they were waited on hand on foot by a coterie of devoted black servants, and it was during a visit here that Coon Dog fell for John Snively's sister, Avis. After a whirlwind, alcohol-fuelled romance, the pair married in March 1944 and two years later, Coon Dog was welcomed into the family business – though he would never be regarded as more than an underling – taking over the Snivelys' box-making factory at Baxley, in Georgia.

The Connors' was not a marriage made in heaven. Coon Dog refused to find a house in Baxley, preferring to put down roots in Waycross, a railroad town some 40 miles over the state border, next to the Okefenokee Swamp where he could indulge in his passions: hunting and fishing. Coon Dog also liked to drink, a costly pastime in those days with Georgia's strict laws on alcohol, which could only be purchased from licensed clubs and restaurants. His alcohol dependency, he claimed, stemmed from his wartime traumas. As for Avis, she spent most of her time socialising, working for numerous charities and running the local ladies' bridge group. It was only when her first child was born on 5 November 1946 – at Winter Haven, for she flatly refused to have the heir to the Snively fortune enter the world in what she considered was a backwater – that the rot set in and she, the first to criticise her husband's habit, began drinking herself into an early grave.

Their son was baptised Ingram Cecil Connor III, though throughout his life he would be known as Gram. In 1951 his sister, Little Avis, was born. Theirs was a reasonably happy childhood, primarily because they were raised by a succession of nannies and relatives. They attended the William Heights School, and on Sundays the local Episcopal Chapel where Gram sang in the choir. He was closer to Coon Dog than he was to his mother, and went on hunting trips with him, but it was Avis who ruled the roost. She never ceased reminding her husband that *her* family were the ones holding the purse strings and wielding the power – that without their benevolence he might easily have fallen by the wayside.

The original Mommie Dearest, Avis Connor is not believed to have been physically violent towards her children, but she was inordinately strict, ignoring them much of the time in favour of her social calendar – then trying to make up for this lack of attention and affection by plying them with expensive gifts. Gram and Little Avis did not just have every latest toy on the market, they had a music room filled with instruments, access to as many lessons as they wanted, and a huge collection of gramophone records which were played on the very best equipment. From Avis' point of view, if the children could amuse themselves, there would be more time in the day for her to socialise with her snooty friends.

By the age of ten, Gram had mastered the piano and drums, and was on course for becoming an accomplished trumpeter. His musical influences, however, did not bode well with the Snivelys: blues and gospel, boogie-woogie and jazz, and rhythm and blues, music primarily associated with black performers. The Snivelys were not intentionally racist; it had simply been bred into them that coloured people were there to be skivvies, not to be socialised with. However, like his greatest early inspiration, an up-and-coming 21-year-old rockabilly singer from Tennessee called Elvis Presley, Gram always treated them as his equals.

In these days before mega-stardom and enforced solitude, Elvis was working the tour-trail the same as his contemporaries, and generally evoking mass hysteria wherever he appeared – though this was not always the case when he was attempting to win over some of the more diehard country music audiences. In November 1972, Gram would recall to Jan Donkers how, as a seven-year-old boy, he had first seen Elvis in Nashville, when he had debuted on the Grand Old Opry show. Topping the bill, he claimed, had been Little Jimmy Dickens (born 1920), famed for producing a string of novelty hits, such as 'May the Bird of Paradise Fly Up Your Nose'. 'Finally he came on, and the whole place went bonkers,' Gram drawled in a voice far sexier than that of his idol, adding that after the performance he had marched through Dickens' dressing room and into Elvis', announcing, 'Hello there, you're Elvis Presley, and I'm a little kid who buys records and I think you're all right!'

In fact, Elvis' only appearance at the celebrated venue (20 October 1954) had been something of a non-event: he had performed just one song, *Blue Moon of Kentucky*, to an unappreciative crowd, and legend has it that the show's producer, Jim Denny, had advised him that if *this* was the best he could do, then he might be better off going back to truck driving! Gram actually first saw Elvis performing 15 months later, at the time he was topping the Country and Western charts with 'I Forgot to Remember to Forget', and had just recorded *Heartbreak Hotel*. On 22 February 1956, he played three 30-minute sets at the Waycross City Auditorium, and sitting in the front row at the last of these were Gram, two female friends – and a chaperone whose job was to prevent her charges from meeting the star after the show and 'becoming perverted'.

Elvis was being denounced from pulpits across the country, and his live television appearances saw him filmed from the waist upwards because his on-stage gyrations and raw, unfettered sex appeal traumatised religious groups and the so-called moral majority. In fact, Gram and his companions did get to spend a moment or two with Elvis, enough time to get his autograph – and for Gram to decide that he wanted a career in music, albeit that he had not yet reached his 10th birthday. The very next day, he bought his first guitar from his generous weekly allowance, and in the music room at home, each evening after school, he would put on Elvis records and jam along with this or on the piano.

In September 1957, apparently against Coon Dog's wishes, Avis enrolled Gram at Bolles, the military prep school (next stop, West Point) some 80 miles away in Jacksonville, Florida. For father and son this was a terrible wrench. Coon Dog lost his young soul mate and anchor, a companion for his excursions away from the wife and family he was starting to despise, the only person he lived for. Similarly, for a boy whose entire life had been spent in a privileged sphere, having to share a dormitory with total strangers was virtually unbearable. The spartan discipline at Bolles, too, made Avis' incessant ranting appear tame. Gram forced himself to stick it out, sharing his misery in a series of letters with his mother, yet never once begging her to get him out of this place, believing that to admit defeat would make him appear that much less of a man in her eyes.

Waycross was experiencing more than its own fair share of drama. Coon Dog had fallen into the deepest depression, yet another condition his doctors blamed on his shell shock. He was just 42, but drink had aged him a good twenty years. The root of his problem, however, was his wife. Since Gram's departure Avis, now also an alcoholic, had become the local society lush, embarking on any number of not so very discreet affairs. Matters reached crisis point on 22 December 1958 when she and her children left Waycross to spend Christmas with her family at Winter Haven, leaving her husband to his own devices. Coon Dog is known to have driven them to the railway station, and Gram later recalled how he had been in a more jocular mood than usual. The next day, he calmly entered his bedroom and put a bullet through his skull.

Avis learned of her husband's suicide the next day, but opted not to tell the children until after the festive season. Gram was heartbroken, more so not just because his mother never mourned Coon Dog, but because she attended a party that same evening instead of staying home to comfort him and Little Avis. To avoid being denounced as insensitive by the local community, the Snivelys –

most of who had loathed Coon Dog – arranged for his body to be brought back to Winter Haven where he was interred in the family plot.

Gram returned to Bolles in January 1959, by which time Avis had already set her sights on husband number two: Robert Ellis Parsons, a spivvish Florida businessman who was no less promiscuous than she was. Employed by the Bechtel Corporation, Parsons was responsible for organising earth-moving projects in South America and Cuba, losing money in the latter upon Castro's rise to power. He was in search of a rich wife to bale him out of a tight corner, and Avis Connor was but one of several women he 'auditioned' for the role, wining and dining her with the panache of an Onassis. Avis fell for the ruse, and introduced Parsons to her children. Gram was initially suspicious and resentful: he had adored his father, and no one would ever take his place. Though he would try to get along with Parsons for his mother's sake, in later years he would scathingly refer to him – whenever possible to his face – as 'The Alligator Shoes-Pinkie Ring Asshole'. The proposed wedding, while he was still mourning his father, took its toll on Gram. He became troublesome at school, got into fights for the sheer hell of it, and soon ended up bottom of his class. Eventually, the principal contacted Avis: unless she removed Gram from Bolles, he would be expelled.

For several months, Avis appeared to change for the better. Rather than punish her son for humiliating the Snivelys, she recognised the errors of her ways and took Gram and Little Avis on a train holiday across America – accompanied by their chaperone and her personal maid. They visited Chicago, San Francisco and New York – taking in the shows and 'bumping into' Nat King Cole and Peggy Lee. The hotels were never less than five-star, the restaurants invariably the most exclusive in town. Avis was getting her offspring on side, ready for when their stepfather moved in. Even when Gram complained bitterly about her decision to dispatch him to another prep school, Avis compromised by enrolling him at St Joseph's, a non-denominational establishment in Winter Haven, so that he could be close to home to continue with his music. He would last here less than a year before being threatened with expulsion – this time for sending dirty letters to the principal, having discovered that his wife was 'turning tricks'. Very much against her will, Avis conceded to the ultimate in humiliation by sending Gram to the local high school. Avis Connor and Bob Parsons married, and within a matter of weeks Parsons legally adopted Gram and Little Avis. The move is supposed to have distressed the boy, which only begs the question – when he turned professional, why did Gram not revert to his birth name? And very soon, Bob Parsons would be playing his wife at her own game: staying faithful only until after the birth of their daughter, Diane, and while Avis drank herself near senseless every day, Parsons began affair with Bonnie, the couple's teenage babysitter.

The Parsons relocated to a new house in Winter Haven's exclusive Piedmont Drive, and the move coincided with Gram falling behind at school yet again – less to do with his change in circumstances than with his increasing passion for music. He had always excelled at English, in essay writing and poetry most especially, and while Avis and his stepfather socialised he, Little Avis and their friends jammed in the basement of their home – anything from Ray Charles to Elvis, from Hank Williams to Buddy Holly.

Gram matured early. His voice broke at 13 giving way to a pleasant, slightly cracked tenor with just the right amount of vibrato. By 14 he was shaving regularly; at six foot he was taller and, as the class photographs reveal, better looking than most of the other boys in his grade. He was possessed of a flawless skin that tanned easily, and rumours of his 'endowment' had enabled him to dispense with his virginity and sleep with at least half a dozen girls. Gram was the envy of everyone at school because he owned a car – despite the fact that he was not old enough to drive – and of course he was popular all around because he was never short of money. Even then, he was a magnet for scroungers. Gram formed his first group, The Pacers – of which little is known – towards the end of 1960. Early the next year, by this time a familiar figure in Winter Haven's tea rooms and restaurants – more of the occasional lounge singer than a hard rocker, accompanying himself at the piano or Hammond organ – he was asked to join the audaciously titled rockabilly outfit, The Legends, founded by Jim Stafford, who played lead guitar. The other band members were bassist Jim Carlton and drummer Lamar Braxton.

Two years older than Gram, James Wayne Stafford hailed from Eloise, a suburb of Winter Haven. The son of an area dry cleaner, he had begun playing guitar with his father during the mid-1950s. 'Gram was thirteen and I was sixteen when we started playing sock hops, Elks clubs, veterans halls, dances, weddings, anywhere we could play,' he recalled. 'We were never any good.' Stafford would later blame the band's shortcomings on lack of rehearsals, and their tendency to perform only the hits of the day, rather than write their own material, though he was doubtless selling himself short. Within a week of joining The Legends, Gram took over as lead vocalist and celebrated by buying a new guitar – an expensive, gold-plated Fender Stratocaster which became one of his most prized possessions.

Jim Carlton would remain a close friend for the rest of Gram's life, and be responsible for the safekeeping of some of his early songs – treasures which would not see the light of day until 2000, when in the wake of Gram being inducted into The Georgia Hall Of Fame, Sundazed Music released *Another Side of This Life*. Carlton had taped the first batch of these on a Sony 500 reel-to-reel machine in March 1965, shortly after Gram's first visit to New York. As such, they represent the kind of material he had performed on the Greenwich Village folk circuit: the first recorded version of 'Brass Buttons', Reverend Davis' 'Candy Man', Lieber and Stoller's 'Searchin'', a near-definitive version of Tom Paxton's 'The Last Thing On My Mind', and Gram's own 'Zah's Blues' – by far his best song from this period.

Unlike most of those who worked with him, Jim Carlton's respect and praise for Gram have been unswerving. Comparing his innate charisma with that of Elvis Presley, Clark Gable and Billie Holiday, he subsequently wrote of their friendship:

> *If you've ever been lucky enough to have been befriended by someone as magnetic and brilliant as he, you know the feeling, because that's a personal experience and largely indescribable – even overwhelming in retrospect . . . To many people he was larger than life and his continued cult-hero popularity and music legacy is testimony to that.*

The Legends developed a sizeable following on the local college-high school circuit, travelling as far afield as Jacksonville, performing Elvis and Everly Brothers numbers for the 'hip' members of the audiences, and slow songs for the kids to smooch to. One tape of them survives: dating from 1961, this is a raw-edged rendition of Ray Charles' 'What'd I Say?' and the earliest known recording of the Parsons voice. The Legends were one of the few bands at the time to own their own PA equipment – courtesy of Gram, for whom money was no object. Such was his charm that, with little or no effort, he invariably ended up with the prettiest girl in the audience, whether she was spoken for or not. Needless to say, he got into many a fist-fight and, despite his size, almost always came off worst.

The Legends' greatest achievement occurred in 1962 when they were offered a three-minute spot on *Hi-Time*, an afternoon children's magazine show on local television. By now they had a manager of sorts, 23-year-old Lewis 'Buddy' Freeman, a friend of the Snivelys who lived in Greenville, South

Carolina. Freeman worked in his father's plumbing factory, but his real passion in life was entering equestrian events. He was hired not by the band, but by Avis Parsons, who hoped he would keep an eye on Gram and steer him clear of trouble.

The Legends' line-up changed almost as regularly as their repertoire: by the end of their first 12 months together, while still leaning heavily on the songs of Elvis and the Everly Brothers, they were also performing Gram's own arrangements of folk songs popularised by The Kingston Trio, Pete Seeger and Peter, Paul and Mary. Gram included a little comedy patter too, which he sometimes slipped in while the others were re-tuning their instruments, and which he described as a cross between Steve Allen and The Smothers Brothers.

As the folk songs began monopolising their primarily rockabilly act, and cracks began forming in the otherwise friendly relationship between the band members, The Legends split: Gram and two friends formed The Village Vanguards, so-named after the New York landmark. When Gram complained to his stepfather about the lack of venues in Winter Haven, Bob Parsons solved the problem – by buying him a nightclub to perform in! The Derry Down was the region's first themed club. It served 'Shakespearean' fare such as Hamlet-burgers and Henry V steaks, *no* alcohol, and quickly became a mecca for Gram Parsons groupies who often scrapped outside the place over which of them would be asking Gram to escort them home after the show. Buddy Freeman was still managing-chaperoning, though not making a very good job of the latter. Gram's reputation as a stud, even at 16, preceded him, and during the summer of 1963 precipitated a family meeting wherein the Snivelys, en bloc, elected to remove him from their midst. In the September he was re-enrolled at Bolles, and his departure put paid to The Village Vanguards.

Forced back into the establishment he loathed, Gram rebelled against the system with a vengeance – organising 'sin weekends' at wealthy friends' houses which involved everyone getting drunk, smoking joints and partaking of the delights of much older prostitutes. As usual, he picked up the tab. This time, however, there was no question of expulsion. Gram had played a blinder by ensuring that one of these women had connections with the school, which in those days would almost certainly have been closed down, had the scandal become public knowledge.

Spurred on by the promise of regular evenings of music and hedonism, Gram ploughed through his studies and looked forward to each weekend, when he would be able to let his hair down. In the autumn of 1963, Buddy Freeman secured him his most prestigious engagement thus far – as MC/headliner in *The Coca-Cola Hi-Fi Club*, a talent show in Freeman's native Greenville. Among the entrants were The Shilos, a three-piece outfit who had styled themselves on The Kingston Trio, and The Journeymen – subsequently remembered for 'San Francisco' singer Scott Mackenzie, and John Phillips, who founded The Mamas & Papas. At the time, The Shilos comprised Paul Surratt (guitar, banjo, vocals), Joe Kelly (stand-up bass) and George Wrigley III (guitar, banjo). All three provided vocals, and the line-up also included two female singers, Margaret and Kathy Fowler. Gram had first come across The Shilos at a folk concert in Cypress Gardens, Florida, and now, upon learning that George Wrigley had been hospitalised after getting beaten up in a fight, he stepped into the breach – effectively breaking the rules by participating in a competition where he was one of the judges! Needless to say, the 'new' Shilos won, and such was Gram's cheek that he personally presented them with the $150 cheque!

The Shilos' base was in Greenville – no problem for Gram, who commuted regularly from Florida in his flashy red MG sports car. Now professionally managed by Buddy Freeman – in other words, paying him a percentage – the band fared well, playing most evenings after school and every weekend at charity events and political functions, in amusement parks, department store flyers and local clubs. Their repertoire was mostly folk, but Gram had begun writing more of his own material, and this was well received. Freeman secured them eight appearances on local television, but their best-paid gigs were at political rallies – earning a regulation $30 fee that was bumped up on several occasions to over $1,000, when Freeman or Gram passed the hat around. At such events, Gram stood out with his fondness for garish clothes and jewellery. Subsequently, he often found himself pursued by as many well-heeled young women (and the occasional man, who was politely dismissed!), and society matrons pampered him on account of his perfect manners and charm. There was no doubting, setting a precedent for the future, that he alone was the star of every show he appeared in.

Unexpected personal support came from Gram's mother, whose second husband was now treating her in much the way *she* had treated Coon Dog Connor – turning a blind eye to her drinking and carousing and spending most of his time with his mistress, Bonnie. Avis financed a trip to New York for herself and Gram, and Buddy Freeman accompanied them. Freeman had connections in Greenwich Village, and was confident of getting The Shilos bookings in some of the folk clubs for the 1964 summer season. In preparation for this, Avis bought Gram a pair of costly guitars, including a Goya 12-string. Everyone who met Gram appears to have been knocked sideways by his innate charisma and confident, persuasive banter. He performed in four of the Village clubs, including the Cafe Wha? and the Bitter End, where he was observed by a talent scout from NBC, then broadcasting Ed Sullivan's top-rating *Tonight* show – the one which had catapulted Elvis Presley to the top of the show-business ladder when he had supported Edith Piaf. Freeman was asked to submit a demo-tape to the producer.

It was rumoured at the time that Buddy Freeman may have had an ulterior motive for being so overtly keen on promoting Gram: Gram acted as a magnet for the most beautiful girls in town and passed on the 'glut' to his friends. Alternatively, it was suggested that he might even have been interested in Gram himself, though there is no proof of this. In July 1964, while Freeman was negotiating a slot for The Shilos on national television, they played a summer season at Fort Caroline – putting on shows on the beach, or under canvas if it rained. Here, the females were wilder than any Gram had seen, and he is said to have never slept alone until Freeman put his foot down and moved him into the house he was renting. For the other members of the group, who only felt miserable when Gram was not around to liven things up, this proved the last straw – particularly as it also emerged that Freeman had rejected an audition for Ed Sullivan's producer, claiming that The Shilos were too young and inexperienced to take on the big time. Freeman was sent packing by Gram – though technically, as Avis had hired him, she should have been the one doing the firing – and never worked in show business again. Gram, 17 and still legally a minor, announced that *he* would manage The Shilos, and the other band members had every confidence in his abilities. In August they accompanied him to New York, where he found them lodgings with a friend he had made during his visit to Greenwich Village. Gram stayed with the singer Odetta, whose reading of the Traditional American folk-song lullaby, 'All the Pretty Little Horses', was among his favourite songs of all time. Sadly, Odetta (1930–2008) is today best remembered for performing 'There's A Hole In My Bucket' with Harry Belafonte. How he came to know her is not known, but it was she who introduced him to his latest idol, Bob Dylan, whose *Another Side Of Bob Dylan* album he had recently bought.

There was to be an important meeting at the Bon Soir Club – the popular gay establishment at 40 West 8th Street where most of the headliners were actually straight: Ethel Waters, Barbra Streisand and the zany comedienne Phyllis Diller were all regular performers there. Among the clientele was former child star Brandon de Wilde. Four years Gram's senior, blond and blue eyed, de Wilde had also enjoyed a privileged upbringing. Born into a theatrical family, he had made a much-acclaimed Broadway debut, aged nine, in *The Member of the Wedding* – his role, which he had played for almost 500 performances, had won him the Donaldson Award, the first time this had been presented to a juvenile, and in 1952 he had repeated his success in the movie version, directed by Fred Zinnemann. The following year he had portrayed the freckle-faced boy who had idolised Alan Ladd's mysterious gunslinger in *Shane*: his heart-rending scenes had opened and closed the film, and earned him an Oscar nomination. This had led to his own, short-lived television series, *Jamie*. His most acclaimed roles since then had been as a younger brother to Warren Beatty in *All Fall Down* (1962) and to Paul Newman in *Hud* (1963). Then, his star had faded somewhat and when he met Gram he was attempting to forge a career as a pop singer. Though married, Brandon de Wilde *was* amorously interested in Gram, but not put out when informed that their friendship could never progress beyond the platonic. Indeed, some of de Wilde's friends have claimed that he was *relieved* at the rejection, considering friendships more important than relationships because in his case they lasted longer. De Wilde introduced Gram to his agent, Marty Erlichman, who just happened to be the manager of Barbra Streisand, who had started out at the Bon Soir Club four years earlier. Erlichman took to Gram at once: he had a similar zany-fearless-extroverted personality to Streisand, and Erlichman asked him to get in touch with him the next time he was in New York.

The New York trip might have proved more fruitful had Gram travelled alone. Though he looked like a man in his early twenties, his companions did not and with no one willing to engage them without parental consent, they were advised to return to the Village once they turned 18. The Shilos would play a handful of venues back home, otherwise their brief but not entirely unsuccessful reign was over. Thankfully, there is recorded evidence of how good they sounded.

In March 1965, The Shilos taped nine songs in a radio studio at Greenville's Bob Jones University: the session was reputedly financed by Paul Surratt's father, Paul Sr, almost certainly aided by a contribution from Avis Parsons – dedications to both appear on the sleeve, along with a dedication to one Mike Bixel, described as 'The Shilos' most devoted fan'. These tracks resurfaced on an album put out by Sierra records in 1979, *Gram Parsons: The Early Years 1963–1965* (not to be confused with the *Another Side of This Life* recordings detailed in the discography at the end of this book). Included were Dick Weissman's 'I May Be Right', Pete Seeger's classic 'Bells of Rhymeney' (subsequently covered by The Byrds), and 'Mary, Don't You Weep For Me'. Representing Gram's faith which was profound but much of the time kept to himself were the traditional 'Oh, Didn't They Crucify My Lord?' and 'On My Journey Home'. There were two Parsons compositions: the singalong 'Surfinany' and 'Zah's Blues', a lengthy ode to lost youth and loneliness, a remarkably mature piece for one so young which has Gram crooning half-a-pitch lower than usual in the style of a young Billy Eckstine.

The other Shilos were bitter about the split, though Gram *had* stood nobly by them, returning to Georgia when he could have stayed in New York and doubtless better himself – setting what would be a career-blighting precedent, always putting others before himself when they were most of the time unworthy of the privilege. In June 1993, Paul Surratt denounced him in *Record Collector*, saying, 'Gram just used us as a stepping-stone, and went on to another style of music. He started deliberately copying some of the old country singers . . . I think he had too many binges when he started to screw up his voice.' Many would agree, of course, that Surratt was speaking out of a profound attack of sour grapes. In September 1964, Gram returned to Bolles for his final year, preparing for his entry to Harvard where he would study theology – hardly the subject, one might think, for a youngster with his Lothario reputation. Some years later, the writer-photographer Eve Babitz would define him as, 'A complicated Christian, an artist who bore within him the magic seeds of the best and worst of our generation. He was in the classic tradition of the fucked-up young lord zig-zagging from purity to debauchery and singing songs.' In the December, almost exactly six years since Coon Dog's suicide, he was informed that his mother had been diagnosed with cirrhosis of the liver – furthermore, that there was no cure. Gram had grown closer to Avis of late, and now supported her as best he could – spending as much time with her as possible on weekends and during the school holidays, while Bob Parsons virtually ignored her in favour of his mistress.

The end came on the morning of Gram's graduation ceremony: Avis Connor Parsons was just 38, and was mourned by few, least of all by her son, who did not believe in such things. In March 1973 he would tell Judith Sims of *Rolling Stone* magazine,

> *Death is a warm cloak, an old friend. I regard death as something that comes upon a roulette wheel every once in a while. It's sad to lose a close friend. I've lost a lot of people close to me. It makes you a little bit stronger each time. They wouldn't want me to grieve. They would want me to go out and get drunk and have one on them.*

Gram had messed up at every school he had attended. His grades had been mediocre, save in English, and it would appear almost certain that the Snively wealth and/or their name were paramount in his being accepted at Harvard in September 1965. His application was supported by the wily Bob Parsons. He and Gram might have barely tolerated one another, but Gram's stepfather had every reason to champion his decision – to allow the boy to run wild if he wanted to, to even turn a blind eye to his excesses. If anything happened to Gram on account of his recklessness, and *before* his 21st birthday, as his legal guardian Parsons stood to inherit Gram's portion of the Snively fortune – vastly reduced since the war, but still worth in excess of $30 million.

Gram's family may have been surprised – shocked even – to learn that this glamorous, spirited young thing with an apparent inability to keep his pants zipped up should nurture a desire to go searching for God, though it is a well-known fact that some aspects of sex and religion go hand in glove. Prostitutes, for example, are frequently pious and keep religious images next to their beds. Gram's faith certainly had no anodising effect on his sex and opiates addiction – such was his libido that it is estimated, before the age of 20, that he was capable of bedding up to four different women in a single day. And for a young man persistently quoting the Bible, he was a compulsive but comical liar. In the handful of interviews he gave, Gram rarely told the same story or anecdote twice using the same facts. Journalists would be told of his father's death in jail, or that the Snively mansion had been used for filming the interiors of *Gone With the Wind* and that Clark Gable had been a friend of the family! Neither was his claim believed that he had chosen to study theology because he had *seen* God, though initially he took his studies very seriously.

While a freshman, Gram's mentor/spiritual adviser was Reverend James Ellison Thomas, a 26-year-old Baptist minister from Virginia who seems to have been only too well aware of his student's hobbies – girls and drugs. Indeed, Jet, as he was more familiarly known, is on record for helping Gram through at least one acid trip and hiding him in his quarters while going through cold turkey. Besides LSD, Gram was experimenting with pills – largely uppers and downers filched from his mother's medicine cabinet after her death. He had no problems with sleeping or with his nerves as she had – quite simply, he enjoyed experiencing the various highs and lows affected by the drugs. His wealth, of course, ensured that he always had a regular supply of what he wanted.

For Gram, drugs and music went hand in glove: he used opiates as a crutch to help him compose, producing some startlingly moving verses which would be stored away in his mental portfolio for future use. Skipping classes, he would ride off on his new motorcycle in search of inspiration – be this some distant, half-forgotten memory, his surroundings, or merely something he had read in the press. More often than not, he would be accompanied by a 'fuck-buddy', riding pillion, just in case such inspiration was not forthcoming and he needed to let off a little steam. At Harvard, certainly for Gram Parsons, threesomes and even foursomes were very much the order of the day.

It was inevitable that Gram should end up exploring the wealth of Cambridge clubs, in those days cornerstones for jazz and folk enthusiasts. And of course, with his hugely extroverted personality he very soon became an integral, albeit temporary, component of this community. He formed a band that he baptised The Like, an outfit which leaned more towards rock than folk, and which lasted all of one month. Then everything changed when he encountered a young English musician named Ian Dunlop.

Chapter Two
High Flyin' Byrd

It was a meeting of intellectuals. Gram and Ian Dunlop hit it off at once, realised how much they had in common musically, and decided to form a rhythm and blues-country band at a time when such outfits were virtually unheard of. First to join them was John Nuese, a folk singer with a local group, The Trolls – later The Youngbloods. Drummer Mickey Gauvin was next, followed by saxophonist Tom Snow. By November 1965, as yet unnamed, the band were playing local clubs, their repertoire consisting of chart songs, the odd number by James Brown, and several fairly green compositions by Gram. One of these was 'Brass Buttons', which had been published that spring in the *Bolles Literary Magazine* under the title, 'Pre-eminence'. The song, of which more later, would subsequently appear in its revised form on Gram's posthumous album, *Grievous Angel*. In January 1966, Gram received a call from Brandon de Wilde. Would he and his band like to spent a few weeks with him in New York, and maybe work with him? Ostensibly, de Wilde was interested only in Gram's input for whatever musical odyssey he had in mind, but did not wish to offend him by suggesting that he leave his 'backing group' at home. The actor had a pleasant singing voice, and was hoping that he and Gram might form a duo in the stamp of the Everly or Righteous Brothers. Moreover, Marty Erlichman was eager to back them all the way, and was already said to have been negotiating a record deal.

By now, Gram's outfit had a name: The International Submarine Band – title courtesy of an episode (The International Silver String Submarine Band) of the popular television series, *Our Gang*. The move had apparently been against Gram's will, for he had wanted to call them The Tinkers. On 28 October 1965, the band recorded an audition tape for RCA, which was believed lost for over 30 years until a technician discovered it in a company vault. After the festive season, once Gram had left Harvard 'by mutual agreement' – in fact, it was his mentor, Jet Thomas, who shopped him to the dean and got him expelled, Thomas claimed for his own good – The Submarine Band returned to New York. During the holidays they had played the clubs in Boston and Cambridge, Greenville and Winter Haven, and now found themselves working in Greenwich Village, Manhattan and New Jersey, besides backing Brandon de Wilde.

Then all of a sudden it turned sour when, for reasons never explained, *they* dropped Marty Erlichman – not a wise move if an act was hoping to avoid show-business blacklisting, for Erlichman was getting to be more powerful and influential by the minute on account of Barbra Streisand's rapid ascension to America's Number One Star. Erlichman's role was taken over by Monte Kay and Jack Lewis, then managing The Modern Jazz Quartet, and under duress they negotiated a skimpy deal with the little-known Ascot label. The contract was for just one single, but so far as the band were concerned it was a start, enough for them to risk putting down roots in the city.

Ascot were in search of a pop group to record 'The Russians Are Coming! The Russians Are Coming!' for the soundtrack of the film of the same name to be directed by Norman Jewison, who had recently triumphed with *The Cincinnati Kid*, a tough gambling drama with Steve McQueen. The critics dismissed the song as puerile, though most of them liked the B-side, Gram's and John Nuese's adaptation of 'Truck Driving Man', a country and western ditty which had been a hit for Bobby Bare. 'The first one where we got to do hard rock, or R and B and country music at the same time,' Gram later told A&R man, Chuck Casell. Despite its failure to sell, the record sufficiently impressed one CBS executive for him to offer The Submarine Band a short-term contract that resulted in another flop neo-hard-rock single, 'Sum Up Broke One Day Week'. And *still* the work offers poured in: television and radio guest appearances, and a support-slot (to The Young Rascals) at New York's Central Park, in front of 15,000 people. Gram adored everything about New York – except its winters. He had braved the one of 1965–6 because of the promise of greater things to come, but in the autumn of 1966, he decided to treat everyone to a little Californian sunshine and sparkle before knuckling down to the bad weather.

In the wake of his success playing John Wayne's son in the widely acclaimed *Harm's Way*, Brandon de Wilde's movie career had taken a turn for the better and he had recently relocated to Los Angeles, and in October Gram spent a few weeks with his friend and his wife to 'suss out' the place, with the view to moving here permanently. In Hollywood he was in his element: there seemed to be no limit to the amount of LSD and cannabis he could buy and the girls, he declared, were the prettiest he had ever seen, including de Wilde's wife – though this time the spouse of a friend was very definitely off limits. De Wilde introduced Gram to some of his movie pals, including Dennis Hopper, Jack Nicholson and Peter Fonda. The fact that these people lived opulent lives did not impress him at all – indeed, with his Snively inheritance he was better off than many of them. He had a brief fling with a much older actress then appearing in the television soap, *The Secret Storm* – for no other reason than her boasting of his prowess between the sheets might have helped him just that little further up the show-business ladder.

There were one-night stands with at least two other starlets, and at a party he fell for Nancy Lee Ross, the ex-wife of Franklyn D. Roosevelt's grandson, and the current 'squeeze' of David Crosby, a co-founder of The Byrds. The fact that Nancy and Crosby were engaged did not perturb Gram unduly: for him, the law of Zarathustra held good in that Woman was the sport of the Warrior and that ostensibly the strongest man walked off with the prize. The pair spent the night together after the party, and when Gram returned to New York, he took Nancy with him.

For a little while, now that he had a voluptuous, breathing incarnation of the California sunshine by his side, Gram shelved the idea of settling down in the West. However, by February 1967, exactly one year since arriving in the Big Apple, he changed his mind and persuaded the other members of The Submarine Band to move with him to the West Coast. The musicians rented a house in Laurel Canyon, while Gram and Nancy took out a lease on a place on North Sweetzer Avenue, a move which more or less sent The Submarine Band into a not-so-slow decline as Gram eschewed rehearsing with them to spend more time with his new celebrity pals. He had never aspired towards making movies, but learned that Peter Fonda – whose films until now had been mostly syrupy vehicles such as *Tammy and the Doctor* – had always dreamed of becoming a singer! Ultimately, it was a case of a little mutual back-scratching: Fonda promised to put Gram in touch with the right people to launch his recording career as a solo star – all Gram had to do in return was write him a song for his new venture!

Peter Fonda was about to begin shooting *A Lovely Sort Of Death*, scripted by Jack Nicholson and directed by Roger Corman, the undisputed doyenne of low-budget teen-exploitation movies. This latest offering was planned as some kind of shockfest centred around LSD experimentation, based on Nicholson's own experiences under controlled laboratory conditions following the break-up of his marriage, though he himself declined the lead part, declaring that it would be better suited to Fonda. The part of his wife was played by Susan Strasberg, and the other leads included Bruce Dern and Dennis Hopper. And who better to provide its theme-tune than Gram Parsons, an acknowledged substances expert? He came up with 'Lazy Days', a bouncy period-piece which Fonda approved of, but which Corman rejected: he wanted 'acid rock', not exactly Gram's forte, though by way of an apology for dropping The Submarine Band from the soundtrack, he offered them a cameo appearance in the film, whose title, having been disapproved of by the censor's board, was changed to *The Trip*. The film dated very quickly, and today is regarded as little more than a curiosity.

The idea for Peter Fonda to enter the recording studio had come from South African trumpeter Hugh Masakela, in New York to record 'So You Want to Be a Rock 'n' Roll Star?' with The Byrds. Masakela had heard Fonda singing at a party, and thought his voice resembled that of Woodie Guthrie. Gram presented Fonda with 'November Nights' – not a new number, but one which had been in his repertoire for a while, which suggests that he did not regard the actor's singing potential as particularly special. His friend, Jim Carlton, had taped him singing this the previous December. Fonda's version, not a patch on Gram's (which would not be released until 2000), was released on the Chisa label. According to him, it was but one of 16 songs he recorded at the time: these included several Parsons compositions, and material written and composed by Roger McGuinn and David Crosby. Following the failure of 'November Nights', Fonda abandoned his proposed album. Even so, the episode contributed to The Submarine Band winning a recording contract for themselves.

As for *The Trip*, when the film was released Gram doubtless wished that he had never heard of the project. In their segment, The Submarine Band were overdubbed by Electric Flag, the psychedelic-style outfit which Roger Corman had hired to replace them on the soundtrack. Not for the first time – and certainly not for the last – someone Gram had cared about and trusted had let him down. The Submarine Band now had a new manager – Brandon de Wilde's new mentor, Steve Aldberg – who found them work in classy establishments such as the Palomino, then the leading country music club in Los Angeles. As Gram was still a minor (the legal age for alcohol consumption was 21) he was supplied with a fake identity card, though he looked considerably older than 20. Here, for the first time, he was heckled. Some of the hard-bitten 'red-neck' country aficionados did not always take kindly to this 'purdy long-hair' with his effete mannerisms, posturing and pouting in his 'ball-crusher' spray-on satin trousers and rainbow-coloured shirts split to the waist. 'He was either fearless or stupid,' his later road manager Phil Kaufman recalled in a BBC interview in 2006, though he did not know Gram at the time. 'You'd show up in a real red-neck bar, long hair and crushed velour trousers and silk scarves around your neck. That's the sign on your back that says "Kick me!"'

The clientele in these establishments soon realised, however, that appearances could be deceptive, and that Gram was just as butch and red-blooded as they were. They still despised him, though, for making a play for their women, snatching girlfriends and wives from under their very noses. Sometimes he would get away with this, but equally the wronged and disgruntled man would turn up the next evening and demand satisfaction – with Gram usually getting out of a fight by inviting his love rival to share a joint and a bottle of tequila, currently his favourite tipple!

Just as Gram had skipped essential rehearsals with The Submarine Band, so there were times when they were compelled to perform without him but, it must be said, more often than not it was when he was out of town meeting agents and record-company executives in an attempt to secure a viable deal which would benefit them as much as himself. One such was Lee Hazelwood (1929–2007), then head of LHI Records. The gravel-voiced singer-producer had experimented with electric gimmickry during the mid-1950s, adding echo to country songs. In 1956 his composition 'The Fool', written for his first wife Naomi Ford, had been covered by Sanford Clark and reached the Top Ten. The following year he had co-founded Jamie Records, the first of several companies, with chat-show host Dick Clark, and been instrumental in promoting Duane Eddy. With the emergence of The Beatles and the Rolling Stones he had threatened to leave show business, but he had stuck out the British invasion and hit a new high: his mid-1960s triumphs had included his 'These Boots are Made for Walkin'', a Number One hit for Nancy Sinatra on both sides of the Atlantic, and several duets with her, including 'Jackson' and 'Summerwine'.

According to the interview he gave in 1972 for Chuck Casell (*Chemical Imbalance, Vol 3:1*) – though one must make allowances for Gram's fondness for bending the truth – he swaggered up to Hazelwood at a Hollywood party and pronounced, 'Let me make an album for you. I won't take any money for it – unless it's a Top Ten album!' – bringing the response from Hazelwood, 'Okay, but my old lady has to produce it!' True or not, the cutting of The International Submarine Band's only album for Lee Hazelwood's LHI label kept them together for a little longer, albeit mostly in name only. Gram is thought to have disliked Hazelwood on account of his brittle, no-nonsense approach – the fact that if he had anything negative to say, personal feelings were rarely spared, though this tough task-master approach usually paid off with the quality of the finished product. The 'old lady' was Hazelwood's girlfriend, Suzi Jane Hokom. The band already had a sizeable repertoire, largely covers of others artists' work, so Gram and John Nuese set about writing new material. Next there was the question of improving the band's line-up. During a visit to Winter Haven, Gram had bumped into Jon Corneal, an old drummer buddy who had played with The Legends. Corneal was now roped in to replace the just-departed Mickey Chauvin. Mississippi-born Chris Etheridge, who had played in the first Monterey Festival, replaced Ian Dunlop – who went on to form the initial line-up of The Flying Burrito Brothers, a name which Gram had purloined several times when performing extant of The Submarine Band with friends on the club trail. The Submarine Band's studio line-up was completed with the addition of Earl Ball, on piano, and J. D. Maness on pedal steel. The first recording session took place in July 1967, from which Hokom and Hazlewood put out a single, 'Luxury Liner', coupled with 'Blue Eyes', both penned by Gram.

Embracing all the styles Gram had encompassed so far, the album was completed by the end of November and would be released in the spring of 1968, by which time The Submarine Band would be no more. Widely regarded as the world's first country-rock album, it was given the title *Safe At Home* – a misnomer if ever there was one, considering the dramas that had ensued during its production. Even so, it is a remarkable piece of work.

Pride of place goes to the two songs that made up the single. Gram's 'Blue Eyes' has him venting his frustration over being away from his girl. 'I bite my nails, and if that fails I get myself stoned,' he proclaims, while 'Luxury Liner' would go on to become a showstopper for later Parsons' disciple, Emmylou Harris. There were definitive covers of Melvyn Endsley's 'Knee Deep in the Blues', Merle Haggard's 'I Must Be Somebody Else You've Known' – and 'Miller's Cave', the Jack Clement country standard which could have been (but was not) especially written for Gram with its reference to Waycross, and the narrator's wayward girlfriend that he shoots dead, along with her lover, shoving their 'cheatin', schemin' bones' in the cave of the title!

Though young and inexperienced in studio matters, Gram proved a tough task-master, knowing exactly which musical sounds he wanted, and never settling for second best or compromise. He disliked working with Suzi Jane Hokom because she treated him like a novice, and by the end of the second session he vowed never to cross her path again, other than tolerating her involvement with The Submarine Band's second single, 'Miller's Cave', which like its predecessor failed to chart, largely through lack of airplay.

There was also a personality clash with Jon Corneal, whom Gram had apparently wooed with the promise that he would be contributing to the band's repertoire. Gram's chance remark to one of the other band members that he was regretting having invited Corneal to join them let loose the proverbial cat among the pigeons. There was a further dilemma when Nancy Lee Ross – Gram's girlfriend had adopted his name, though they never married – announced that she was pregnant. The band's manager, Steve Aldberg – in the middle of putting together a tour and fearful that Gram might now want to stay home – suggested that Nancy might be better off having an abortion. Gram reacted to this by declaring that he did not care what she did because he had no way of saying that the baby was even his.

This swift progression of dramas, culminating with the curtain coming down on the International Submarine Band, placed Gram on the edge of a nervous breakdown. He coped the only way he knew how, by increasing his intake of drink and drugs, though with tremendous inner strength he did not allow this to affect his work. With an album about to hit the stores and with no band to promote it, Gram began planning his next project – which meant looking for another band. Why he had to have a band, as opposed to turning solo and hiring session musicians, is unclear. Maybe he enjoyed the camaraderie of being part of an outfit, or maybe he was just afraid of taking the risk. He certainly possessed the ability to branch out on his own. When one listens to his work today, no matter which outfit he is fronting, one hears only the voice of a brilliant young singer backed by good musicians and half-decent, syrupy vocals – for it is *his* voice that captivates. Like Freddie Mercury with Queen, or Morrissey with The Smiths, one mostly cares only for the frontman and the others, unfortunately, are but also-rans. Above all, Gram was more than capable of providing his own material without having to rely on anyone else, and would have had no fear of letting himself down, as others had let him down. Whatever the reason, during the spring of 1968 he elected to 'help out' The Byrds – or rather what was left of them.

The Byrds, arguably one of the most original and influential bands of their generation, was founded in 1964 by Jim (subsequently Roger) McGuinn and Chris Hillman and augmented by David Crosby, Michael Clarke and Gene Clark. McGuinn (b. 1942), had previously worked with The Limeliters and The Chad Mitchell Trio, and had also written songs for Bobby Darin. Crosby (b. 1941) had started out as a promising drama student; his father, Floyd, was an

Oscar-winning cinematographer who worked on *High Noon* and Corman's *The Pit and the Pendulum*.

Michael Clarke (Michael James Dick, 1946–93) had run away from his Washington home at 17 and hitchhiked to California where he was discovered, it's been said, by David Crosby, playing bongos on the beach. Similarly, it's alleged he was only invited to play with Crosby on account of his uncanny resemblance to the Rolling Stones' guitarist, Brian Jones. Gene Clark (1944–91), a hugely talented songwriter-musician who made and squandered a great deal of money, yet achieved little commercial success during his lifetime, had cut his first record at just 13 with Joe Meyers & The Sharks, and performed with several folk ensembles in his native Missouri before being discovered and taken on by The New Christy Minstrels. After a short spell with these, he had met Roger McGuinn and they briefly worked as a duo, playing at The Folk Den, before meeting David Crosby. They formed a trio and renamed themselves The Jet Set: their best-known song, though not a success, was 'The Only Girl I Adore'. Soon afterwards, drummer Michael Clarke and bassist-vocalist Chris Hillman joined them.

Managed by Jim Dickson, the quintet, temporarily renamed The Beefeaters, rehearsed and recorded at the World Pacific Studios in Los Angeles, and put out a single, 'Please Let Me Love You', on the Elektra label. In November 1964, now billed as The Byrds, the group signed a contract with Columbia and released Bob Dylan's 'Mr Tambourine Man', which catapulted them to international fame and topped the charts on both sides of the Atlantic. Another of their hits, Pete Seeger's 'Turn, Turn, Turn', had previously been covered by Marlene Dietrich, who performed it around the world as a companion piece to Seeger's 'Where Have All the Flowers Gone?' As musicians and harmonists, The Byrds were arguably second-to-none, but as individuals their varying temperaments would leave much to be desired over the years and result in an almost ever-changing line-up. In June 1967, in the wake of several very successful albums, The Byrds played at the Monterey Pop Festival, where David Crosby caused a stir by making public comments in favour of drugs and, it is alleged, the Kennedy assassination. True or not, Crosby was fired. Only weeks later, Gene Clark left the group under a dark cloud – not just on account of his fear of flying, as was stated in the press at the time, but because of antagonism from the other members of the group who are said to have resented him, as the composer of most of their original songs, earning more than they did. Michael Clarke soon followed, reducing the group to a duo, and all this on the eve of the release of their new album, *Notorious Byrd Brothers* and a European tour. On the positive side, McGuinn and Hillman were joined by bluegrass guitarist, Clarence White.

Widely regarded as one of the finest guitarists of his generation, Clarence White (Clarence LeBlanc, 1944–73) hailed from Madawaska, Maine, where in 1958 he and his brothers had formed a band called Three Little Country Boys. They appeared regularly on local radio, cut a single and guested several times on *The Andy Griffith Show*. In 1962, they changed their name to The Kentucky Colonels, folding three years later in the wake of the British invasion when bluegrass had gone temporarily out of fashion. Since then, White had earned his crust as a session musician, notably on early recordings by The Monkees. McGuinn and Hillman, meanwhile, had already met Gram by way of Peter Fonda, and had apparently had their eye on him *before* the departure of their colleagues. Gram was invited to join them around the time they enlisted a new drummer – Hillman's cousin, Kevin Kelley.

According to Hillman, he and Gram bumped into each other while standing in line at a Beverly Hills bank, and sealed their fate there and then with a handshake. The move cost Gram his uneasy friendship with Lee Hazelwood. With *Safe At Home* now on general release, and with no band left to promote it with, Gram was left with no choice but to move on. What he probably did not realise – or maybe he hoped the situation might be overlooked – was that he had signed a contract with Hazelwood wherein the producer actually owned his vocal rights. Over the years, Chris Hillman has expended a gamut of emotions recalling his experiences with Gram – love, admiration, jealousy, disrespect, anger, spite – all connected to the fact that, while The Byrds and The Flying Burrito Brothers may be remembered collectively, despite his great talent, Hillman will never figure among the rock icons of the 20th century.

Born in Los Angeles but raised in San Diego County, Hillman developed an early interest in bluegrass. At 16, shortly after his father's suicide, and already a familiar name on the local folk circuit, he had joined The Scottsville Squirrel Barkers. These had stayed together for almost two years and cut one independent album, *Bluegrass Favorites*. When the band split in 1963, Hillman joined The Golden State Boys, one of county's leading bluegrass ensembles – soon afterwards, impressed by his input, they had changed their name to The Hillmen, and had made numerous television appearances. Next he had played with The Green Grass Revival, billed as a spin-off from The New Christy Minstrels . . . and then had come The Byrds.

Many years later, interviewed for *The Gram Parsons Project* Internet website, Hillman boasted of how *he* had offered Gram the opportunity of a lifetime. 'We had just hired this kid to join The Byrds,' he pompously declared. 'He was never a *member* of The Byrds. He was hired as a sideman, an accompanist, as an extra singer.' It is an undisputable fact, however, that in all Byrds and Parsons retrospectives, the name heading the credits *is* Gram Parsons.

Chris Hillman's attitude towards Gram was entirely different, back in early 1968. His and Roger McGuinn's intention was that, with Gram's input, The Byrds might attain the same status as the Beatles and the Rolling Stones, but in the new country-bluegrass-rock-ragtime-folk style. Not only this, Hillman and McGuinn were anticipating a double album that, they claimed, would 'chronicle the history of 20th-century American music'. Obviously, they were not asking for much! Gram suggested that the only way to cut an album of such varied genres would be by heading to Nashville, where they would at least have the requisite ambience. This was true, but he is also thought to have been using this as an excuse to get away from all the rows with his girlfriend, Nancy. Gary Usher, who had just produced the Beach Boys' latest album, was hired to spearhead the project that was given the title, *Sweethearts of the Rodeo*.

The first recording session, featuring Clarence White on guitar, took place on 9 March 1968 at the CBS Studios, and apparently went well.

The next evening, The Byrds performed two songs at the 2,400-seater Ryman Auditorium (formerly the Grand Ole Opry, on Nashville's Fifth Avenue) as part of a 30-minute radio programme that was relayed across the United States to an estimated audience of 15 million. CBS had arranged this at the last minute to promote what would be the band's debut single, 'You Ain't Goin' Nowhere', taken from the album.

Introduced by regular host Tompall Glaser, The Byrds performed the song, trying to ignore the sprinkling of hecklers mocking the way they were dressed. Then, after a moderate applause, Glaser returned to the platform and announced that the band would be closing with Merle Haggard's 'Sing Me Back Home'. Gram strode up to the footlights and countered, 'As a matter of fact, we ain't. We're gonna do a song I wrote for my grandmother. We used to listen to the Grand Ole Opry together when I was little. This one's called 'Hickory Wind'!' Glaser waved at Gram from the wings, trying to get him off the stage – though with a live broadcast, filling the four-minute gap would have proved tricky. The other Byrds were just as taken aback: though 'Hickory Wind' had been earmarked for their album, they were yet to hear it! Therefore, they had no option but to follow Gram's lead – and he brought the house down with the beautiful song that henceforth would be regarded as his signature tune.

Gram had co-written this magnificent pastiche with Submarine Band session-man Bob Buchanan, during a lengthy Florida–Los Angeles train journey that had seen the pair busking for kicks. The lyrics centred around the hickory trees, tall pines and oaks close to his grandparents' home which he and Little Avis had climbed as children. It is effectively a hymn to lost innocence and the regret of growing up too fast. 'I started out younger at most anything,' Gram laments, 'All the riches and pleasures – what else could life bring?' Then he concludes, 'It's a hard way to find out that trouble is real in a far away city, with a far away feel.' Effectively it is a potent example of how it feels to be homesick, of longing to return to one's roots when fate has forced one into a world one may not comprehend or wish to be in.

Drama erupted midway through the *Sweetheart of the Rodeo* sessions when Lee Hazelwood served Gram with an injunction, reminding him of his LHI contract, prohibiting him from recording lead vocals with any other label. This was possibly sour grapes. By the time he received the writ, Gram had already laid down eight tracks, and an uneasy 'compromise' was reached. Three of these would be permitted to appear on The Byrds' album: 'Blue Canadian Rockies', 'You're Still On My Mind' – and 'Hickory Wind', which would have been a sacrilege to tamper with.

Gram would go to his grave believing that some of his most astonishing vocals had been wiped and replaced by Roger McGuinn's. In 1990, however, these 'mysteriously' reappeared when Columbia released *The Byrds*, a 4-CD boxed set. Included were Gram's superior renditions of several songs now regarded as country-rock classics: Gram's 'One Hundred Years from Now', his tongue-in-cheek reading of William Bell's soulful 'You Don't Miss Your Water', the George Jones standard 'You're Still On My Mind', and The Louvin Brothers' 'The Christian Life'. Gram, the devout Christian, had thought the (then) non-Christian Roger McGuinn a hypocrite to even attempt this inspirational number.

Between recording sessions – these took place in 'down time', when no one else of greater commercial importance had booked the studio – The Byrds left Nashville and embarked on a promotional tour of the East Coast. As had happened with The Submarine Band, no sooner had the outfit re-formed than they began the slow, agonising and acrimonious process of falling apart, largely on account of Gram's being their most popular member with the public, coupled with his searing professionalism. Just as he had pushed himself forwards at the Ryman Auditorium, aware that *all* groups needed a frontman to prevent them from being regarded as bland, so he was the centre of attention now. Audiences found him sparkling and different, even though they did occasionally give him a hard time because of his choice of apparel.

Initially, the other members of The Byrds were content to have Gram as the centrepiece as their crown was starting to tarnish. However, when the tour transferred to the West Coast in April 1968, the situation changed radically. Rumours circulated that Roger McGuinn and Chris Hillman could have persuaded Lee Hazelwood to drop his lawsuit (which in any event would amount to nothing), but that instead *they* had engineered to have Gram's vocals removed from the album tapes because, they claimed, he was getting to be too big for his boots. 'Roger didn't want the album to turn into a Gram Parsons album,' producer Gary Usher later told biographer Johnny Rogan *(The Byrds: Timeless Flight Revisited*, 1998). The sessions concluded, and with the album set for an autumn release, The Byrds crossed the Atlantic for a brief European tour: one show in Rome, three in London. This, they claimed, would be a 'taster' for a future, more thorough tour that would take in France, Germany, more dates in England and a landmark visit to South Africa. By and large, fans were initially confused. The band's last album, *Notorious Byrd Brothers*, had just been released – yet here they were with a brand new line-up, promoting a totally different sound, and boasting a frontman!

The Byrds' concert at Covent Garden's Middle Earth was a sell-out, and over-hyped. During their stay in London, they were championed by the Rolling Stones' Mick Jagger and Keith Richards, and their rock-chick partners, Anita Pallenberg and Marianne Faithfull, who were captivated by the 'polite young Southerner'. Gram had been raised with manners: to open a door for a lady, to hold out her chair as she took her place at the table, to stand up if a woman entered the room – something he did all his life. But just as Marianne and Anita were fascinated by him, so he was initially star-struck to find himself suddenly included in the Stones' entourage. A chance remark that he had always wanted to see Stonehenge at night saw everyone piling into two cars and taking him there, then sleeping out under the stars after an orgy of cannabis and Johnnie Walker whisky.

The Byrds' second London show was at Blaises, another full house, but it was at the Roundhouse, shortly before the band were scheduled to fly back to America to add the finishing touches to their album, that Roger McGuinn made a rod for his own back – by demanding that Gram take centre stage for a solo version of 'Hickory Wind'. The audience went wild, made him sing it again, and the fans remembered this two months later in July when The Byrds headlined *Sounds 68*, a Boys' Club benefit at the Royal Albert Hall, with The Move and The Bonzo Dog Doo Dah Band. Sitting in the front row were John Lennon and George Harrison, Mick Jagger, Marianne Faithfull, Keith Richards – and Jimi Hendrix! The Byrds, or rather Gram, received the evening's biggest applause. Nick Logan observed in that week's *New Musical Express*, 'A good section of the 4,000 audience was there to see *them* alone – and let them know it!' Gram had by now had enough of playing second fiddle to an outfit who did not appreciate him, and was well aware that the fans were only interested in him. The next morning – having spent most of the night having his ear bent by Jagger, Richards and Hendrix during a pot-and-booze symposium, he informed Roger McGuinn that he would not be going to South Africa, effectively bringing his four-months stint with The Byrds to a not unexpected conclusion.

All manner of excuses were fed to the press as to why Gram had dropped out of the tour. Two of The Byrds cited a clash of egos. One arrogantly declared that he had 'served his purpose as an employee', therefore the band had elected to let him go. The *real* reason was that, having been raised in a blacks-friendly environment, Gram simply could not stomach apartheid and the thought of being compelled to perform to segregated audiences. He told *Melody Maker* at the end of July, 'I knew very little about South Africa before the tour was mentioned. I *knew* there was an intense problem, but I didn't know what it was based on. I began to talk to people, and I found out.'

The tour would prove disastrous. Various members of The Byrds made unwise and uncalled for comments about the South African administration, which saw them heckled on stage, jeered in the street outside the venues, and besieged by death threats. An anonymous tip-off to the police that they were doing drugs in their Durban hotel room finally saw them making a hasty exit from the country without collecting their pay. Later, when they tried to sue, they were informed by the promoter that in order to get what was owing to them, they would have to return to South Africa and face the music – even if this meant standing trial for the drugs charges laid against them. All told, Gram had had a lucky escape.

Chapter Three

That's the Bag I'm In!

Gram spent the summer of 1968 at Redlands, Keith Richards' mansion near Chichester, West Sussex, which he shared with Anita Pallenberg, his common-law wife between 1967 and 1977. Something of a loose cannon with an unpredictable temper, Pallenberg (b. 1944) had first become involved with the Stones guitarist in 1965 and then Mick Jagger while filming *Performance*. She and Richards would have three children – their first, Marlon, was named after Brando. Theirs would also, maybe not inadvertently, set a precedent for impossible-to-live-with/ impossible-to-live-without rock couples: in years to come Sid Vicious and Nancy Spungen, Kurt Cobain and Courtney Love, and Pete Doherty and Kate Moss would all follow their destructive example.

This was, however, no idle sojourn: Gram taught Richards all he knew about country music, which was considerable, and it was this enlightenment that would subsequently influence the Rolling Stones' *Beggar's Banquet* album, which the group had just begun working on. For the rest of his life, Gram would remain one of Richards' closest confidants. In April 2005, the guitarist told *Rolling Stone* magazine,

> *We both loved that melancholy, high-lonesome shit. We were always looking for the next heart-tugger, looking to pull that extra heartstring. As a songwriter Gram worked very much like I do . . . knock out a couple of chords, start to spiel and see how far it can go. Rather than sitting around with a piece of paper and a pen, trying to make things fit neatly together, if you just get on the microphone things come to you. Lines come to you that you wouldn't dream of, because they have to come to you in a split second.*

Regarding Gram, the man, Richards added,

> *He was fun to be around, great to play with as a musician. And that motherfucker could make chicks cry. I have never seen another man who could make hardened old waitresses at the Palomino Club in LA shed tears the way he did. It was all in the man.*

A mutual friend was Pamela Miller (later Des Barres), aka Miss Pamela of The GTOs – the first two initials of the all-female group stood for Girls Together, the 'O', they claimed, for Outrageous, Oral, Orgasm, or anything else beginning with the letter. The other members went under the names Miss Sparky, Miss Lucy, Miss Christine, Miss Sandra, Miss Mercy and Miss Cynderella. Billed as 'performance artists' because they could neither dance, sing, nor play instruments, The GTOs had been formed by Frank Zappa and employed by him to open his concerts with The Mothers of Invention. Even so, in 1969, one month before disbanding following a charge of drugs possession, they would release an album, *Permanent Damage*, a puerile mish-mash containing such instantly forgettable tracks as *The Eureka Springs Garbage Lady* and *I Have a Paintbrush in My Hand to Colour a Triangle*, and which would achieve little more than showcasing the talents of Zappa, guitarist Jeff Beck, and The Monkees' Davy Jones.

Miller, something of a super-groupie, confessed a long list of show-business conquests which included Zappa, Mick Jagger, Chris Hillman, Jimi Hendrix, Noel Redding, Keith Moon, Ray Davies, actor Don Johnson and, quite possibly, Gram. She had first seen him at the premiere of the Beatles' film, *Yellow Submarine*, when he had worn a suit decorated with yellow submarines – more to do with The International Submarine Band than the Fab Four. Pamela Miller and Gram had been properly introduced after a Byrds concert at the Kaleidoscope. 'He was a really mellow, laid-back, bedroom-eyed guy,' Miller told *The Gram Parsons Project*. 'He had this incredible charisma, and glamour and shine. He was very unlike anyone we'd met in Hollywood, that's for sure. He brought his weeping willow tree, Southern consciousness into Hollywood.' Of Gram's adherence to Keith Richards, she observed, 'They were literally becoming each other. They were inseparable. I think they were in love – not anything physical, though they did hang all over each other. They were just in each other's faces and arms all the time. It was an unbelievable vision.'

Gram was in England in the August when *Sweetheart of the Rodeo* was released, providing The Byrds with their least successful album so far – courtesy of a half-failed tour and broken line-up. It just scraped into the *Billboard* chart, though today opinions have changed and it is regarded as one of the most influential country-rock albums of all time. Chris Hillman, who had cursed and criticised Gram for backing out of the South Africa tour, himself left The Byrds, leaving the outfit to slowly flounder. He then grasped with both hands the opportunity to work once more with Gram when the call-to-arms came. 'I was ready to murder Gram,' he told Sid Griffin, who published Gram's biography in 1985, 'and then we made up and became friends again. The South African tour was a farce, and he was right. We shouldn't have gone, but he shouldn't have let us down by copping out at the end.' At around the same time, Gram was reunited with Submarine Band bassist Chris Etheridge.

The rift between Gram and Nancy Lee Ross had widened beyond repair, probably exacerbated by the birth of their unplanned-for daughter, Polly, in December. Though there is more than a slight physical resemblance to Gram, the rumour persists to this day that she may not have been actually fathered by him. In the spring of 2006, Phil Kaufman somewhat ungallantly told a BBC radio programme, 'There was a little groupie girl hanging out, and somebody knocked her up. Instead of pointing to the guy who did it, she pointed to the guy with the money.' According to Kaufman, Gram contested the child's paternity, though the matter never reached arbitration. He concluded, 'When we got to the court, it was either hang around the court, or go for a beer. So he opted for the beer and he ended up with a kid.' Interviewed for the same retrospective, and with no mother present to back her up, Polly was unfazed: the story changed, she said, depending upon whose version one listened to. 'When you talk to people that were there,' she added, 'they are dead against the fact that Gram was anything but a completely loving father who was very, very much a part of my life. However, it was not appropriate to him becoming a father, business wise, so the spin in the camp was that he was not going to embrace the fact, publicly. I'm fine with it either way. If it is, that's wonderful – if it's not, *that's* wonderful.'

Gram moved out of the North Sweetzer Avenue house and into a property on DeSoto Avenue, Resada, in the picturesque San Fernando Valley. Chris Hillman, recently divorced, moved in with him and Chris Etheridge practically lived there, too. Thus in a haze of pot-smoke, yet another milestone of country rock would be created: the perhaps not inappropriately titled, *The Gilded Palace of Sin*. Gram's ex-colleague, Ian Dunlop, had formed The Flying Burrito Brothers West early in 1968, but aside from a few sporadic appearances on the local circuit the band had achieved little. Dunlop had returned to England around the time Gram had arrived back in Los Angeles, apparently permitting his friend to use the name *and* handing over his (also ex-Submarine Band) drummer, Jon Corneal.

The Flying Burrito Brothers was a complicated set-up, with so many comings and goings that is hard to keep track of what was going on. Initially, the trio of Parsons, Hillman and Etheridge worked on new material by day, and came up with some pretty stirring stuff. Few would argue that among the best songs The Burritos produced – if not *the* best – were Gram and Etheridge's stunning 'Hot Burrito #1' and 'Hot Burrito #2'. In the former, Gram rips his heart out and unreservedly lays bare his soul, the crack in the voice this time suggesting that the tears are for real. His lover may have left him for someone else, but he assures her that whatever happens, she will only ever belong to him: 'I'm your toy, I'm your old boy, and I don't want no one but you to love me.' The pleading continues in the song's more upbeat companion piece, though by now Gram's heartache merges with anger as he warns her, 'You better love me – Jesus Christ!'

By night, The Burritos played as many as the country clubs as could contend with them. Just as England had had its Mods-versus-Rockers phase, so California was currently going through its red-necks-versus-long-hairs phase. Basically, the rednecks saw themselves as the archetypal, hard-drinking, hard-loving heterosexual males pursued by all the pretty girls – while the long-hairs were stereotyped as effete, weakling homosexuals. In fact, in many instances these roles were reversed! Gram's music was very definitely aimed at the red-necks crowd, while he personally fitted into the longhairs category – though his hair was not yet as long as it would be later on.

The red-necks may have secretly liked The Burritos' music, even sniffling at Gram's rattling crescendo in 'Hot Burrito # 1', but to impress their womenfolk they had to act tough and show a little hostility towards this quartet of oddities wearing what appeared to be women's blouses and skin-tight pants which in Gram's case left nothing to the imagination. The band was bombarded with insults such as 'faggot' and 'ass-bandit'. It was only when these loudmouths realised that The Burritos were just as 'normal' as themselves – chiefly by observing Gram leaving the venue each night with a different girl on his arm – that they gave them a little space. Even so, the 'faggot' incidents troubled Gram, to such an extent that he is thought to have begun doubting his own sexuality. Though propositioned by Brandon de Wilde, and later by producer Terry Melcher, there is absolutely no evidence that he ever even thought of having a gay relationship – though with his fondness for experimentation, particularly with opiates, anything might have been possible. He is also known to have been something of an exhibitionist, proud of flashing his 'legendary appendage', and for not always closing the door to the bedroom when he was vociferously entertaining a lady friend. The unfounded rumour and Gram's alleged concern over what some might have been saying behind his back about his living arrangements with Chris Hillman, may explain why Gram executed a volte-face and persuaded Nancy Lee Ross to move in with them, despite the fact that they had been on the verge of splitting up.

Of late, Nancy and her daughter Polly had been living with Brandon de Wilde and his wife, and Gram attempted to woo her back into his life – it must be said in typical old-days Hollywood tradition – by asking her to marry him. A date was set for the ceremony: 31 January 1969. Meanwhile, Gram received his draft notice. He had always nurtured pacifist tendencies, and was virulently opposed to the war in Vietnam, so how he would have reacted if ordered to fight may only be assumed, as is whether the Snively millions would have got him off the hook, as they had allegedly got him into Harvard. In any event, he was declared 4F unfit by the medics who examined him. Gram's friends always assumed that he failed his medical on account of the opiates within his system, or that he had merely spun the examination board another of his yarns. In fact, it later emerged that he was discovered to have a heart-murmur and high blood pressure, a condition he kept to himself. The incident led to him and Chris Hillman penning a rare protest song, 'My Uncle' – the uncle in question being Uncle Sam himself, whom he berates for sending a draft board questionnaire asking for personal details of his parents. 'So,' the conscientious objector concludes, 'I'm heading for the nearest foreign border!'

Satisfied that all was quiet on the home front, at least for the time being, Gram and Hillman completed their band's line-up by hiring pedal-steel guitarist Sneaky Pete Kleinow (1934–2007), a former special-effects man who had worked on the big and small screen – notably on *The Outer Limits* series – an employment he would subsequently return to, after Gram's death. They then put together a demo-tape and began doing the rounds of the record companies. Gram used one of his 'tall tales' – that Keith Richards had promised to produce their debut album, allegedly backed up by a telephone call from Richards himself – and on the strength of this they were offered a deal by Reprise, most famous for recording Frank Sinatra.

The fact that Gram was given the responsibility of accepting or rejecting the deal suggests that the other Burritos, like The Byrds before them, were well aware that *he* was the band's mainstay: he turned the offer down, and eventually settled for A&M. The advance was a paltry $10,000 to share between them, along with a clothing allowance, but they had at least been welcomed into a stable which housed The Carpenters, Joe Cocker and Procul Harum. The album was completed in just 15 days. Of the 11 songs, only two were not Parsons collaborations with Hillman or Etheridge: Dan Penn's 'Dark End of the Street', a minor hit for Aretha Franklyn, and his 'Do Right Woman', with David Crosby on uncredited backing vocals. Of the others, 'Christine's Tune', unflattering towards its subject, is about Christine Hinton, Crosby's girlfriend and a former president of The Byrds' fan club. When she was killed in a car crash, Gram changed the title to 'Devil in Disguise', though the sentiments remain the same. 'Wheels' is a modern take on 'Swing Low, Sweet Chariot', juxtaposing Gram's and Hillman's passion for motorcycles and fearlessness of death. It is difficult to discern whether the narrator wishes to escape the monotony of life by ending it all or by merely driving off somewhere, when he pronounces, 'Come on wheels, take this boy away.' 'Hot Burrito #1' and 'Hot Burrito #2' have been mentioned. 'Juanita' recounts the story of the 17-year-old 'angel' who rescues her older, wasted lover from an existence of drink and drugs. 'Sin City' is a drawled, tongue-in-cheek attack on the Vietnam War, credit-free transactions, the San Francisco earthquake and Larry Spector, the manager The Burritos accused of duping them – he who lives on the First Floor, behind the gold-plated door that will not keep out 'the Lord's burning rain'. Brilliant!

As had happened with The Submarine Band and The Byrds, with the perfectionist Gram at the helm, The Burritos began experiencing line-up problems before their album was released. Jon Corneal had left midway through the recording sessions: his replacement had stuck it out for just three weeks, and now The Byrds' Michael Clarke stepped into the breach. Chris Etheridge would walk out in July 1969 and be replaced by Bernie Leadon. Born in Minneapolis in 1947, Leadon had, like Hillman, been raised on a diet of bluegrass, and had played with numerous outfits, including with Hillman in The Scottsville Squirrel Barkers. He will remain best known, perhaps, as a founding member of The Eagles.

Meanwhile, for one who had been 'cut deep' by the 'faggot' taunts at The Burritos' early concerts, Gram sailed dangerously close to the wind by hiring fashion guru 'Nudie' Cohen, who ran Nudie's Rodeo Tailors on Hollywood's Sunset Boulevard, to supply the band with their stage outfits. This hugely extroverted character had been born Nutya Kotlyrenko in Kiev, Russia, in 1903.

A Jew, he had arrived in the United States in 1913, become interested in the fashion trade, and by the 1930s had become the first designer to attach rhinestones to his creations. In the early 1940s he had relocated to California and begun designing elaborately embroidered cowboy suits for flamboyant music stars such as Roy Rogers, Lefty Frazell and Hank Williams. His real *coup de grace*, however, had come in 1957 when he had designed the infamous $10,000 gold lamé suit worn by Elvis Presley: riots had ensued when Elvis had worn this in Chicago and St Louis. No less over-the-top than his creations, Nudie could be seen driving around town in a Cadillac customised with pistol door handles, steer horns and Winchester rifles. Many years later, Gram's biographer, Jason Walker (*Gram Parsons: God's Own Singer*) would aptly describe these garish creations as, 'The kind of suits that only Hank Snow or Porter Wagoner would be seen dead in.'

Gram's Nudie suit would be his statement to society, his less-than-subtle way of describing the kind of man he was to those who did not already know. Nudie's assistant, Manuel Cuevas later claimed (but only in retrospect of the tragedy which no one foresaw at the time) that the suit was Gram's way of saying how he wanted to die: the flames creeping up his legs and consuming him, the large red cross on the back of his jacket which signified his faith, the pills and marijuana embellishments and the naked women on his lapels declaring that he had lived life to the full. Complementing the outfit was a matching cream cowboy hat decorated with large blue stars. Gram was also sufficiently certain of his sex appeal to ask Nudie to cut his jacket shorter than those of the other Burritos – to enable his 'tight buns and man's fist crotch' to be displayed to their best advantage.

The music press, particularly the tabloids, were merciless. To their largely unintelligent way of thinking, *no* straight man would even think of stepping on to a stage looking like what one journalist described as 'country rock's equivalent of Liberace'. A few years later, of course, Elvis would go one step further and turn rhinestones and silks into an art form – and few entertainers came more butch than him. In an interview conducted at the end of 1968, but not published until the following spring to coincide with the album's release, Gram attempted to defend these attacks against himself and The Burritos, telling *Fusion* magazine,

> *They're so uptight about our sequinned suits! I just can't believe it! Just because we wear sequinned suits doesn't mean that we think we're great. It means we think sequins are great! I'm using clothes because clothes are the most obvious*

> *things you can point at to see what a person is doing. And the other side uses clothes, too. Richard Nixon and Governor Reagan see a bunch of little girls in pea-jackets and wearing Onks, and think they're the enemy of educational wisdom. Maybe everyone would be a lot safer wearing sequins! We're wearing them because they're bullet-proof! . . . Country music is going through its fad. It's been affected by the Nehru shirt scene. Glen Campbell is a very, very good guitar player but he's been hyped, ruined, destroyed! So many country artists are trying to pick up gimmicks. Conway Twitty's back! He's better than all of us new country groups because he's paid his dues. He's older!*

But, the editor of *Fusion* wanted to know, had The Burritos been happy recording a country album in Los Angeles, as opposed to Nashville? And what did Gram have in mind as a follow-up? Cursing the city's smog problem, which had been so bad at one stage that he had had to wear an oxygen mask, Gram explained,

> *We went through Hot Burrito #1 and #2, and saw that we had the highly polished musical thing by the nuts. My piano and organ playing came back to where it was before The Byrds. I started getting funky again . . . it was time to end the album, time to get out of LA . . . We would love to have our next album called Ray of Hope. We'd like to find some place over in Europe where we're really happy, where we could write about all the funky farmers!*

The Burritos' record company publicly praised them for capturing so much attention, but privately condemned them for running up such a costly bill. When A&M had given Gram carte blanche to organise their stage clothes, they had not envisaged him spending almost $4,000 on four suits – almost half the advance they had paid the band! Even so, they looked great – though Michael Clarke might have benefited from a tidier hairstyle, a wash and a shave – and Gram emerged from the exercise looking more attractive and macho than ever. The Nudie suits were worn for the first time during the photo shoot for The Burritos' album cover. Witnesses may have been excused for thinking that the band and their team – art director Tom Wilkes, his photographer and technical assistant, numerous A&M representatives, a clapper boy and a pair of voluptuous models – were about to participate in a Russ Meyer epic, or an actual porno flick rather than grabbing a handful of publicity shots for an album. All of these people clambered into a Volkswagen truck to trail The Burritos' hired limousine for the three-hours drive to the town of Joshua Tree, out in the Mojave Desert – one of Gram's favourite spots, which sadly will always be associated with him for all the wrong reasons.

The morning was chilly and blustery when the convoy stopped off at Cap Rock for the first part of the shoot. Just about everyone was stoned, including the cameraman who seemed more interested in the girls than the band, while The Burritos desperately tried to protect the valuable Nudie suits from the dust and swirling leaves. Gram camped it up a lot, strutting around with his hands on his hips and posturing in front of the Joshua trees. The shot chosen for the album cover displays none of this affable humour – quite the reverse, for The Burritos look like they are posing against their will after a particularly nasty argument. 'There were other pictures from that session that were good, one where we were standing in front of a Joshua tree that's a lot better,' Gram later told Chuck Casell. 'So why did they pick *that* one?'

The Gilded Palace of Sin tour kicked off in January 1969, and certainly lived up to its name as an extended orgy of drugs, booze, sex, and poker-playing. A&M had wanted it to begin in mid-February, giving Gram and Nancy time to recover from their honeymoon, but Gram insisted that the tour would *replace* his nuptials. All the plans had been made for the wedding, including the $900 rhinestone gown designed by Nudie Cohen, which Gram had audaciously asked to be put on The Burritos' 'professional tab'. Whether A&M actually paid for the gown is not known: it was never collected, and Nudie kept it for years, displayed on a dummy in his store. Neither is Nancy's reaction towards being jilted on record. She and Polly moved out of Gram's house, but he continued to support them from the Snively trust fund and saw them regularly even though he still frequently insisted to close friends that he was convinced Polly was not his daughter.

For three weeks, The Burritos cut their teeth playing the Los Angeles clubs and high school auditoriums, mostly to unappreciative audiences, but thankfully free of rednecks. Now, though, A&M were anxious to recover their investment, and insisted on the band travelling further afield to play selective, larger venues. Gram had always been terrified of flying: he had coped with the long flight to London, he told one journalist, because the prospect of meeting the Rolling Stones had made the anguish worthwhile. This was untrue, for when he had flown to London with The Byrds, he had had no idea he would meet the Stones. Even so, the return flight from London *had* put the fear of God into him, and he would never be the same again. Before boarding the plane at Heathrow, he had been in such a state of paranoia that a doctor had been summoned to administer a tranquilising injection, and he had remained semi-comatose throughout the flight. Later, he would be taken aboard one plane in a wheelchair. Now, he flatly refused to fly, and threatened to boycott the tour unless A&M arranged for The Burritos to travel by train.

The Burritos were 'chaperoned' by their new road manager (or 'mangler', as he referred to himself), Phil Kaufman, who had formerly been employed as 'executive nanny' to the Rolling Stones. Gram personally paid his wages. The two had met during the Stones' *Beggar's Banquet* sessions: Kaufman later claimed that he had not been impressed because he had disliked country music – moreover, that with his silk scarves and crushed velvet pants, Gram had struck him as being effeminate. He had since revised his opinion and the two had become good friends. However, there would soon come a time when Gram's loved ones and fans would be wishing that he and Kaufman had never met at all.

Equally vital to The Burritos' entourage was A&M man Michael Vosse, armed with an 8mm camera to capture the highlights of the trip – and around $10,000 worth of various drugs to keep everyone content on the lengthy journeys between venues. These included mescaline crystals, a potent hallucinogenic obtained from a variety of Mexican cactus, and one of the few substances Gram had never experimented with. The first time this was doled out by Vosse, The Burritos ran amock, and rather than eject them from the train, the purser – for a suitable fee paid by Gram – found them and their entourage a private carriage-dining room where they could 'have fun' without disrupting the other passengers. This scenario resulted in Gram and Chris Hillman penning 'The Train Song', a chug-along piece which begins almost as a German drinking-song, not exactly one of their better collaborations. A&M's big mistake was in rushing it out as The Burritos' debut single – and unforgivably putting 'Hot Burrito #1' on the B-side!

The tour took in New Mexico, Chicago and Detroit, where the band played in a black suburb that had been near-ripped apart by riots the previous week. They supported Procul Harum and, wearing their Nudie suits, received such abuse from the crowd of hard-bitten onlookers outside the theatre that they had to be escorted in and out of the building by the National Guard, still patrolling the area. In Boston, between 20 and 23 February, Gram caught up with several buddies from his Harvard days – including Jet Thomas, whom he appears to have forgiven for getting him thrown out of the establishment. This was the week of the annual Boston Tea Party, and with Procul Harum performing elsewhere, The Burritos found themselves sharing the bill with The Byrds' new line-up.

Fireworks were anticipated, considering the acrimonious parting of the ways on the eve of the South African tour, but Gram and Roger McGuinn hugged each other on stage, seemingly with genuine warmth, and their four appearances saw the two bands combining, thrilling the capacity crowds. And each time, 'Hickory Wind' stopped the show.

From Boston, The Burritos travelled to New York, then Philadelphia – where Gram hit on the idea of having everyone perform in a turban, each with a different jewelled brooch to match his Nudie suit. Needless to say there was a return to heckling with cries of 'faggot'. It was also an unnecessary expense, charged to A&M's account, and very nearly the last straw: Gram was ordered to curb his spending, or risk the rest of the tour being pulled. His extravagances had cost them a staggering $70,000 so far, and the figure was mounting every day – while A&M had received less than half of this back in ticket sales. Gram reluctantly drew in the reins, but after The Burritos' 6 April show at San Francisco's Aragon ballroom was savaged by the critics, he himself came close to calling it a day.

The album was released later that month. To draw attention to its content and style, A&M hired a vacant lot at MGM and attempted to recreate the ambience of Elvis Presley's 'Tumble-weed' sketch when he had appeared on *The Steve Allen Show* back in the fifties. The idea was to have The Burritos lounging upon straw bales in a mock-Western setting, and the theme was extended to the invitations for the live audience – to each one was clipped a few strands of hay.

Unfortunately, the gimmick backfired when one media representative had his analysed in a laboratory, genuinely believing that the record company had sent him marijuana! *The Gilded Palace of Sin* was applauded by *Rolling Stone* magazine who, having singled out Gram as The Burritos' leading light, called the album, 'The statement of a young man who must feel at home nowhere,' concluding: 'Perhaps Parsons, coming from the country, feels more deeply than most of us the strangeness and hostility of the modern world – but he speaks of it, and for all of us. Gram Parsons is a good old boy!'

Sadly, the album shifted less than 50,000 copies, which was less to do with the quality of the product than through lack of decent airplay. Like the later Jeff Buckley and Nick Drake, Gram's work was not easy to categorise. Nashville did not consider him authentic country, yet the FM radio stations starting to spring up across the United States considered him *too* country for most of them. Shortly after the album's release, Gram left the house he had been sharing with Chris Hillman, and moved into the chic but costly Chateau Marmont complex, where he shared a bungalow with Tony Foutz, a film director friend. Actress Fay Dunaway was a neighbour. Gram was still seeing Nancy Lee Ross, off and on, but there was a new love in his life: Linda Lawrence, the ex-girlfriend of Rolling Stone Brian Jones. Gram boasted to friends of how he enjoyed having sex all the more with Linda because one of his idols 'had been there first'.

Tony Foutz had supposedly been commissioned to shoot a low-budget science fiction movie, title undecided, with Gram, Linda Lawrence and another close friend, Mamas & Papas singer Michelle Phillips. There is virtually nothing on record to support this, other than these four and a cameraman spent several days in the Mojave Desert until whoever was allegedly financing the project backed out. On 4 July 1969, Gram and Linda received a telephone call with the devastating news that 27-year-old Brian Jones had been found dead at the bottom of his swimming pool at his Sussex home. An asthmatic, his inhaler had been found at the side of the pool, and initially he was thought to have suffered an attack, an epileptic fit to which he was also prone, or that he had merely overdosed on a cocktail of pills and booze and drowned. The coroner would plump for the latter, but many years later Jones' companion-lover, Frank Thoroughgood, would confess on his deathbed to having murdered him – though the truth has never been confirmed. Gram and Linda held a wake for the dead rhythm-guitarist at the Chateau Marmont.

The following day, Gram received a call from the Woodstock promoters. Would he and The Burritos like to participate in the first ever free-admittance rock festival, to be held near Bethel, New York State, over three days in August? The Grateful Dead, Jimi Hendrix, The Who and Jefferson Airplane had already been booked for the event which would be filmed and feted as *the* landmark of America's sixties youth-hippie culture. Gram, with his unswerving anti-war stance, would have suited the Woodstock bill perfectly. Rather than make up his own mind, he called Keith Richards in England and asked his advice. When he learned that the Rolling Stones had turned the festival down, in the same way that he had heeded his friend's advice and dropped out of The Byrds' South African tour, so he turned down Woodstock and what, in retrospect, would almost certainly have proved *the* cornerstone event of his career.

At some stage during Gram's brief spell with The Byrds, Joan Baez had heard him performing 'Drug Store Truck Driving Man', penned with Roger McGuinn in just 30 minutes after one of their shows. Baez's version of the song would end up in the *Woodstock* movie, and earn Gram his very first royalties cheque – which he framed for a week before cashing! There were but a few good Burritos moments left. In September 1969, the band entered the studio to begin work on their second album, *Things*. Recording was beset by problems. Gram's heart no longer seemed to be in it: A&M had not unexpectedly tightened the purse strings – and the Rolling Stones were in the United States. Prior to entering the studio, The Burritos supported Bread at the Aquarius, on Sunset Boulevard. Gram had thankfully got over his turban phase: on this occasion his Nudie accessories included a lurid green silk scarf and pointed-toe cowboy boots studded with rhinestones. The audience was a mixture of placid Bread fans and rednecks, and this time there was one 'faggot' cry too many. After just three songs, Gram walked off the stage – and made matters infinitely worse by bursting into tears in the wings.

On the days when he was in top form, Gram produced some pretty sparkling material for A&M which, though not always well received and appreciated then, has since enhanced his legend. He wanted his *pièce de résistance* to be '$1000 Wedding', which tells the story of his aborted nuptials with Nancy. Several versions were taped, ranging in length between 10 and 14 minutes. When he refused to trim these, they were assigned to an A&M vault.

The Rolling Stones were in the United States to complete their new album, *Let It Bleed*, and to prepare for a nationwide tour. For over a month, Gram and Keith Richards were virtually inseparable. A deep bond had formed between them. Gram neglected his own group to hang out with the Stones at the Sunset Sound Studios. When not working, Richards rode pillion on Gram's new Harley-Davidson. Alternatively they spent weekends with Anita Pallenberg and Marianne Faithfull at Joshua Tree, sitting in Gram's car at Cap Rock, half-bombed on magic mushrooms and staring into the night sky in search of UFOs, which Gram was convinced he had seen many times.

As a friend and mentor, Keith Richards was regarded by Gram as a godsend in the wake of the personal and professional dramas of the last few months. Richards also used Gram as a crutch to help get over Brian Jones' death. To The Burritos and the A&M executives, however, Richards was a pariah and a bad influence – for whereas Gram had always been staunchly independent, if not stubborn, now, whenever an important decision had to be made, he always made a point of 'consulting the oracle'. It was courtesy of Keith Richards that Gram ditched Linda Lawrence and acquired a new girlfriend: eighteen-year-old Gretchen Burrell, a pretty blonde actress he had met at one of the Stones' shindigs. Gretchen had just been assigned to *Pretty Maids All in a Row*, the one Rock Hudson film which would never crop up in Hudson retrospectives owing to the increasing number of such real-life stories in recent years. Directed by Roger Vadim and co-starring Angie Dickinson, Hudson played Tiger, the high-school counsellor who seduces the prettiest girls on the campus, then murders them when they become too clingy. Gretchen was his first victim, which is said to have tickled Gram, who later on in their stormy relationship joked with a friend that maybe *he* should have taken a leaf out of Hudson's book and done the same!

Gram also asserted his influence on the Stones. One of the tracks on their new album was *Country Honk* which, though not written by him, so borrows from his Cosmic American style that it might just as well have been. The Burritos covered the Stones' 'Honky-Tonk Women' and some years later the title 'Honky Tonk Heaven' would apply to a double-album of Burritos rarities. Similarly, the Stones gave Gram one of their new songs, 'Wild Horses', which certainly shows how much Keith Richards cared for his slightly younger friend and, unlike most of those about him, recognised Gram's enormous potential. The song was not, however, as has been stated, composed especially for him, and is said to have been regarded by Mick Jagger as unlucky, owing to the manner in which it had been conceived. The phrase, 'Wild horses couldn't drag me away', is said to have been muttered to Jagger by Marianne Faithfull in 1969 while she was coming to after a barbiturates overdose in Australia, so maybe Jagger was pleased to have someone take it off his hands, at least for the time being. Whatever the reason for its ending up in their repertoire, the other Burritos were thrilled about 'Wild Horses', which they recorded before the Stones. Though they had criticised Gram for spending too much time with someone else's band, they felt that he had come good in the end by acquiring something from them which would assure them their first chart success. Gram loathed their hypocrisy and was relieved – despite the fact that he too would lose out – when Keith Richards and Mick Jagger asked him not to release 'Wild Horses' as a single. Suddenly, The Burritos revised their opinion about it. What had once been described as a 'brilliant piece', was now dismissed by Chris Hillman as, 'The most maudlin, depressing song I've ever heard.'

As the Rolling Stones swept across the United States like a tidal wave, The Burritos had a tour of their own to contend with – on a much smaller scale, of course, but essential if the band wanted to pay off the enormous bill they had run up for A&M, currently standing at around $85,000. Gram rarely turned up for rehearsals, but he was always on good form for the shows themselves. One of these took place at the Atascadero State Penitentiary, which housed some of the country's most hardened criminals. Gram insisted on playing there, even though A&M tried to persuade him otherwise. He turned up at the venue wearing red 'ball-crusher' pants, a red blouse, and a pink bush-hat into which he had inserted a bird-of-paradise flower, and was advised by the governor to 'dress down' for the concert unless he wanted to instigate a riot. Gram told the governor not to worry: he would be performing in his 'best suit'. Obviously the man had never seen photographs of The Burritos in action. The Nudie suits and rhinestone boots would have been problem enough, but by now part of Gram's between-songs patter saw him impersonating Mick Jagger, wrapping a feather boa about him, thrusting his ample crotch forwards, and pouting his lips – which he did on this occasion for an audience of no-nonsense, hardened criminals! 'He looked like a cross between a bad drag queen and some country guy,' Chris Hillman later told *The Gram Parsons Project*. 'It certainly didn't enhance The Burritos' reputation.' Hillman could not have been more wrong. The band were not heckled once, though some of the prisoners' asides to Gram – what they would like to do to his 'purdy ass' should he still be among them after lights-out – saw him speeding for the exit once the show was over. Needless to say, he never played another penitentiary!

Gram was so close to the Rolling Stones, and they sufficiently enamoured of him, that he almost joined the band. He was also behind their next important career move, though not one he would be ultimately proud of. As an artist, from Gram's point of view, getting paid for performing had always been secondary to the performance itself – he did not need the money because he was raking in a small fortune each month from his Snively trust fund. Since his death, several of his bandmates have accused him of selfishness because of this – *he* may have been financially secure, but most of them had had families to support. In fact, Gram was more than generous to his entourage: a great many of the expenses incurred by whichever band he fronted, except for The Burritos' *Gilded Palace Of Sin* tour which was covered by A&M, were paid for directly out of Gram's pocket. Even so, he firmly believed that *every* entertainer had a duty to give something back to their fans every once in a while – from the 'dirt-poor' Flying Burrito Brothers to the mighty Rolling Stones.

For some time now, the Stones' management had been accused of ripping off fans by 'hiking' the ticket prices for their concerts. On average, it cost twice as much to see the Stones as it did American contemporaries such as Jimi Hendrix and The Doors. This had nothing to do with the band themselves, who had always left such decisions to others, but they now effected a remedy of sorts by announcing, following Gram's suggestion, that they would give a *free* concert, providing a suitable venue could be found to accommodate a predicted crowd of 200,000. Additionally, they would pay out of their own pockets the 'going rates' for their support acts: Crosby Stills Nash & Young, Santana, Grateful Dead, Jefferson Airplane – and The Flying Burrito Brothers. The consultant supervising the event was to be Chip Monck, who had been partially responsible for Woodstock, and the proceedings would be filmed for posterity.

On 11 December 1969, the Stones announced their venue: the Altamont Speedway, a stock-racing ground at Livermore, some 50 miles east of San Francisco. Pandemonium erupted, however, when the promoter further declared that the concert would take place the very next day! The first obstacle to overcome was security. Rather than recruit from a reputable agency, the organisers hired hundreds of Hells Angels. These had been used before, notably for Grateful Dead concerts, and there had been little trouble. By mid-morning of 12 December, an unprecedented 500,000 fans had poured into the 80-acre Altamont site, and there were 10-mile traffic jams in all directions. The Stones had arrived the previous evening, and Keith Richards has always maintained that Gram was with them. So too did Mick Jagger, in a subsequent interview. Perhaps to discredit him, and once again accuse him of thinking only of himself, The Burritos told a different story. According to them, when their van became stuck in a traffic jam, Gram hitched a lift with a friendly biker who zipped him through the long line of cars – arguably hammering one of the final nails into the band's coffin, for (they alleged) he was making it clear that if push came to shove, he would perform without them. Whatever the real story, by the time The Burritos' van reached the site, chaos had erupted. An 'acid chemist' had provided backstage 'refreshments', which included fresh orange juice laced with LSD, and this was being doled out free to the artists and Hells Angels. Another dilemma concerned the stage itself, almost at ground level. When fans attempted an invasion to get to the openers, Jefferson Airplane, the now-high Hells Angels began beating them with pool cues and baseball bats – some even lashed out with bicycle chains. The band's lead singer was sent sprawling and knocked unconscious during the scuffle. By the time Crosby Stills Nash & Young came on, the Hells Angels had waded into the crowd, bashing anyone who got in their way.

Astonishingly, the violence subsided once Gram and The Burritos took to the stage for their 35-minute set. Their music was quieter, non-political, and seemed to calm the savage beasts. Very wisely, they had decided not to wear their Nudie suits – though Gram still looked every inch the 'pretty boy' in his split-to-the-waist Nudie rhinestone shirt and crushed velvet pants which were so tight, according to one journalist onlooker, 'that you could work out his religion'. They also received a mighty roar of appreciation from the crowd after their definitive rendition of the Bee Gee's 'To Love Somebody' – Mick Jagger and Keith Richards walked on to the platform to join them. 'The simple verities of their countrified electric music soothed the warriors,' observed *Rolling Stone* magazine.

According to eyewitness Pamela Miller, after The Burritos' performance, Gram and Richards swapped clothes. 'They were leaning into each other,' she told *The Gram Parsons Project*, 'Gram had Keith's eye make-up on, Keith had Gram's cowboy belt and scarves on. Gram had Keith's bracelets on. It was just incredible.' Arguably it was the shock of this scenario – the fact that Gram had been welcomed with open arms into the Stones' inner sanctum while they had not – that caused the other Burritos to see red and leave Altamont immediately after finishing their set, while Gram hung around to watch his friends' performance, from the comparative safety of the wings. By now, the Highway Patrol had arrived, less interested in the Hells Angels than they were in spiriting the Stones away from Altamont if the trouble flared up again, whence the riot police would move in. It did, the instant the Stones plugged in their instruments, though Mick Jagger had made it clear from the offset that the band would not be leaving until *they* were ready – after all, this was why everyone was here!

The Stones' set was halted for 10 minutes when someone set fire to one of the Hells Angels' motorcycles and its tank exploded. Those on the stage were too involved with the excitement of the performance to witness the *real* drama: a black youth named Meredith Hunter pulled a gun when one of the Hells Angels began harassing his white girlfriend, and was stabbed to death, while three other fans died in the early evening violence. Ironically, the Stones' closing number was 'Street Fighting Man'. One of the journalists covering Altamont was Memphis-born Stanley Booth, who had met Gram two months earlier in Los Angeles. Booth had been following the Stones around, gathering material for a biography, and Gram had invited him and the GTOs to a party at his Laurel Canyon home. Gram had singled out Booth to 'chronicle' the party because he had given *The Gilded Palace of Sin* a decent review in *Rolling Stone*. The two men had hit it off at once, 'chewing the fat' over Gram's sore throat, of all things. In *The True Adventure of the Rolling Stones* (Heinemann, 1985), the biographer recalled how Gram had filled him in on the 'Parsons Health Plan' – the fact that, in his opinion, drugs cured all ills and guaranteed one good health. 'That's what I tell all my health-food friends,' he had concluded.

At Atamont, Gram and Stanley Booth discovered that they had another thing in common besides a fanatical devotion to the Rolling Stones – they had both been raised in Waycross, Georgia. Booth would subsequently describe Gram as, 'The best-looking white person of the male gender I had ever seen – the first heterosexual male I ever saw wearing running shoes.' It was he who helped spirit the two of them away from the venue, once the Stones had left the stage. A helicopter had been laid on to transport everyone to Livermore airport, where a private plane had been chartered to fly them back to San Francisco. By the time Gram and Booth reached the helicopter – to avoid the carnage taking place about them, they had to scramble through a hole in the perimeter fence, then crawl on their stomachs to the summit of a hill – it was already full, and they were still being hoisted into it when it began taking off.

'Wild Horses' was one of the highlights of The Burritos' second album, released in May 1970 under the revised title, *Burrito Deluxe*. Essentially, having been 'stung' by the band to the tune of $100,000 on account of the tour fiasco and its aftermath, A&M were now seen to be cutting corners. The rushed production resulted in an 'economy' package containing material left over from *The Gilded Palace of Sin*, a few covers such as Bob Dylan's 'If You Gotta Go' (released as a single), the traditional *Farther Along*, Harlan Howard's tearjerker, *Image of Me* – and just two new songs.

The stomping 'High Fashion Queen' was reputedly about a transvestite – or even Gram himself as some perceived him, camping it up as a neo-Rolling Stone, hitting the same seedy club each night to mix with others of his/her kind. 'Man in the Fog' is a hoedown, noisy but resplendent with Carbajal on the norteno accordion. 'Older Guys' is a rockabilly number which starts out like The Monkees' 'I'm A Believer', but soon rushes off into Rolling Stones camp-hard-rock. One only has to close one's eyes to visualise Gram's Mick Jagger emulation! 'Cody, Cody' has The Burritos actually impersonating The Byrds, arguable better than The Byrds themselves. There is also an authentic Byrds song, 'Lazy Days', written by Gram for 'The Trip' – discarded, subsequently recorded by The Byrds, but now re-polished and sounding better than ever. Then there is Bernie Leadon's 'God's Own Singer', the title later used for Gram's graveyard epitaph – the story of the ageing singer, past his prime but still capable of holding his own for the patrons of the downtown bar he has long frequented. And finally there is Gram's 'Down in the Churchyard'.

The remaining numbers recorded by The Burritos during these sessions would, like much of Gram's work with The Byrds, be released posthumously. There was Merle Haggard's 'Sing Me Back Home' and 'Tonight the Bottle Let Me Down', and covers of country standards 'Your Angel Steps Out of Heaven', 'Crazy Arms', and 'Close Up to the Honky Tonks' – itself the title given to a later Burritos' compilation. Also there was an audacious version of the Stones 'Honky Tonk Women' – and a slightly off-key rendition of Sheb Wooley's 'Green, Green Grass of Home', an earlier hit for Tom Jones.

By the time the album hit the stores, The Burritos were all but finished. Gram's enthusiasm for the band had waned to such an extent that he was no longer interested in performing with them. The way he saw things, he had expended far too much of his time and talent on an enterprise which he believed was going nowhere: he had never disputed the other musicians' abilities, just their lack of dedication, and as such was in search of new horizons. His own extravagance while promoting the band's debut album had almost put A&M into the hands of the receivers, yet by drastically reducing publicity costs for its successor, the company had effectively shot themselves in the foot, for it had sold just 25,000 copies.

Now, Gram was plunged into the blackest depression. Had he been an artist struggling to make a living, of course, instead of one of the heirs to a $30 million fortune, he may not have allowed things to have gone this far – he might have put more effort into pursuing his career, instead of just sitting back and waiting for things to happen – not always *caring* what happened because there was always his trust fund to fall back on. He would have been compelled to utilise his talent to its best advantage, striking out for a successful solo career instead of wasting his time on one doomed outfit after another.

Chris Hillman may also have had a valid point in blaming The Burritos' disintegration on Gram's continuing involvement with the Rolling Stones. Some years later, Stanley Booth told *The Gram Parsons Project*, 'Chris had a chip on his shoulder,' adding that Hillman could have joined in with the fun he was having, had he so wished. Phil Kaufman also scoffed at Hillman's irrational comment that Gram was 'just another star-struck Stones' groupie', telling the same publication, 'Gram was their *teacher*. He was their *equal* – not a straphanger. They *respected* him.' While The Burritos struggled to stay afloat, Gram fought his demons the only way he knew how to – his weapons, an over-indulgence of drink and drugs. His doctor prescribed antidepressants, but rather than stick to an authorised regime Gram doubled up on the dosage, mixing these with downers. When his supply ran out, he simply bought more from his regular dealer, Sid Kaiser. Against his will, he embarked on a half-hearted tour with The Burritos, performing mostly in colleges and high schools. The shows were well received, but there were none of the usual post-performance high-jinks. On the road these days, Gram slept alone.

A great source of pride and comfort to Gram at this time was his customised Harley-Davidson, with its coffin-shaped fuel tank and starry-skies bodywork. At Harvard, he had looked forward to his out-of-town excursions on his first motorcycle, accompanied by his 'fuck-buddy', notebook and guitar – tools that had enabled him to evade student drudgery. The new machine was much bigger and more powerful than the one back then. Contrary to what has been said and written, Gram was no weakling: he was a little over six feet tall, well built, and *could* handle it, though roaring around the Mojave Desert without a crash helmet and over-medicated *was* irresponsible.

Inasmuch as Gram hated doctors and never went near one unless absolutely necessary, so he appears to have had an aversion towards mechanics touching his 'baby', attending to minor repairs and servicing the machine himself. This included securing his loose front forks with a wire coat hanger, a quick fix which almost cost him his life. He and an unidentified female pillion passenger were riding through Bel Air – well within the speed limit – when the coat hanger snapped, causing Gram to swerve and his front wheel to hit the kerb. The handlebars gave way, throwing him forwards and smashing his face into the tarmac. For a while, it was touch and go. Gram was rushed to St Joseph's Hospital, in Burbank, where he underwent emergency surgery to relieve pressure on his brain. He remained in intensive care for two weeks, and it was another two weeks before he was allowed home to the Chateau Marmont bungalow. Astonishingly, just days later he was back on stage with The Burritos, which was *way* too soon. The band had accepted a short season at the Jam Factory, in San Antonio, and Gram would not hear of cancelling – he felt he had let The Burritos down too much in the recent past to do so again. The after-effects of the accident had left him confused, and occasionally he dried up, mid-song. He also began having very bad attacks of the shakes which everyone, including himself, assumed must have had something to do with drink and drugs. It was only when he was rushed back into St Joseph's that he learned the truth: the shock of the accident combined with the after-effects of the operation had left him with epilepsy, and his heart-murmur had worsened. For three more years, in refusing to compromise and cut down on his substance abuse, Gram would be walking around with a time bomb ticking away inside him.

According to Chris Hillman, Gram finally overstepped the mark at the end of June 1970 during a Burritos concert at the Bravo Ring, in the San Fernando Valley – by playing the wrong intro, and off-key, to their opening number. Hillman later claimed that Gram's lack of professionalism had left him and Michael Clarke with no option but to fire him – hardly likely, for Gram and Hillman were equal partners in their enterprise and Clarke but a late-addition backing musician, one whose own drugs and drink episodes were legendary. He would die in 1993, aged 50, from related liver failure. Less forgivable was Hillman's spiteful act, after the show – smashing Gram's costly Gibson J-200 guitar against the dressing-room wall. In the autumn of 1972 Gram would confide in the journalist Chuck Casell how he had always been wary of expressing his opinion to the volatile Hillman, terrified that they might end up in a fist-fight. In the same interview he also confessed that, though he loved him like a brother, Michael Clarke had never fitted into the category of country drummer.

Chris Hillman has rarely missed out on an opportunity to denounce the best thing that could have ever happened to him. Speaking to ABC Radio's Richard Kingsmill in 1999, and yet again laying The Burritos' split at Gram's door, he declared that Gram had been getting too far into self-abuse for anyone to help him any more. 'I think his major failing as far as being a member of the group was concerned was that he lacked the sense of professionalism, discipline, reliability and responsibility you must have if you work with others,' he told Kingsmill. This was grossly unfair. Gram's behaviour at this time may have bordered on the erratic, but he was never *less* than the consummate professional, and there is little doubting that Hillman was jealous of his legend, while he himself was largely a forgotten quantity in the world of country rock.

Following Gram's departure, Hillman found himself another vocalist: Florida-born Rick Roberts. His self-composed 'Colorado' and some of the songs on The Burritos' next album, it must be said, showed tremendous promise. Without Gram, however, the outfit lacked sparkle. Bernie Leadon and Sneeky Pete Kleinow threw in the towel, and Hillman left to work on a variety of projects, including a spell fronting The Desert Rose Band – leaving Rick Roberts at The Burritos' helm until they finally gave it up as a bad job.

Chapter Four

Hearts on Fire

The Burritos now firmly behind him, Gram made a valiant attempt to pick up the threads of his life and career. He moved out of Tony Foutz's Chateau Marmont bungalow, into one of his own with new girlfriend Gretchen Burrell. Then he called producer Terry Melcher (1942–2004), whom he had met just before his accident when he had dropped in on The Byrds' latest recording session, sparking off rumours that he may have been thinking of rejoining them. Gram and Melcher had three things in common – a privileged upbringing, the love of good music, and the hatred of their respective stepfathers. Melcher was the son of actress Doris Day to her second husband, trombonist Al Jorden, and had been legally adopted by her next husband, Marty Melcher, who had mentally and physically abused him. An aficionado of the surf-rock craze, he had first recorded under the name Terry Day, then with future Beach Boy Bruce Johnson he had formed Bruce and Terry: they had scored a minor hit in 1963 with *Be a Soldier*. He had since co-written songs with Randy Newman and Bobby Darin before producing The Byrds' 'Mr Tambourine Man' and 'Turn, Turn, Turn', though his tenancy with the group had been a mostly acrimonious one. One critic had labelled his involvement with their album, *Byrdmaniax*, as 'Melcher's Folly'.

Taken on by Columbia as a record producer, Melcher was currently earning in excess of $250,000 a year, and he never took on a new project unless he was 100 per cent assured of its success. He had worked with Paul Revere and the Raiders, and performed on the Beach Boys' album, *Pet Sounds*. Additionally he was on the board of the Monterey Pop Foundation. Terry Melcher was fascinated by the Parsons voice, as was Doris Day, and swore that he would make him a household name. Much of his enthusiasm is thought to have stemmed from the fact that he was also interested in the man himself.

Like Gram, 28-year-old Terry Melcher had recently suffered trauma, having made the grave mistake of becoming involved with Charles Manson, the self-styled 'Jesus Christ Reincarnation' who in August 1969 had ritually slaughtered eight-months pregnant actress Sharon Tate and four others at 10,050 Cielo Drive. This was the farmhouse built for French film star Michele Morgan and some years later purchased by Melcher, who had lived here with his actress girlfriend, Candice Bergen. Melcher had agreed to audition some of Manson's compositions, with a view to offering him a record deal if he deemed them marketable. A hard-headed businessman with no patience with time-wasters, Melcher had dismissed them as 'below average nothing', and because of this, according to the FBI theory at the time, Manson had gone all out for revenge. By this time, Melcher and Bergen had moved out of Cielo Drive, and it was being rented out to Polish film director Roman Polanski and his wife, Sharon Tate. Manson and several members of his so-called 'Family' had turned up here looking for Melcher – though one of the witnesses said at the trial that he had known Melcher's new address, in Malibu – and, finding Melcher no longer here, had killed its other occupants instead.

Melcher had subsequently hired round-the-clock protection for himself and his mother: he later claimed that the stress had driven him to drink and drug addiction. Soon after the killings, like Gram, he had almost died in a motorcycle accident but now, after six months in hospital and six more in plaster casts – and with the Manson gang caged for ever – he was back on track, immensely wealthy and living in a huge house in Benedict Canyon. Swapping their tales of woe, Gram and Melcher became close friends – but only after Gram assured him, as he had Brandon de Wilde, that there would never be anything physical between them. For the first time, Gram had it hammered into him that he did not need to be part of a band and squabbling incessantly. A co-produced solo album project was discussed, for which Melcher quickly acquired backing from A&M – the very company which had vowed *never* to work with Gram on account of his extravagant spending! Some of those who had had first-hand experience of this – notably The Burritos' producer Jim Dixon – argued with Jerry Moss, the head of A&M, that the company might only be heading for financial ruin by effectively giving carte blanche to a pair of hedonistic rebels whose project might never see the light of day. Such advice was ignored: Gram had the talent, and Melcher the chutzpah to make it work.

Terry Melcher was not in the habit of doing things by halves. Recently, Gram had guested on Delaney & Bonnie's new single 'Motel Shot' – according to the husband-and-wife honky-tonk duo, 'off his face' with cocaine and blind drunk – though if this was the case, he had put in a sterling performance just the same.

Little remembered today, Delaney & Bonnie were renowned at the time for their ability to woo some of the best 'accompanists' in the business, including Eric Clapton and George Harrison. The fact that they had hired a man with Gram's albeit more-fabricated-than-actual reputation meant a lot to Melcher, who followed their example by recruiting some of the ablest musicians *he* knew to support Gram in the studio: Ry Cooder, Clarence Spooner and Clarence White. Ten tracks were taped around November–December 1970, but not mixed and completed. These included a much shorter version of '$1000 Wedding', a cover of the Jim Reeves hit, 'She Still Thinks I Care', and Boudleaux Bryant's 'Sleepless Nights', pencilled in by Gram as the album's title because, he claimed, he had had enough of those to last him a lifetime! In fact, Bryant and his wife Felice had been so moved, hearing Gram perform their 'Love Hurts' that they had written this especially for him, along with 'Brand New Heartache'. There was also said to be terrific reading of Roy Orbison's 'Dream Baby'. In fact, Terry Melcher soon decided that there were too many covers and not enough Parsons originals. A&M, who had promised Gram a substantial advance (but not actually committed anything to paper), then dropped the bombshell that they were no longer interested in the project and the album was aborted. This was not entirely Melcher's fault, but so far as Gram was concerned, forever regarding himself as the victim, yet again someone he had trusted and leaned upon had unceremoniously whipped the rug from under him. He abruptly ended his friendship with Terry Melcher.

Not one to give up easily – though *someone* should have taken him to one side and persuaded him to seek help for his now crippling depressions and the accident-related migraines which had begun plaguing him – Gram fronted up to his abject terror of flying by accepting Keith Richards' offer of an extended holiday in England. To Richards' way of thinking, if A&M no longer appreciated his friend, then *he* would put him in touch with someone on his side of the Atlantic who would.

In February 1971, Gram dropped in at A&M's Hollywood offices, sweet-talked the pretty receptionist into loaning him the keys for the company vaults – and promptly filched the tapes he had worked on with Terry Melcher, leaving a note that he would 'square things up' later. At the end of the month, he and Gretchen flew to London to find out exactly what Keith Richards had in mind for his 'Cosmic American Music'. Such was Gram's influence on the Rolling Stones that, since meeting him, they had included at least one Parsons-style country-rock number on each of their albums, and would do so for years to come. Now, it appeared very likely that he would soon be recording his own album for Rolling Stone Records – Richards' only condition being that the studio work would have to take place when the Stones were not recording themselves, or about to tour, which certainly ruled out the next four months at least.

Richards invited Gram to sit in on the Stones' recording sessions and production meetings, an idea which was opposed by Mick Jagger who believed that he and Richards were getting professionally a little too cosy. 'Mick and Gram never really clicked, mainly because the Stones are such a tribal thing,' Richards told *Rolling Stone* in April 2005. There were also personality clashes between Gretchen and Anita Pallenberg. According to press reports later, reconfirmed by both women, the pair hated each other from the word go, though Gretchen did say that on the rare occasions that the feisty Pallenberg was not high and throwing knives around, she could just about tolerate being near her. Gram failed to comprehend the media intrusion which all too frequently marred the lives and careers of celebrities on the British side of the Atlantic – the official reason the Stones had given regarding their decision to leave England for good, though essentially what they were doing was going into tax exile.

Gram had experienced problems with the press just once, when trailed by a nosey reporter – taking a short cut to avoid him, he had been arrested for jaywalking in Los Angeles. In London, each time the Stones ventured out of doors they were pursued by the paparazzi – who were now just as interested in the 'Southern beau' as they were in his more famous friends. Journalists were fascinated by his impeccable manners, the fact that unlike the Stones, Gram could string a sentence together without swearing. On top of this, the rough-edged element of the music press were frequently 'thrown' by his always addressing them as 'sir' or 'ma'am'. Elvis had behaved exactly the same way.

Gram tagged on to the Stones' 'Goodbye Britain' tour, his sunny disposition lighting up the backstage drudgery at Liverpool, Manchester, Leeds, Newcastle, Edinburgh, Glasgow and London. Fearful that drugs would be harder to come by in the South of France, Keith Richards and Anita Pallenberg attempted to curb their substance ingestion by booking a half-hearted cure at a detox clinic – with Gram joining in, he said, for the experience. In April, when the group headed for their £8,000-a-month rented villa near Villefranche – and to prepare for Mick Jagger's wedding, a few weeks later, to Bianca Perez de Macias – Gram rented a plush apartment in Kensington's Abingdon Villas, and reapplied himself to his aborted album. Keith Richards had secured him an audition at the

Olympic Studios with Rolling Stones Records' Trevor Churchill – though when Churchill began deliberating over the financial aspects of completing the A&M tapes and only thinking about releasing an album, Gram footed the bill himself.

Once the project was completed, Gram himself deliberated over accepting a brief tour of the Home Counties to test out his reworked material – then just as quickly changed his mind, fearful that British country music fans might disapprove of his revolutionary style. Later he would regret his decision and tell Jan Donkers, 'In England, they seem to be ready for country music in a big way – but in the main all they ever get to hear is Jim Reeves and old Patsy Cline records, and I think that's terrible.'

Gram and Gretchen joined the Stones at the Villa Nellcote, near Villefranche – finding the place so overrun with hangers-on that Keith Richards, who was picking up the tab, is said to have hardly recognised anyone. The French cooks worked around the clock, never knowing who was going to drop in: Keith Richards' infamous 'round-the-table' meetings would see him holding court to two or 22 each meal time. People would just drift through the gates claiming to be friends, and the security never asked questions. So long as they appeared to know *someone* connected with the Stones, or if they were found to have drugs on them, this was fine.

The group were putting together their new double album, *Exile On Main Street*, in the basement studio: Gram was invited to join in with the rehearsals and jamming sessions. When they were not working, jazz blasted through the loudspeaker system, or monologues by Noël Coward. This was eccentricity in the extreme and the whole circus was magnificently captured by the photographer Dominique Tarle, who lived at the villa for four months and documented every crazy, drugs-induced moment. Though Gram may clearly be heard augmenting the backing vocals in 'Sweet Virginia', for many years, intimates of the Stones denied that Gram had actually contributed to this classic album, but in June 2006 Richards put paid to the rumours, telling contactmusic.com:

> *We were sitting around playing all day, writing two songs a day which we would record in the evening. Gram was intimately involved with it, let's put it that way.*
>
> *He was seeing what kind of impact the Stones could have on an audience and was definitely soaking it up. He would be asking me about rock 'n' roll. It was a two-way street.*

When Gram was not playing with the Stones, he and Gretchen argued a lot. She could not bear being near Anita Pallenberg, and Gram refused to throw kindness in Keith Richards' face by moving out of the villa. Eventually, as the drugs were ferried in, courtesy of the Stones' connections in Marseilles, over-indulgence caused so much friction among their houseguests that the group's manager, Jo Bergman, effected a clearout of all the spongers. Unfortunately, Bergman was unable to distinguish between these and the Stones' genuine friends – and with Richards on a 'cotton-candy' (uncut smack) bender, Gram and Gretchen were among those shown the door. The couple returned to London, where they rented another apartment in Kensington. Gram collected his master-tapes from the Olympic Studios, and was about to book a flight back to Los Angeles when he received a call from his old friend, Ian Dunlop.

Since leaving the pre-Gram Burritos' line-up, Dunlop had kept his hand in with the music scene, but his primary income these days came from an organic farm in Tregidden, Cornwall. Gram and Gretchen spent two months with Dunlop and his wife. By day they roared around the rugged Lizard Point on Dunlop's motorcycle with its two-adult sidecar. On evenings the trio frequented the Prince of Wales pub in nearby Newton, then afterwards jammed the night away, planning a musical enterprise which would never materialise. There was an empty cottage in Tregidden – the owner had relocated to Malaysia, and Gram seriously considered renting the property for the rest of the year. He is also claimed to have undergone treatment for heroin addiction at a clinic in Truro, though there is no record of this, and no real proof that he ever took heroin – if he did seek medical attention for a drug problem, it was under an alias. Ian Dunlop later confessed that he and Gram *had* experimented with psychedelics at the time, but swore that he had never witnessed Gram taking Class A drugs. Having worked out that nothing would come of his plans with Ian Dunlop, Gram and Gretchen travelled to Sussex, where they spent several weeks with another friend.

Born in Bordeaux and four days older than Gram, Rik Grech was an accomplished cellist and violinist who began his career with the Leicestershire Symphony Orchestra, though he will be remembered as a highly accomplished songwriter and rock musician. In 1965 he joined a local combo, The Farinas, playing bass guitar. They subsequently changed their name to Family, and signed to the UK Liberty label before winning a contract with Reprise: their 1968 debut album, *Music in a Doll's House*, made a big impact on the underground scene and its successor, *Family Entertainment*, containing three

Grech compositions, put the musician on the map. One of these, 'How-Hi-the-Li', a pun on the standard, 'How High the Moon', pondered if the then Chinese premier, Chou En-Lai, ever got high on tea! In fact, virtually all of Grech's songs would contain drug references. In 1969, Grech left Family to join ex-Cream guitarist Eric Clapton and Stevie Winwood (the frontman from the recently dissolved Traffic) and formed Blind Faith, though he proved disappointing on account of his drug dependency and was frequently disorientated on stage and unable to play adequately. Soon afterwards, the group split and re-formed with Grech, Winwood and ex-Cream drummer Ginger Baker as Ginger Baker's Air Force. When this group folded, Winwood re-formed Traffic, recruiting Grech, Chris Wood and Jim Capaldi. Grech stayed long enough with the new band to cut two albums, *Welcome to the Canteen* and *The Low Spark of High-Heeled Boys*, but owing to his drug problem was then dismissed. In 1971, he started out on his own as one of Britain's most sought after session players.

Gram had first met Grech at the Chateau Marmont and this reunion, like the one with Ian Dunlop, gave way to grandiose plans. The pair jammed and smoked joints on the Sussex Downs, collaborated on several songs, and there was talk of a joint album. Again, certainly for the time being, these plans amounted to nothing. Gram attributed 'home cooking and good English ale' to his increase in girth at this time. His weight rose by 30 pounds in two months, and even close friends jumped to the conclusion that drugs were involved. He was also suffering from migraines and night sweats. Returning to London, he rented a house in Holland Park and consulted a Harley Street specialist. Tests reconfirmed cluster-migraines, but also a thyroid problem – like Gram's epilepsy directly related to his motorcycle accident. Gram is not thought to have told Gretchen about his health problem, though he did confide in Rik Grech, who suggested that he get a second opinion from Sam Hutt (aka Hank Wangford, b.1940) and put him in touch with the renowned doctor-musician whose practice was in Exhibition Road, near Kensington Gardens. 'If Daniel O'Donnell is the brightly scrubbed face of British country music,' one critic recently observed, 'then Hank Wangford is its guilty conscience, its dark and troubled grubby soul.' Gram kept the real reason for his visit to Hutt a secret, claiming that the doctor was treating Gretchen for a minor gynaecological condition. In fact, it seems very likely that Gram's consultation with Hutt had nothing to do with his illness. In his autobiography (*Hank Wangford: The Middle Years*), and speaking to *The Gram Parsons Project*, Hutt confessed his unorthodox methods for helping drug addicts, and rock stars in particular, who trusted him not to report them to the police, by prescribing 'psychedelic Marmite' – cannabis – in tincture form.

Figuring among his clients were The Who, Grateful Dead and the Rolling Stones. According to Hutt, when Gram first entered his consulting room, a record by Fred Neil (1937–2001), the songwriter best known for *Midnight Cowboy*'s, 'Everybody's Talkin'', was playing on the turntable – though why this should have been here, and why Gram had been present during Gretchen's examination is baffling. Similarly, Hutt claimed not to have known who Gram was until halfway through the consultation – odd, when Rik Grech is supposed to have set up the meeting. Hutt also explained how Gram had told him he was an ex-Byrd, then grabbed Hutt's guitar, which also happened to be handy, and entertained him with a chorus from 'You're Still on My Mind'. 'That was it, my road to Damascus!' Hutt enthused. He also claimed he admired Gretchen's forceful character, for one so young, writing of her, 'I recall a hardness about her . . . but if you're going to have to deal with someone like Gram, you have to be strong, you have to be hard.'

Sam Hutt's 'fee' for treating Gretchen – or Gram – was a course of lessons in country rock. He also later confirmed Gram's alleged heroin problem, of which, as will be seen, there was no substantial proof. Though Gram appeared to be in good shape when they met, Hutt claimed that on at least three occasions he had been summoned to wherever Gram was staying and found him unconscious, slumped on the toilet with the syringe still sticking out of his arm. 'Really terminal,' he observed. 'Really getting himself to the edge. To me that was one of his darker sides, getting as far out of it as he could and everybody rushing around him. It was a very distorted way of finding out how much people loved him, rather than any kind of death wish.' And in the midst of this turmoil, Gram asked Gretchen to marry him.

Since leaving Los Angeles, Gram had not once contacted his family and friends, though with customary devilment he had had others call them to relay a series of tall tales. Subsequently, the last six months had seen him on an extended detox programme, living with a new wife and child somewhere in Europe, hiding in a Tibetan refuge – or, best of all, converted to Buddhism and doing voluntary work in a monastery! Now, Gram contacted his former Harvard mentor, Jet Thomas, and asked him to officiate at the September ceremony. Then he threw a spanner into the works by announcing that this would take place at the New Orleans home of his stepfather, Bob Parsons. Why Gram wished to spend what potentially should have been the happiest day of his life in the company of a man he loathed is baffling. Bob Parsons had done little to adhere himself to Gram, or the Snivelys, over the last few years. Firstly he had married Bonnie, the teenage babysitter with whom he had cheated on Gram's mother – though Avis had behaved as badly, in this respect. Next he had punished Gram's sister, Little Avis, for getting pregnant by having her committed to the DePaul Hospital, a local psychiatric institution.

It may be that Gram, an innately genial, fun-loving person, liked to turn the tables on himself every now and then by wallowing in needless self-inflicted drama. Joan Crawford, Montgomery Clift, Rock Hudson and Judy Garland had all had selfish, megalomaniac mothers, yet largely on account of in-bred family loyalties they had relentlessly forced themselves to contend with the misery. Neither did Gram have any involvement with the guest list. Deliberating over which friends and music associates to invite, he compromised by inviting none of them! The honeymoon likewise was no great shakes – just a few days in Disneyland, after which the newlyweds returned to the Chateau Marmont.

No sooner had he arrived back in Los Angeles than Gram was contacted by Eddie Tickner, an ex-manager of The Byrds who was now handling The Flying Burrito Brothers. Chris Hillman was about to hand over the reins to Rick Roberts, and wanted to know if Gram would like to play with his old band one last time for old times' sake. Anyone else might not have wished to see Hillman again after his reputedly odious behaviour, but as with everyone else who had hurt him, Gram had long since forgiven him. He and Gretchen travelled to Baltimore and he squeezed into his Nudie suit: contrary to what has been written, Gram was not fat and bucolic looking. Photographs taken at the time reveal him to have a slight paunch, and it was true that he had piled on the pounds, but he was a tall man and the excess weight was well spread out. Once they had hugged, and Chris Hillman had doubtless swallowed a huge wedge of humble pie, Gram's former partner began raving about an attractive young folk singer he had recently chanced upon. Her name was Emmylou Harris, and Hillman suggested that rather than form another group, Gram might be better off auditioning Emmylou with a view to forming a duo. It all sounds very far-fetched, considering the acrimony in the wake of Gram's last encounter with Hillman, but Emmylou later confirmed that this is exactly what happened.

Born in Birmingham, Alabama, in April 1947, Emmylou Harris spent much of her early life travelling between one military base and the next – like Coon Dog Connor, her father served as a Marines pilot during World War II. In 1952, while serving in the Korean War, he was reported missing in action but had actually been incarcerated in a POW camp and tortured. Upon his return home the following year, he was awarded the Legion of Merit. Unlike Coon Dog, however, he offered his family kindness and stability, supporting his daughter's every decision.

An accomplished musician, Emmylou played clarinet, saxophone, flute and piano, but always felt more comfortable strumming a guitar. Therefore it came as no surprise to her family when, having attended the universities of Boston and North Carolina, after falling under Bob Dylan's spell she dropped out and headed for Greenwich Village, where she performed on the folk circuit. This was in 1965, at around the time Gram was coming to the end of his term with The Shilos. In 1969, Emmylou relocated to Nashville, married a songwriter named Tom Slocum, and cut her debut album. *Gliding Bird* contained numbers by Slocum, Bob Dylan and Hank Williams but, like her marriage, didn't amount to much. When she met Gram, Emmylou was divorced and living at her parents' home in Washington DC with her infant daughter, Hallie. She had joined forces with local musicians Gerry Mule and Tom Guidera, and was also resident chanteuse at Clyde's. Opened in 1963 and still going strong today, Clyde's of Georgetown was designed along the lines of an old-fashioned American saloon. It comprised a lengthy, oak-panelled bar decorated with vintage railroad posters and original oil paintings, and in the early seventies is said to have possessed an ambience second to none. Emmylou is reputed to have been offhand towards Gram the first time he called her to invite her to join him 'for a little jamming' at an unspecified location. She had never *heard* of Gram Parsons, and declared that if he wanted to meet her so badly, then *he* would have to make the trip to Baltimore. He was also warned to keep his trousers zipped because Emmylou already had a man in her life, bassist-songwriter Tom Guidera. This had never stopped Gram before, of course – he is known to have begun cheating on Gretchen within days of their wedding.

Well aware of Gram's Lothario reputation, Gretchen accompanied him on the train journey to Washington. When they arrived at Clyde's Bar, Gram's name had been added to the makeshift playbill, listing him as 'special guest'. Emmylou had three15-minute spots. Gram watched two of these from the back of the bar, worked out a few vocalising ideas inside his head, then disappeared into the singer's dressing room – leaving Gretchen alone and wondering what else the pair might have been getting up to instead of discussing country music. One of the songs Gram and Emmylou duetted on that evening was 'That's All it Took', a fairly complex number which Gram said she 'sung like a bird'. He later told

Chuck Casell that Emmylou had picked him up at the railway station (there was no mention of Gretchen) and that the audition had taken place in her kitchen, which may have been another of his yarns. He was, however, accurate in describing to Casell how he always directed Emmylou when they were on stage:

She's got fantastic eye contact. She can sing anything you're doing in perfect harmony so long as you look at her. And if you raise your eyebrows when you're going up a note she goes right up on it with you in perfect pitch.

It was this 'eye contact' that worried Gretchen, ignominiously referred to by Gram's friends as 'the child bride'. She was therefore relieved when, after the brief set in Washington, Gram and Emmylou merely exchanged telephone numbers and promised to stay in touch. Gretchen's apparent distrust of her husband, however – and she had every reason to feel this way, when as a part-time member of the Rolling Stones' entourage she had witnessed first hand what some rock stars could be like – had already cast a dark cloud over the Parsons' marriage. Gram reminded Gretchen that at 20, she was not old enough to go into clubs and bars, so he left her at home, though her age had not stopped him a few years before from taking Gretchen to Clyde's Bar. Gram hit the town every night, not always womanising but more often than not getting drunk as he searched for that elusive mentor who might help get his long-standing solo project off the ground. Through Eddie Tockner, the man who had inadvertently led him to Emmylou Harris, Gram met Mo Austin, the head of Warner Brothers' Reprise label: the company had had his name on their books since almost signing him with The Burritos. Austin listened to the A&M tapes, liked what he heard, and agreed to take him on. At long last Gram was in sight of that elusive crock of gold at the rainbow's end.

Gram spent the winter of 1971–2 looking for a reputable producer, a thankless task it seemed. Though he had boasted for some time how Keith Richards had promised to spearhead the project, he now knew this would never happen. A call came through from Reprise that country legend Merle Haggard was eager to work with him. Haggard had always admired Gram's covers of his songs and Gram spent some time at Haggard's Bakersfield home, rearranging some of the songs he had taped with Terry Melcher. Things appeared to be going swimmingly until Mrs Haggard walked out of her marriage after a blazing row, the build-up to which Gram was party to – though Haggard would later loan him his engineer, Hugh Davies. Rejected once more, Gram hit the bottle with a vengeance, and the combined effect of the liquor and his medication resulted in him flaking out at the most inopportune moments – once in the studio, when technicians genuinely believed that he had overdosed on heroin.

In May 1972, Rik Grech called from England. He was thinking of making a country album with Sam Hutt/Hank Wangford, and wanted Gram to co-produce it with Robert Stigwood. Gram and Gretchen booked themselves on the next flight to London, and a few days later they set up base in the Sussex farmhouse where Gram had spent a pleasant sojourn the previous summer. 'Ademo' was recorded with Grech on bass, The Who's Pete Townsend on lead guitar, and Spooky Tooth's Mike Kellie on drums. Then, according to Hutt, heroin abuse sent the project haywire. 'Rik and Gram just got really stoned,' he recalled. 'Rik was so stoned he couldn't get his recording machine to work. For hours and hours he and Gram would get higher and higher, and nothing happened.' Returning to London, Gram rented a mews house in Belgravia and attempted to clean himself up. Sam Hutt prescribed Lomotil, an anti-diarrhoea medicine. 'You take vast overdoses of it,' he told *The Gram Parsons Project*. 'Forty-eight pills on the first day, and decrease them over four or five days. You come off the smack without any withdrawal.'

From his posh new address, and very much out of character, Gram threw a series of dinner parties. One was presided over by heroin-addict novelist William S. Burroughs (1914–97), whose *The Naked Lunch* had established him as a spokesman for the late-1950s beat generation founded by Jack Kerouac. Gram was fascinated by this extremely odd character and had him repeat his 'William Tell story' at the dinner table: in 1951, Burroughs had placed a glass atop his common-law wife Joan Vollmer's head, shot at it, missed, and killed her. Since then he had lived in a male brothel in Tangiers, and when asked to bring a guest to Gram's party brought his boyfriend, Ian Sommerville, who ran Paul McCartney's studio in London's Montagu Square, allegedly to fix him up with Gram – a ruse which failed. Burroughs – he figures as Old Bull Lee in Kerouac's novel, *On the Road*, was similarly intrigued by Gram's adaptation of 'Streets Of Baltimore', written by Tompall Glaser, whom Gram had crossed swords some years earlier at the Ryman Auditorium. The song tells of a man who sacrifices his farm in Tennessee, and his family, to buy a one-way ticket to Baltimore because this is where his wife wishes to be. 'Well, a man feels proud to give his woman what she's longing for,' he opines, before ruefully adding how the ruse backfired when she ended up turning to prostitution, loving the city lights far more than she ever loved him!

Armed with the A&M tapes, and what little had been salvaged from Rik Grech's farmhouse sessions, Gram returned to Los Angeles. His dream of a solo album about to be realised, and with enough signatures on legal documents to ensure there would be no turning back this time, he called Eddie Tickner and reeled off the list of musicians he wanted to back him. His excitement appeared to have made him appear over-audacious at the time, though in retrospect this was merely Gram's supreme professionalism coming to the fore. And of course, if the record company refused to submit to his demands, he had the wherewithal to finance the project himself. Gram asked for guitarist James Burton, drummer Ronnie Tutt, and pianist Glen D. Hardin – all currently employed by Elvis Presley! At around this time (though the interview would not be published until the November) he told Dutch journalist Jan Donkers:

> *I ain't into the whole group thing any more. I like working as a solo artist, and there are a couple of people I like to sing with. If they want to stick around fine. But I think a lot of musicians these days feel that they don't want to be tied into an organisation inside a record company. It's like being in a penitentiary. People should understand, you can't stick together as Billy, Buzzy and Boppy for very long without losing part of your mind!*

Prior to working with Elvis, this trio had already acquired an impressive pedigree. Hardin had worked with The Crickets, and Delaney & Bonnie. Burton had provided the stunning solo for Ricky Nelson's chart-topper, 'Hello, Mary Lou'. Tickner made the necessary enquiries and was pleasantly surprised when Elvis agreed to the loan-out. Rik Grech and Hugh Davies were hired to co-produce the album with Gram. Emmylou Harris – after waiting almost a year in the wings – was roped into a project that, courtesy of Gram Parsons, would set her on the path towards international stardom.

Chapter Five
In My Hour of Darkness

Gram suffered a tremendous personal tragedy when, on the evening of 6 July 1972 his close friend Brandon de Wilde was involved in a car accident in the Denver suburb of Lakewood, en route to appear in the stage play, *Butterflies are Free*. Swerving to avoid a vehicle travelling on the wrong side of the road, his truck collided with a trailer parked on the grass verge and de Wilde was trapped under the wreckage for several hours before paramedics cut him free and took him to the Denver University Hospital. He died shortly before midnight, aged just 30. Gram was devastated, and never really recovered from his loss.

Early in August 1972, 'the Parsons gang' were guests of honour at one of Elvis Presley's shows at the Las Vegas Hilton, with passes to meet Elvis himself after the performance. By the time they arrived, Elvis had changed his mind: one week earlier, his wife Priscilla had acquired a formal separation order, and he was about to file for divorce. Therefore, he was in no mood for socialising. Elvis *is* known to have spoken encouragingly to Gram over the telephone, which must have boosted his confidence no end.

A visit to a casino after Elvis' show inspired Gram and Rik Grech to come up with a new song for the album, pleasing Reprise who had already criticised Gram for having too many covers in his repertoire. Declaring, accurately in his experience, that luck is never on his side, Gram opines in this albeit upbeat number, 'Ooh, Las Vegas, ain't no place for a poor boy like me . . . The Queen of Spades is a friend of mine, the Queen of Hearts is a bitch!' In the September, with sessions for the new album imminent, and with Gretchen said to have been suffering from 'widow's blues' on account of the comings and goings at the Chateau Marmont which rarely involved her, Gram decided to put down roots – though most of his friends were of the opinion that his marriage should never have occurred in the first place. The couple moved into a house on Laurel Canyon Boulevard, within a stone's throw of the movie stars on Mulholland Drive.

Gram hosted a leaving party in the lounge of the Marmont Hotel. Accompanying them at the piano, he and Emmylou Harris gave a preview recital of the songs from the new album. The most popularly received was 'We'll Sweep Out the Ashes in the Morning', a stomping, neo-blues piece composed four years earlier by Joyce Allsup. The theme is adultery: the couple in the song know what they are doing is wrong and persistently say this will be the last time, but such is their desire – 'Out of your arms, I'm out of my mind!' he declares – that though they *want* to stop, they know it will only happen again. The song summed up Gram completely. To Gretchen's way of thinking, leopards very rarely changed their spots, and she must have felt uncomfortable watching her husband performing the number with a pretty young woman – staring into her eyes all the time to give her direction, doubtlessly with no hidden agenda, but giving outsiders the impression that they were considerably more than just singing partners. The Parsons were experiencing marital difficulties, but finding it hard to keep these private. One particular incident made the newspapers, in which Gretchen was alleged to have hit Gram over the head with a coat hanger, perforating his eardrum and causing him agony for several days when he sang. If this was true, then in the wake of his motorcycle accident and the onset of epilepsy, the consequences could have been far worse.

The first day of recording at the Wally Heider studio had to be aborted when both Rik Grech and Gram were taken ill. Grech was already into the lengthy, drugs-fuelled downward spiral of physical debilities that would kill him in March 1990, and now found himself hospitalised with suspected renal failure. Gram had quaffed one tequila too many to calm his nerves and this had reacted with the medication he was taking for his epilepsy: he passed out during the first take of the album's opener, 'Still Feeling Blue'. Gram had written this following his split from Nancy Lee Ross, and even Byron Berline's jaunty fiddle accompaniment and Gram's tongue-in-cheek approach does little to camouflage the longing. 'Every time I hear your name I want to die,' he sings, though he bears no malice now and only hopes she is happy with her new lover. Gram should have received hospital treatment – would have done, had those about him known the truth about his illness – but as such he was merely shunted into an ante-room and allowed to 'sleep off' his excesses, returning to the studio a few hours later to complete the take.

Chronologically, the next song on the album is 'A Song For You'. Bud Scoppa, who wrote a review for *Rolling Stone* in March 1973, observed, 'The song is absolutely hopeless, beyond despair, the saddest song I've ever heard.' It is a poignant, beautiful pastiche within which Gram's voice cracks intermittently, and not inadvertently, as he philosophises the ups and downs of life. He berates those closest to him for letting him down, the most familiar pattern of his life, of course, as he pronounces, 'Some of my friends don't know who they belong to . . . Some can't get a single thing to work inside.' 'She' evokes Gram's tremendous admiration for Mahalia Jackson and Eartha Kitt, black entertainers who suffered racial prejudice and persecution, yet kept going for the love of their art. Kitt hailed from South Carolina, familiar Parsons territory. Gram juxtaposes the two to present us with the archetypal figure who spat in the face of adversity to triumph against the odds, like himself spurred on by their unyielding faith: the girl from the cotton fields, the great gospel singer.

After 'That's All It Took' comes Gram's 'The New Soft Shoe', an oddity inspired by William S. Burroughs within which he adopts the novelist's oft-incomprehensible style of merging the past with the present. Gram sings about automobile magnate Erratt Cord, but no sooner has he explained who he is than he moves on to shopping-mall preachers and the advent of colour television. Baffling but beautiful! 'Kiss the Children' is without any doubt one of Gram's most poignant creations since 'Hot Burrito #1'. Backed by a superb quartet of male voices (Tom Bahler, Mitch Gordon, Lewis Morford, Ron Hicklin) which almost puts The Jordanaires to shame, its theme once more is adultery. A bar-room chanson-noir from Rik Grech, and reminiscent of Kenny Rogers' 'You Picked a Fine Time to Leave Me, Lucille', this sees Gram telling the mother of his children how tough his life has been – but that she should never have expected too much from their relationship because she knew from the start what kind of a man he was. Even so, he is tired of her mind-games – 'One more night of this'll put me six feet under!' – and points to the gun hanging on the kitchen wall. Just which of them he intends putting out of their misery is revealed in Grech's original lyric for the song, which Gram occasionally performed live, but which was considered too strong for the record release. For while Gram describes the gun as 'pointing straight to Satan's cage', Grech had intended the weapon to be 'smoking when they find the rest of me'.

'Cry One More Time' sees Gram brilliantly emulating Fats Domino's usually inimitable style, drowning his sorrows after his girl has walked out on him. 'How Much I've Lied' has him donning the proverbial hair shirt to enter the confessional, so to speak, before begging his lover to see sense and ditch him before it is too late. 'I've been living deep in sin,' he says. 'I don't know just what's right or wrong.' Declaring this to be yet another example of Gram being torn between the moral codes of his Southern upbringing and the immoral show-business world he had been thrust into, his friend Bud Scoppa observed in *Rolling Stone*, 'He realises that both are corrupt, but he survives by keeping a hold on both while believing neither.' The album closes with Gram's 'Big Mouth Blues', not entirely insipid, but another excursion into William S. Burroughs territory that for some reason sees him denouncing New York, through the eyes of a local.

GP was released in March 1973, housed in an attractive gatefold sleeve, depicting Gram sitting in a high-backed chair. His Nudie Cohen days behind him, he wears candy-striped pants and a turquoise over shirt. Another nice touch was Gram's insistence that Emmylou Harris' name should appear immediately below his on the cover. Gram was suddenly in the lap of the gods, having finally realised his dream, though with his customary blighted luck, all would not be plain sailing. Reprise released a single, 'She/That's All It Took' (GB: 'The New Soft Shoe/She'). Astonishingly, both failed to chart, though *GP* has gone on to sell millions of copies, worldwide, and is regarded as perhaps the best country-rock album of all time.

Aided by Phil Kaufman, who once more had agreed to be his 'road mangler deluxe', Gram set about collecting the musicians who would accompany him on a promotional tour now that Elvis' backing-group had returned to the fold. These included guitarist Gerry Mule and Neil Flanz on the obligatory pedal steel. Rehearsals were sparse and amounted to little more than a few jamming sessions at Kaufman's house on Chandler Boulevard where Gram was lodging in the wake of one fight too many with Gretchen. Gram seems to have genuinely been of the opinion that, as had happened at the Ryman Auditorium with The Byrds, it was simply a matter of everyone following his lead. Gram and Emmylou Harris had worked out a set-list comprising the 11 songs from *GP*, and around a dozen numbers selected from Gram's back-catalogue with the various outfits he had fronted. Each evening they were played on stage with Neil Flanz's instrumental, 'Flint Hill Special'. Gram's original moniker for his band had been The Wild Turkeys – until someone had enlightened him that in critics' circles, the word 'turkey' meant flop. Subsequently he had come up with the Fallen Angels.

Gram was convinced, and perhaps a little *too* confident, that his shows would embrace a wider range of audiences than any of his successors – the 'long hairs and short hairs' travelled in a converted Greyhound bus driven by a shady character named Lance, who it later emerged was an escaped convict. First stop on the road was Boulder, Colorado, where six shows had been organised at the curiously named Edison Electric Company, a rock club within a shopping mall. Only recently the venue had experienced problems when an adjacent motel had obtained a noise abatement order: when this had been ignored, the local Chief of Police had closed the establishment down. It had just won its appeal to re-open when Gram and his troupe arrived.

On opening night, Gram's nerves got the better of him. This was a big step for him after two years in the wilderness, and he swapped several of the songs on his set-list, fearful of forgetting the words, for a Chuck Berry medley and ditties such as 'Hang on Sloopy' – which went down like a lead balloon. The audience, many of whom had heard tracks from *GP* on the local radio station, booed. On top of this, a backstage row had resulted in Gerry Mule walking out of the tour in a huff and the next morning, after the Edison Electric Company contacted them to cancel the five remaining shows, Gram received an angry call from Reprise. He was ordered to clean up his act or risk the company withdrawing their support for the rest of the tour. On the plus side, by the time the Fallen Angels left Boulder, Gram had found a replacement guitarist – ten times better, he said, than Mule. Jock Bartley had played with local band Zephyr, and would later augment Firefall.

Several days ahead of schedule, the Fallen Angels arrived in Austin, Texas. Because they had time to spare, Gram put this to good use – he hired the Armadillo World Headquarters, where they would be performing, for essential daytime rehearsals. In Austin there was an encounter with Rusty Bell, a surly DJ who seems to have gone out of his way to antagonise Gram during a live interview on KOKE-FM Radio. Bell asked Gram and Emmylou Harris to define their style of music, arguing that it could be pigeon-holed as 'country' or 'rock', but not both. When Gram made an attempt to explain how he hated the term, and that his music defied categorisation, Bell muttered a few personal comments which led to Gram saying nothing at all throughout the remainder of the broadcast – bringing the acid response from the DJ when it was over, 'Thanks for the worst interview of my life!'

The rehearsals paid off. The Texas show was a resounding success, the 2,000-plus audience clamouring for so many encores that the Fallen Angels performed all the *GP* songs twice. The same thing happened in Houston, Texas, where there were eight shows. One was filmed by a local television station: Gram looks heftier than usual, thought not overweight, sings for much of what remains of the footage with his eyes closed and his head thrown back, and wears bright red nail varnish.

In another show, two of the 'groupies' who joined the band on stage were Linda Ronstadt and Neil Young, in town for a concert at the Coliseum. There was also a new phenomenon – the Sin City Boys, a group of mostly gay Parsons camp followers, so named after the song he had performed with The Burritos – and who henceforth would trail around after him and heckle, albeit with appreciated good humour, until he had performed 'their' song!

In Blytheville, Arkansas, the Parsons' crumbling marriage took a nosedive when the police were called to an incident at the Holiday Inn. Rather than retire early with the rest of the troupe after the exhausting two-day bus journey, Gram honoured the management's request to perform several of the *GP* songs at the grand piano in the lounge bar. Some of the Sin City Boys had followed on from Texas, and the bar stayed open an hour longer than usual when residents began coming downstairs for the free show. Gretchen seems to have taken exception to this extensive interest in her husband and afterwards laid into Gram in their room. When the police arrived, an inebriated Gram pulled one of his 'party tricks' – bunching his massive fist, aiming it at the cop's nose, but stopping a fraction of an inch from his target. The cop, not seeing the funny side of this, laid into him, knocking him to the floor, then beating him with his night-stick before arresting him. Phil Kaufman later claimed that when he turned up at the precinct to bail out his friend, he heard officers still beating Gram in his cell. Gram's lawyer advised him to press charges, but he never did.

Next stop was Chicago's Quiet Knight Club, where Gram earned himself a mighty cheer when he walked on to the stage sporting a black eye. It was here that he and Emmylou performed 'Love Hurts' for the first time, the old Everly Brothers hit which with one fell swoop they turned into their personal anthem. Its heartfelt lyric fitted Gram's fragile psyche like a second skin, and many regard it as the finest song he and Emmylou sang. Written in 1960 by Everly stalwarts, Felice and Boudleaux Bryant, it will be forever associated with Gram. Three decades later, writing the booklet notes for *The Gram Parsons Anthology*, Bud Scoppa summed it up exactly and definitively:

> *Harris's soprano flutters angelically, caressing Parsons' earnest tenor, to heart-wrenching effect. It still kills me. To say that Gram and Emmy made these songs their own would be an understatement.*

It was back to the rough-and-ready element a few evenings later when the Fallen Angels played The Smiling Dog, in Cleveland, Ohio. The audience were appreciative but rowdy, and one section did not take too kindly to the sentiments expressed in 'How Much I've Lied'. After the song, several cowboy rednecks – Parsons-friendly, one report declared, now that he no longer appeared on stage 'looking like a fruit' – fired guns into the air, and there was a catfight in the middle of the auditorium between two 'saloon girls' when one accused the other of having an affair with her husband.

In New York, the Fallen Angels played three shows to capacity audiences at Max's Kansas City – the infamous watering hole favoured by The Velvet Underground and Andy Warhol's Factory crowd. This led to the band being offered a deal with WLIR-FM Radio in Hampstead, Long Island – a 60-minute live broadcast for which they would be granted exclusive recording rights. The tape of this would resurface in 1982, be cleaned up and released on an album, and in 1991 be re-released in its complete, unedited version, exactly as listeners had heard it back in the spring of 1973. Then critics and fans who had never had the privilege of seeing Gram live would learn that if he had been first class in the studio, he had been no less enigmatic in front of an audience.

The album would also help dismiss stories circulated by detractors that Gram had frequently appeared on stage the worse the wear during this final tour, by way of drink, drugs or both. His voice is in tremendous form throughout the set – from the boisterous opener, 'We'll Sweep Out the Ashes in the Morning', to Merle Haggard's rip-roaring 'California Cotton Fields', which closed the proceedings. There is also a refined dig at some of those former colleagues who had accused him of 'wronging' him when, introducing 'Drug Store Truck Driving Man', he drawls, 'This is an old song I did with The Byrds, when I was in fear of getting my life taken away from me.' And if the studio version of 'Love Hurts' brings a lump to the throat, the one here makes the listener cry.

The tour progressed to Philadelphia, with three shows at the Bijou Café. From here the Fallen Angels travelled to Boston, where they installed themselves at the Fenway Boylston Motor Hotel for the week. Back on his old stomping ground, Gram felt more relaxed than he had for some time. Between the five concerts he caught up with old friends and hired a car to drive Emmylou and the musicians around the countryside he loved. Word soon spread that they were having an affair, which they strenuously denied. Gram's intimates went one step further by declaring that, such was his honesty, that if they *had* been an item he would have admitted it, inasmuch as he admitted to a whole string of liaisons at the time.

Gretchen certainly believed the stories which winged her way, and the massive row which took place in the Parsons' hotel suite very nearly led to the whole troupe being evicted from the premises. The drama resumed the next evening, when Gretchen approached the front of the stage while Gram and Emmy were in the middle of 'Love Hurts'. Allegedly deliberately mistaking her husband's 'eye-contact direction' for something else, she attempted to disrupt the performance. Back at the hotel, a show of hands – Gram's included – decided that Gretchen would have to go. Though the tour only had a few days to go, she was put on the next plane for Los Angeles.

The tour completed and with Gram working on the songs for his next album, he attempted to salvage what was left of his marriage. His biggest dilemma, of course, was that he probably should never have tied himself down in the first place, but like his near-marriage to Nancy Lee Ross, it had been born of a moment's impetuosity. Neither was trying to patch things up in the unsettling company of Bob and Bonnie Parsons, aboard their sailboat bound for the West Indies, a good idea. It ended in disaster, brought about not on account of Gram fighting with his wife, but because his stepfather chose the most inopportune moment to come clean about his past.

During a particularly heavy drinking session, Bob Parsons opened his heart and confessed that Avis Connor's death had occurred directly as a result of his negligence – that while she had lain desperately ill in hospital, the doctors had told him that under a detox programme she might live a little longer or even pull through, but that he had purposely hastened the end by sneaking her miniature bottles of vodka. Gram had never hit anyone since flooring a rival during his wild Burritos days, but he later told friends that if Parsons had not dropped him and Gretchen off at the nearest port, he would have *killed* him. The couple returned to Los Angeles, arguing over someone else for a change, and moved back in together. Speaking to Barney Hoskyns (*Mojo*, July 1998) 25 years after the event, Gretchen claimed that Gram had begun having 'terrible seizures' at around this time which resulted in his being hospitalised three times. 'He just wasn't there, mentally, any more,' she concluded, 'and it scared the shit out of me.'

These attacks had of course been debilitating Gram for some time, without Gretchen's or anyone else's knowledge. First there had been the epileptic fits, mostly occurring when Gram had been 'on the razzle' with friends – which they had put down to drug abuse, effecting a cure by putting him to bed until he came around. Then there had been the incident in the studio when he had been recording *GP*, a direct result of mixing alcohol with medication. It appears that Gretchen had never been made aware of the situation either because Gram had not wanted her to know, for whatever reason, or because his friends had disliked her so much. Indeed, some of Gram's friends genuinely believed Gretchen to have been the *cause* of his malady, which was not the case: it all stemmed from the blow he had received to the head at the time of his accident. The shaking, the slurred speech wrongly misinterpreted by many as a sexy drawl, and the slight facial paralysis followed by sudden, inexplicable recovery were, in the words of a hospital spokesman, 'symptoms of TIAs' – trans-ischemic attacks, a kind of temporary mini-stroke, in Gram's case often exacerbated by drink and/or substance abuse. At this point in his life he is known to have been popping amphetamines concurrently with his epilepsy medication – and washing these down with tequila, unaware of the danger.

Emmylou Harris told *The Gram Parsons Project* that she had never been in the company of a heavy drinker before, but that at the time she had been too naive to pick up on the damage Gram might have been inflicting upon himself. 'I look back on it now and think, how could I *not* have known he was in trouble,' she reflected. Gram's singing partner must have been sufficiently concerned at the time, however, to wish to temporarily relocate to Los Angeles to be near him. She and Tom Guidera rented a suite at the Portsmen's Lodge Hotel – a move interpreted by Gretchen that Gram and Emmylou were now carrying on right under their respective partners' noses. Whether Gram actually asked her to leave – according to one friend, because Gretchen's jealousy was 'really starting to fuck with his head' – is not known. She flew to Hawaii for a holiday with her parents, only to become an even bigger thorn in his side far from home, according to Rik Grech, calling him several times every day and screaming abuse down the phone. Gram came to the conclusion that there could only be one solution – divorce – though for the moment his hectic work schedule prevented him from taking matters further.

In June 1973, the Fallen Angels embarked on what was promoted by Reprise as 'The First Country-Rock Roadshow' – a title Gram unsuccessfully fought against using. This was a travelling festival comprising several acts that took it in turns topping the bill. Augmenting Gram's entourage was his friend, Clarence White. Gram caused a minor controversy each evening by hanging a Confederate flag behind the drum kit. Though not as widely covered by the media as the band's previous tour, the shows were reported to have been well attended, with curtain calls after every performance. Unfortunately, the period was marred by a tragedy from which Gram would never recover.

On 5 June, the Fallen Angels headlined at Philadelphia's Tower Theater: Gram and Emmylou were so enthusiastically received that he told the audience their next album would see them sharing equal billing. Clarence White, who had just formed the bluegrass combo Muleskinner with a group of friends, was in the audience, and Gram asked him to join them on the stage – it was a little after midnight, and the guitarist's 29th birthday. Gram was photographed with one arm around each of these precious friends, grinning shyly, unaware that the three of them would never share the same spotlight again.

On 14 July, Clarence White and his brother were loading their instruments into his car after a Colonels reunion show in Palmdale, California when they were struck from behind by a vehicle thought to have been travelling on the wrong side of the road. The drunken driver, Yoko Ito, would subsequently receive a 12-months suspended jail sentence, and lose her licence. Though his brother only suffered minor injuries, White died instantly. Gram took his death very hard – probably because it had come only weeks after that of his regular dealer, Sid Kaiser, and only a week after the first anniversary of Brandon de Wilde's fatal car crash. He attended the funeral, but refused to go inside the church. At the graveside he, Chris Hillman and Bernie Leadon led the mourners in a few choruses of 'Farther Along', one of the last songs he and Hillman had written for The Burritos, and also the title given to The Byrds' last album. Phil Kaufman, also at White's funeral, has recalled countless times how Gram walked up to him after the ceremony and said, of his alleged terror of being placed in the ground, and of not wishing people to be stood around weeping over *him*, 'If this happens to me, I don't want them doing this to me. You can take me to the desert and burn me. I want to go out in a cloud of smoke.'

One might add that Gram was coming down from a four-day bender brought about by his grief – that under such circumstances people say all kinds of things which they would not normally say, and which they may not mean. So far as is known, there were no witnesses to this conversation, which Kaufman subsequently amended when speaking to Jason Walker (*God's Own Singer*): 'Gram and I had gotten very drunk and made a pact whereby the survivor would take the other guy's body out to Joshua Tree, have a few drinks, and burn it. The burning was the bottom line.' What also should be considered, in support of Kaufman honouring Gram's wishes if he *had* made such a pact, was that Gram had been 'deeply wounded' by what he considered the lack of respect shown to Brandon de Wilde, after his death. De Wilde had once told him how, when his time came, he wanted to be buried in Hollywood, so that his friends would be able to visit his grave. This had happened, but then his parents had his body disinterred and reburied in Pinelawn Memorial Park, in New York's Suffolk County, to be closer to their Long Island Home.

Gram paid tribute to this trio of cherished friends by collaborating with Emmylou Harris on one of their finest songs. 'In My Hour of Darkness' is in every sense a hymn divided into three segments, one for each tragedy. 'Who'd have thought they'd build such a deadly Denver bend/ To be so strong, to take so long as it would till the end?' he laments of Brandon de Wilde, while Clarence White is revered as, 'Just a country boy . . . and the music he had in him, so very few possess.' Of Sid Kaiser, whose death he says was expected, though he had not been particularly old, Gram observes, 'He read me just like a book, and he never missed a page,' concluding that he had loved him like a father and a friend. The supplementary vocals on this truly inspired piece were provided by Linda Ronstadt, who was already a sizeable name with two successful albums under her belt.

Clarence White's death appears to have drilled it into Gram how truly precious life was and, momentarily shelving his divorce plans, he attempted another reconciliation with Gretchen. The couple moved back into the Laurel Canyon house and are even thought to have considered trying for a family. They had been here but a few days when the place was gutted by a fire believed to have been started by Gram falling asleep – or passing out – with a lighted cigarette in his hand. His entire Nudie wardrobe was destroyed and, it is believed, his copies of the master-tapes that he had worked on with Terry Melcher. Gram and Gretchen attempted to save their possessions, but were overcome with smoke inhalation. They spent the night in St James' Hospital, Burbank, before being collected by Gretchen's parents, who insisted on them staying with them until Gram found them another place. For Gram, being stuck in the same house as the people he referred to as 'Attila and Mrs Hun' – and a wife he no longer loved – this was the last straw. Phil Kaufman came to Gram's rescue, allowing him to stay in the small cottage within the grounds of his home, and it was here that the shoot took place for the new album cover. Gram had kept his promise that he and Emmylou Harris would have equal billing: they were photographed astride his Harley-Davidson. Hung over the foot-pedal was a Sin City jacket given to Gram by gay fans from Texas.

The album was to be called *Sleepless Nights*, the title Gram had wanted for the aborted one with Terry Melcher, and a term he was familiar with of late. He began working on the songs – a daunting task blighted by health problems and recurring writer's block. Effectively, of the 11 songs eventually selected for the album, aside from 'In My Hour of Darkness', only one was a new Parsons composition, and even this had been part-written by a fan. 'Return of the Grievous Angel' had started out as a lyric poem penned by Tom Brown, a young Bostonian who had *almost* met Gram during the Fallen Angels tour – prevented from doing so because, as he had been about to walk into the dressing room, he had caught Gram and Gretchen in the middle of a furious row.

Centred around Brown's courtship of his first wife (the 'sweet Annie Rich' he asks to scratch his itch in the opening stanza!), the song juxtaposes this with Brown's fanatical admiration of Gram, the 'King' with the 'amphetamine crown'. Indeed, the phrase 'unbuckling the Bible belt' may allude equally to sexual attraction as it does Gram's leaving behind of his Southern connections to embrace the rock 'n' roll drink-drugs culture. As such, the subject of the song – Gram/Brown – finds himself torn between past and present: the calico bonnet of the woman he has left behind (Nancy Lee Ross/Annie Rich) and 'the truckers and the kickers and the cowboy angels' of this thrilling new life which both have discovered since hitting the road – Gram on the tour bus, Brown the camp follower.

With Gram about to file for divorce, and Gretchen out of the picture completely, the recording sessions (at the Wally Helder and Capitol Studios) were relaxed, and Gram felt no shame in letting the world know how she had messed up his life – though it must be said that there were two sides to their story, with Gram messing up equally and having the advantage of better getting his say by way of his music. The song was 'Hearts on Fire', penned by Emmylou's partner, Tom Guidera. 'My love for you brought only misery,' he opines. 'My love has turned to hatred, sleep escapes me still.' The fact that Gram harmonises so well with the young woman he was suspected of having an affair with only adds poignancy to the piece. 'I Can't Dance' was a cover of a Tom T. Hall song. 'Brass Buttons', a companion-piece-of-sorts to 'Return of the Grievous Angel', had been in Gram's repertoire since 1965 – this is the reworked, tightened-up version of his poem, *Pre-eminence*, which had been included in that year's *Bolles Literary Magazine*. Composed in honour of his mother, it recalls her few redeeming qualities as perceived through the eyes of the doting youth, and the items he has retained in his mind's eye to remember her by: the silver shoes, the comb next to her bed, the pins she wore in her hair. 'The sun comes up without her – it just doesn't know she's gone,' he sings in a moment's genuine heartbreak, which suggests that he had long since forgiven Avis for sending him away from home.

Gram had lambasted his wife and eulogised his mother, therefore it seemed obligatory that ex-girlfriend Nancy Lee Ross, the mother of the daughter he now hardly ever saw, should be paraded in his pantheon of personal reminiscences. In '$1,000 Wedding', he confuses the issue by recounting the incident in the third person, blaming Nancy for walking out on *him* – yet he only seems concerned about his child, demanding, 'But where are the flowers for my baby?' Then he sums up the farcical 'happy' event by concluding, 'Supposed to be a funeral . . . it's been a bad, bad day!'

In the absence of the trio of studio songs which Gram had decided not to have on the album – including 'Sleepless Nights', though Gram was insistent that this title should stay the same – Reprise substituted these with 'live' versions of 'Hickory Wind' and 'Cash on the Barrelhead', listed as having been recorded in North Quebec. In fact, this was Gram taking everyone for a ride. The two songs had been cut in the studio, complete with Gram's 'on-stage' giggles, to which had been added applause and crowd noises! Though written by the Louvin Brothers back in 1956, the latter number tickled Gram because it reminded him, he said, of the time he had mouthed off at a cop who had arrested him for some minor indiscretion – and who had subsequently frisked him and discovered his secret stash of weed. Hauled before a judge, Gram had been given the choice – pay the fine, or go to jail. Gram had coughed up the money, but in the song the narrator opts for the latter. After 'Love Hurts' and 'Ooh, Las Vegas', Gram closed the proceedings with 'In My Hour of Darkness', hardly knowing that this would serve as his epitaph. The sessions completed, and with the album scheduled for release at the end of the year, Gram, Eddie Tickner and Phil Kaufman drew up rough plans for a promotional tour – not just of the United States and Canada, but taking in Britain and Europe where, though none of his records had charted, he was starting to build up a sizeable fan base.

During the afternoon of Monday 17 September 1973, Gram booked himself into Room 8 at his favourite out-of-town hangout, the Joshua Tree Inn, situated at 19 Palms Highway, just outside the desert location. This was a cheapish, unpretentious breeze-block establishment, perfectly matched to the vicinity with its wealth of 'druggy shacks' and derelict-looking bars. With Gram were Margaret Fisher – an old friend from his Bolles days – and Dale McElroy and her boyfriend, Michael Martin, friends of Phil Kaufman who had tagged along with the Fallen Angels tour. The quartet spent the evening drinking in the town. Despite his wealth and class, Gram was no snob and had always preferred the rough-and-ready watering holes, particularly the Hi-Lo, where in the past he had often put on free impromptu shows for the locals.

The next day, according to sketchy reports, mostly told in retrospect and which may or may not be true, Michael Martin drove back to Los Angeles to stock up on their marijuana supply, leaving Gram to go exploring with the two women. Dale McElroy returned to the Joshua Tree Inn, complaining of feeling unwell. Gram and Margaret Fisher returned here later in the afternoon and Gram took his epilepsy medication and lay down for a nap. Margaret Fisher stayed with Gram, and a few hours later observed what appears to have been him having a seizure in his sleep. She fetched Dale McElroy from the room next door and, finding Gram unconscious and virtually colourless, rather than summon a doctor they effected an old 'junky remedy' – pulling down Gram's denims, they inserted ice cubes into his rectum, the theory being that the sudden cold would send his internal organs into shock and increase the blood flow to his heart and lungs. This appears to have worked. Gram staggered to his feet, walked around the room, then lay down again. Not long afterwards, he arrested again and this time McElroy attempted to resuscitate him. When this did not work, the hotel manager was called, but refused to administer mouth-to-mouth, claiming he could smell morphine on Gram's breath. Finally, *several hours* after his first attack, someone called an ambulance – but instead of trying to revive him, the paramedics decided to wait until they reached Yucca Hospital, 20 minutes down the highway. Gram never made it.

Chapter Six
Farther Along

Gram Parsons was certified dead at 12.31am on Wednesday 19 September 1973. His was an utterly pointless demise, one which almost certainly could have been avoided on that night, though there is no real guarantee that he would have lived much longer. Since his motorcycle accident in May 1970, Gram may have presented the appearance of a strapping, hale and hearty perfect specimen – in truth, he had been a desperately sick young man. Just *how* sick, only he may have known.

The music press was monopolised by the death, the next day in an air crash, of Jim Croce. Though not as well remembered today as Gram, Croce's album, *You Don't Mess Around With Jim*, had recently topped the *Billboard* charts, and Frank Sinatra and French singer Sylvie Vartan had had massive hits with his 'Big, Bad Leroy Brown'. The tabloids invented a sleazy, undignified deathbed scenario: shot through with drugs in a tawdry hotel room, Gram's trousers about his ankles while being 'serviced' by two probably disreputable ladies. Phil Kaufman only added to the drama and speculation by declaring (in a statement which he repeated to *The Gram Parsons Project*) that Gram had overdosed on a cocktail of alcohol, cocaine, and 'some sort of downer' – claiming that, upon hearing of Gram's death, he had headed straight for the Joshua Tree Inn and removed the evidence before the police had arrived.

For more than 30 years, more often than not sporting his Fallen Angels T-shirt, Kaufman has vociferously 'dined out' on the events at Joshua Tree. 'I've always said that death is a great career move,' he said in a BBC radio interview of 2005. 'In retrospect, Gram's records didn't do too well, but more people became familiar with him, so I think that there's a double-edged sword there – and both sides are okay.' Interviewed for the same radio retrospective, and relying only on what she had been told (she was little more than a toddler at the time), Gram's daughter Polly observed, 'The truth of the matter is that my father was a bit of a renegade and, fortunately or unfortunately, a very mythical creature. I think that mythical creatures tend to go out in mythical ways . . . If he'd been able to choose the way that things went down, I doubt that things would have gone down much differently.'

Phil Kaufman and the gutter press could not have been more wrong. The only drugs found in Gram's system were the phenobarbital he had been taking for his epilepsy. The coroner's report observed that he had mostly ingested this in tablet form, but in extreme cases (such as if he felt an attack might be imminent), by injection – which may explain Dr Sam Hutt's theory that he had several times found Gram unconscious with a 'heroin' syringe sticking out of his arm. A fairly high level of alcohol *was* found in his bloodstream, but not enough to cause him serious harm. The cause of death, the inquest concluded, had been acute heart failure.

While his friends and colleagues mourned him, Gram's relatives began squabbling over his fortune, even before his body had been removed from the hospital mortuary. He had filed for divorce from Gretchen, but his lawyer had not got around to dispatching the papers, therefore she and Gram's daughter Polly were officially his next of kin – but only so far as his properties and possessions were concerned, otherwise the legal heirs to the Snively fortune were Little Avis and Bob Parsons.

The size of the Snively inheritance was never made public, but thought to have been around $25 million, much less than when Gram's parents had been alive, but a tidy sum all the same. And as he had had Gram's sister certified 'unfit', and sent her to live with a paternal uncle in Tennessee, Parsons was hoping to grab the lot. His only requisite was that he put in a claim that Gram had been a resident of New Orleans at the time of his death. He had not, but at some time, for reasons unknown, he had inadvertently helped his stepfather by giving Bob Parsons' home as his forwarding address, and forgotten to change it. Parsons also learned that if this ruse backfired, he could posthumously put in another claim for Gram's New Orleans residency – by having him buried within the city.

Phil Kaufman, who had spent hours listening to him beefing about this man, and who claimed that he had loved Gram like a brother – though the way he subsequently behaved, one might suggest that he had a strange way of showing it – now made up his mind that Parsons would not receive one cent of his friend's money. In principal, Kaufman was acting solely in Gram's interests: there would be no personal gain for himself, just one final display of one man's love for another out of respect of the great bond which had formed between them. Unfortunately, the way Kaufman went about this made for some of the most salubrious headlines of the decade.

After the autopsy, Gram's body had been taken to a funeral parlour in Yucca Valley, where arrangements had been made to transport it to Los Angeles International Airport, where it would be flown to New Orleans. Phil Kaufman, recalling their pact at Clarence White's graveside, called Dale McElroy and Michael Martin. McElroy owned an old hearse that she had bought for camping trips. Kaufman borrowed this, and set off with Martin for the Yucca Valley. As to exactly what happened next, we only have Kaufman's word, though there seems to be no reason not to believe the story he has repeated in countless interviews, and included in his memoirs. Wearing ordinary clothes, Kaufman and Martin drove to the offices of Continental Air Mortuary Services, and somehow acquired the documentation required to release Gram's body from the funeral parlour. Loading the casket into the back of the hearse – it was almost dark and they aroused no suspicion – they drove to Joshua Tree, drinking heavily en route and stopping off at a service station to buy a can of gasoline. Their journey ended at Cap Rock, Gram's favourite spot where he had often slept out under the stars, or spent the night gazing up into the sky, looking for UFOs.

Kaufman recalled – it has to be said unfeelingly, though in his defence he *was* speaking 30 years after the event – how he and Martin had unloaded the casket from the hearse, removed the lid, pinched Gram's cheek and joked how 'hung' he had been – then poured gasoline over his naked corpse and set it alight. 'We looked down,' he observed. 'He was very dead and very burned. There wasn't much left to recognise.' Gram's gruesome, horrendous cremation proved all the worse for his family because it had taken place on his half-sister Diane's birthday. Speaking in Gandulf Hennig's groundbreaking documentary, *Fallen Angel*, she confessed that the event still caused her tremendous pain and that with every passing year she was forced to relive the agony. One may therefore only sympathise with her and with Gram's widow, Gretchen, who had he lived a little longer would have become his ex-wife, and who attacked Kaufman in the same film. 'You just don't take a friend, pour gasoline on him and light a match,' she said, choking back the tears. 'How does anyone with any morals, any *heart*, begin to make a pact with a friend like that? It's insane. You don't do it.'

Unashamed, if not proud of their actions because, they claimed, this is what their friend would have wanted, Kaufman and Martin handed themselves in to the police. They were bailed and at the subsequent hearing – held on 5 November 1973, on what would have been Gram's 27th birthday – were charged with nothing more than the 'wanton destruction of a casket'. Ordered to pay $708 in costs, both walked free from the court. Bob Parsons had his way and Gram's remains – or the 35 pounds of him salvaged from the desert inferno – were interred in the Garden of Memories, within New Orleans' Metaire Cemetery. Gram's revenge on this greedy, detestable man would come from beyond the grave: Parsons died less than two years later, like Avis Connor from cirrhosis of the liver, and *before* his inheritance came through. The 'insanity' order he had had bestowed on Little Avis was reversed, and it was she who received the bulk of the Snively fortune, the balance being shared out equally between Gretchen, Nancy Lee Ross and her daughter, Polly.

For 10 years, none of these loved ones seemed to care about remembering him. He lay in an unmarked grave until – shortly before her death in a boating accident in 1993 – Little Avis commissioned the tiniest brass memorial. Around the base reads the inscription: GRAM PARSONS – GOD'S OWN SINGER. It is a simple epitaph that he richly deserves, for there was no better way of describing him.

Gram died believing that so much of his work had been lost or destroyed: the 'wiped' songs with The Byrds, the A&M tapes. One finds it hard to believe that Terry Melcher did not make copies of these tapes, which for three decades fans have prayed might some day resurface – though it's less likely since Melcher's death from skin cancer in November 2004. The new album, which to his dying day Gram had still wanted to call *Sleepless Nights*, and over which Gretchen Parsons now had near-complete artistic control, was released in January 1974. Its title had been changed to *Grievous Angel*, and needless to say the artwork had also been changed: the commissioned photograph of Gram and Emmylou Harris, astride his Harley-Davidson and showing them a little too close for comfort so far as Gretchen may have been concerned, was replaced by a head-and-shoulders shot of Gram.

Gram's death had dealt Emmylou Harris a double blow. Not only had she lost a dear friend, but the anchor for her career. 'All I could see was the future,' she later told *The Gram Parsons Project*, 'all the great music we were going to make. It just seemed like the beginning and never occurred to me that it could be the end. I had found my voice through Gram. How could I possibly think of singing without him?'

The connection with Gram continued when, while going through his personal effects, Phil Kaufman came across Gram's favourite Martin New Yorker guitar. Knowing that Gram would want her to have it, and without even consulting his family, Kaufman gave the instrument to Emmylou. Out of respect for his dead friend, he even became her road manager. With the passing of time, Gram's singing partner has also come to terms with her then very closely guarded personal feelings – confessing to *The Gram Parsons Project* of how, two weeks before his death, she had finally accepted the fact that she had been in love with him. Moreover, now that Gram and Gretchen had split up, she had planned telling him this to his face the next time they met, rather than impersonally over the phone.

Since Gram's death, Emmylou has never failed to sing his praises, as an artist, a friend, and as a human being. In 1974, their 'Love Hurts' was released as a single, though it is perhaps ironic that only inferior versions of the song charted – Scottish rock band Nazareth's in the USA, Jim Capaldi's in Britain. It had not been written for Gram and Emmylou, but it will remain their 'property' song (it would be Emmy nominated in 1982), and only sound inadequate when performed by anyone else.

Many of Emmylou's albums since 1973 have included Parsons or Parsons-related songs. The first, *Elite Hotel*, released in 1975, contained cracking covers of 'Sin City', 'Ooh Las Vegas', and 'Wheels', and boasted the presence of the same Elvis Presley musicians that had complemented GP. That same year, she composed a song in Gram's honour, 'Boulder to Birmingham' which proclaimed of her sadness, 'The last time I felt like this, it was in the wilderness and the canyon was on fire,' and concludes, 'I would walk all the way from Boulder to Birmingham, if I thought I could see your face.'

The ultimate tribute to Gram, many believe, came in 1985 with the release of Emmylou's self-composed (with Paul Kennerley) concept album, *The Ballad of Sally Rose*. Based on her relationship with Gram and expressing some of the personal thoughts she never got around to sharing with him, this told the story of Sally Rose, the singer whose mentor and lover – a hard-drinking, hard-loving musician – is killed on the road. Harmony was provided by Linda Ronstadt and Dolly Parton, who had much admired him.

In the spring of 2006, Emmylou told Phil Sutcliffe of *Q* magazine, 'I lived with the ghosts for a long time. I embraced them. I was holding onto them not only to make my peace with losing someone, grieving for him, but also to feel closer to him by playing his music. But I think the ghosts have moved on, now. They've got other things to do.'

The music critic Marley Brant observed in the CD liner notes for *GP/Grievous Angel*:

Gram Parsons based his life's work on one honest premise: he believed that all people, despite their differences, should talk, attempt to get along and always try to live in the peace and harmony God had intended for Mankind. Out of this basic belief came the music.

Gram's close friend Jim Carlton said,

Too many people think of him as the shy Southern boy shit-kicker with a slow drawl, but he had an enviable qui vive and zest for life that belied the tragic circumstances of his death.

The last word will be left to Emmylou Harris, who observed in 2004,

In the case of Gram, his work stands the test of time. The greatest PR stunt you can perform is dying young, but Gram would be a bit bemused by all this worship stuff. He'd probably have a good laugh about it!

Gram Parsons Discography

The following represents the known commercial output of Gram Parsons. Unless otherwise stated, all are US releases and appear in the order they were recorded. Guest appearances are not included.

GRAM PARSONS

The Early Years Volume 1: 1963–65 (1979)
Posthumously released album of Gram's work with The Shilos, dedicated to Mrs Parsons, Paul Lewis Surratt Sr, Mike Bixel (a fan).
I May Be Right/ Big Country/ Zah's Blues/ Mary Don't You Weep/ Bells of Rhymney/ Goin' Away, Don't You Wanna Go/ They Still Go Down/ On My Journey Home/ Surfinnanny/ Oh, Didn't They Crucify My Lord
(LP) SIERRA/BRIAR SRS 8702

Another Side of This Life (2000)
Subtitled: The Lost Recordings of Gram Parsons 1965–6.
Codine/ Wheel of Fortune/ Another Side of This Life/ High Flyin' Bird/ November Nights/ Zah's Blues/ Reputation/ That's the Bag I'm In/ Willie Jean/ They Still Go Down/ Pride of Man/ The Last Thing on My Mind/ Hey Nellie, Nellie/ She's the Woman I Love/ Good Time Music/ Brass Buttons/ I Just Can't Take it Anymore/ Searchin'/ Candy Man
(CD) SUNDAZED MUSIC SC 11092

GRAM PARSONS AND THE INTERNATIONAL SUBMARINE BAND

The Russians Are Coming! The Russians Are Coming!/ Truck Driving Man (1966)
(Single) ASCOT 2218
Sum Up Broke/ One Day Week (1967).
(Single) COLUMBIA 43935

Safe at Home (1967)
*Blue Eyes/ I Must Be Somebody Else You've Known/ A Satisfied Mind/ Medley: Folsom Prison Blues & That's All Right Mama/ Miller's Cave/ I Still Miss Someone/ Luxury Liner/ Strong Boy/ Do You Know How it Feels to Be Lonesome/ Knee Deep in the Blues**
* added for CD reissue of 2004
(LP) LHI RECORDS LHI (S) 12001

Luxury Liner/ Blue Eyes (1967)
(Single) LHI RECORDS LHI 1205
Miller's Cave/ I Must Be Somebody Else You've Known (1968)
(Single) LHI RECORDS LHI 1217

GRAM PARSONS AND THE BYRDS

*You Ain't Goin' Nowhere/ Artificial Energy** 1968
(Single) COLUMBIA 44499
* Gram sings on the A-side only

Sweetheart of the Rodeo (1968)
You Ain't Goin' Nowhere/ I Am a Pilgrim/ The Christian Life/ You Don't Miss Your Water/ You're Still on My Mind/ Pretty Boy Floyd/ Hickory Wind/ One Hundred Years From Now/ Blue Canadian Rockies/ Life in Prison/ Nothing Was Delivered/ You Got a Reputation/ Lazy Days/ Pretty Polly/ The Christian Life (Take #11)*/ *Life in Prison* (Take 11)*/ *You're Still on My Mind* (Take #43)*/ *One Hundred Years From Now* (Take #2)*/ *All I Have Is Memories* (instrumental)
(LP) COLUMBIA CS9670
* added to reissue of 1997 CK 65150

Pretty Boy Floyd/ I Am A Pilgrim (1968)
(Single) COLUMBIA 44643

*Bad Night at the Whiskey/ Drug Store Truck Driving Man** (1969)
(Single) COLUMBIA 44746
* B-side only co-written with Gram

Dr Byrds and Mr Hyde (1968)
Compilation, includes *Drug Store Truck Driving Man*
(LP) COLUMBIA CS9755

The Byrds (1990)
4-CD boxed set which includes several out-takes from the *Sweetheart of the Rodeo* sessions with Gram's vocals on:
The Christian Life/ One Hundred Years From Now/ You Don't Miss Your Water/ Reputation/ Lazy Days
COLUMBIA 44773

GRAM PARSONS AND THE FLYING BURRITO BROTHERS

The Train Song/ Hot Burrito #1 (1969)
(Single) A&M 1067
If You Gotta Go, Go Now/ Cody, Cody (1969)
(Single) A&M 1166

The Gilded Palace of Sin (1969)
Christine's Tune (Devil in Disguise)/ Sin City/ Do Right Woman/ Dark End of the Street/ Wheels/ My Uncle/ Juanita/ Hot Burrito #1/ Hot Burrito #2/ Do You Know How it Feels?/ Hippy Boy
(LP) A&M 4175

Burrito Deluxe (1970)
Lazy Days/ Image of Me/ High Fashion Queen/ If You Gotta Go, Go Now/ Man in the Fog/ Farther Along/ Older Guys/ Cody, Cody/ God's Own Singer/ Down in the Churchyard/ Wild Horses
(LP) A&M 4258

Down in the Churchyard/ Older Guys (1970)
(Single) A&M 1189

Close Up to the Honky Tonks (1974)
Compilation, plus previously unreleased material: *Close Up to the Honky Tonks/ Sing Me Back Home/ To Love Somebody/ Here Tonight* (sung by Gene Clark)
(LP) A&M 3631

Sleepless Nights (1976)
Compilation of rarities, issued under the title he wanted for his second solo album.

Gram with the Flying Burrito Brothers: *Tonight the Bottle Let Me Down/ Sing Me Back Home/ Your Angel Steps Out of Heaven/ Crazy Arms/ Close Up to the Honky Tonks/ Together Again/ Honky-Tonk Women/ Green, Green Grass of Home/ Dim Lights*

Gram with the Fallen Angels: *Brand New Heartache/ Sleepless Nights/ The Angels Rejoiced Last Night*
(LP) A&M 4578

Dim Lights, Thick Smoke and Loud Music (1987)
Compilation
(LP) EDSEL ED197

Farther Along: The Best of the Burrito Brothers (1988)
Christine's Tune/ Sin City/ Do Right Woman/ Dark End of the Street/ Wheels/ Juanita/ Hot Burrito #1/ Hot Burrito #2/ Do You Know How it Feels/ Break My Mind/ Farther Along/ Cody, Cody/ God's Own Singer/ Wild Horses/ Dim Lights/ Just Because/ Six Days On The Road/ To Love Somebody/ Close Up to the Honky Tonks/ Sing Me Back Home/ I Shall Be Released
(CD) A&M 5216

Hot Burritos: The Flying Burritos Anthology (2000)
Featuring Gram: *Christine's Tune/ Sin City/ Do Right Woman/ Dark End of the Street/ My Uncle/ Wheels/ Juanita/ Hot Burrito #1; Hot Burrito #2/ Do You Know How it Feels/ Hippie Boy/ The Train Song/ Lazy Days/ Image of Me/ High Fashion Queen/ If You Gotta Go, Go Now/ Man in the Fog/ Farther Along/ Older Guys/ Cody, Cody/ God's Own Singer/ Down in the Churchyard/ Wild Horses/ Six Days on the Road/ Close Up the Honky Tonks/ Break My Mind/ Dim Lights/ Sing Me Back Home/ Tonight the Bottle Let Me Down/ To Love Somebody/ White Line Fever*
Featuring Rick Roberts: *Colorado/ Hand to Mouth/ Tried So Hard/ Just Can't Be/ To Ramona/ Four Days Of Rain/ Can You Hear Me Calling/ All Alone/ Why Are You Crying/ Ain't That a Lot of Love* (live)/ *Losing Game* (live)
(2 CDs) A&M 069-490-610-2

Out of the Blue (1996)
Sing Me Back Home/ Hot Burrito #2/ Break My Mind/ Dark End of the Street/ Cody, Cody/ Wheels/ Hot Burrito #1/ Sin City/ Do Right Woman/ God's Own Singer/ Older Guys/ Train Song/ Lazy Day/ Christine's Tune/ Close Up the Honky Tonks/ Do You Know How it Feels/ High Fashion Queen/ Man in the Fog/ To Love Somebody/ My Uncle/ Hippie Boy/ Juanita/ Image Of Me/ Farther Along/ If You Gotta Go/ Bonie Moronie/ Six Day on the Road/ Wild Horses/ Down in the Churchyard/ Wake Up Little Susie/ Pick Me Up On Your Way/ Just Because/ Lodi/

Money Honey/ I Shall Be Released/ White Line Fever/ Ain't That a Lot of Love/ Don't Fight It/ Losing Game/ Tried So Hard/ All Alone/ One Hundred Years From Now
(CDs) A&M 540408-22

GRAM PARSONS: SOLO PROJECTS

Cosmic American Music: The Rehearsal Tapes (1995)
Various recordings, part-songs, jamming sessions etc, of varying quality
A Song For You/ Kentucky Blues/ Streets of Baltimore/ Folsom Prison Blues/ Lovesick Blues/ The New Soft Shoe/ How Much I've Lied/ Still Feeling Blue (part & full-versions)/ *Ain't No Beatle, Ain't No Rolling Stone/ Medley/ How Can I Forget You/ Cry One More Time/ A Song for You/ Streets of Baltimore/ That's All it Took/ Somebody's Back in Town/ More and More/ Teaching Emmy To Sweep Out the Ashes/ Daddy's Fiddle/ We'll Sweep Out the Ashes in the Morning/ Cold, Cold Heart/ That's All it Took/ A Song for You*
(CD) SUNDOWN/ MAGNUM MUSIC GROUP CDSD 077
Re-released 2003 by Cowboy Music under the title, **Gram Parsons: The Lost Recordings**

GRAM PARSONS AND EMMYLOU HARRIS

GP (1973)
Still Feeling Blue/ We'll Sweep Out the Ashes in the Morning/ A Song for You/ Streets of Baltimore/ She/ That's All it Took/ The New Soft Shoe/ Kiss the Children/ Cry One More Time/ How Much I've Lied/ Big Mouth Blues
(LP) REPRISE 2123

She/ That's All it Took (1973)
(Single) REPRISE 1139
Cry One More Time/ Streets of Baltimore (1973)
(Promotional single) REPRISE PRO-557
The New Soft Shoe/ She (1973)
(Single) REPRISE K14245 (United Kingdom only).

GRAM PARSONS, EMMYLOU HARRIS AND THE FALLEN ANGELS

Love Hurts/ In My Hour of Darkness (1974)
(Single) REPRISE 1192

Grievous Angel (1974)
Return of the Grievous Angel/ Hearts on Fire/ I Can't Dance/ Brass Buttons/ $1000 Wedding/ Medley: Cash on the Barrelhead & Hickory Wind/ Love Hurts/ Ooh, Las Vegas/ In My Hour of Darkness*
* Credited *Live in Quebec* but actually a studio recording with audience embellishments
(LP) REPRISE MS 2171

Return of the Grievous Angel (alternative take)/ *Hearts On Fire* (1981)
(Single) WARNER BROTHERS 5001

Gram Parsons and the Fallen Angels: Live 1973 (1982)
The performance given for Long Island's WLIR-FM Radio 13 March 1973
We'll Sweep Out the Ashes in the Morning/ Country Baptizing/ Drug Store Truck Driving Man/ Big Mouth Blues/ The New Soft Shoe/ Cry One More Time/ Streets of Baltimore/ That's All it Took/ Love Hurts/ California Cotton Fields/ Six Days on the Road/ Bony Moronie/ Forty Days/ Almost Grown
(LP) SIERRA RECORDS 6003

Love Hurts/ The New Soft Shoe (both live) (1983)
(Single) SIERRA/ BRIAR GP105

Warm Evenings, Pale Mornings, Bottled Blues 1963–73 (1991)
A compilation album covering Gram's career from The Shilos to the Fallen Angels
Zah's Blues/ Blue Eyes/ Strong Boy/ Truck Driving Man/ Hickory Wind/ The Christian Life/ Reputation/ One Hundred Years From Now/ Hot Burrito #1/ Christine's Tune/ Sin City/ The Dark End of the Street/ Wild Horses/ She/ The New Soft Shoe/ We'll Sweep Out the Ashes in the Morning/ Brass Buttons/ Return of the Grievous Angel/ Drug Store Truck Driving Man/ Brand New Heartache/ Love Hurts
(CD) RAVEN RECORDS (Australia) RVCD-24

The Gram Parsons Anthology 2001

Gram and the International Submarine Band:

Blue Eyes/ Luxury Liner/ Do You Know How it Feels to Be Lonesome/ I Must Be Somebody Else You've Known/ Miller's Cave/ Knee Deep in the Blues

Gram and The Byrds:

Hickory Wind/ You're Still on My Mind/ The Christian Life/ You Don't Miss Your Water/ One Hundred Years From Now

Gram and the Flying Burrito Brothers:

Christine's Tune/ Sin City/ Do Right Woman/ Dark End of the Street/ Wheels/ Juanita/ Hot Burrito #1/ Hot Burrito #2/ High Fashion Queen/ Older Guys/Cody, Cody/ Wild Horses/ Sing Me Back Home/ To Love Somebody.

Gram, Emmylou Harris and the Fallen Angels:

Still Feeling Blue/ We'll Sweep Out the Ashes in the Morning/ A Song for You/ Streets of Baltimore/ She/ The New Soft Shoe/ Kiss the Children/ How Much I've Lied/ Drug Store Truck Driving Man/ That's All it Took/ California Cotton Fields/ Return of the Grievous Angel (remix)/ *Hearts on Fire/ Brass Buttons/ $1000 Wedding/ Love Hurts/ Ooh Las Vegas/ In My Hour of Darkness/ Brand New Heartache/ Sleepless Nights/ The Angels Rejoiced Last Night*

(2 CDs) WARNER BROTHERS/RHINO 8122-76780-2

The Complete Reprise Sessions (2006)

Promoted as, '3 discs celebrating Gram Parsons' 2 highly acclaimed solo albums, containing 16 never-before-heard alternate takes from **GP** and **Grievous Angel**, plus a rare radio interview with Gram and Emmylou Harris

Disc One: contains all the songs from **GP**, plus: *Love Hurts/ Sin City* (live on WBCN RADIO) and interview with Maxine Sartori

Disc Two: contains all the songs from **Grievous Angel**, plus: *Return of the Grievous Angel* (instrumental) and interview with Gram

Disc Three: contains alternate takes from both albums:

She/ That's All It Took/ Still Feeling Blue/ Kiss The Children/ Streets of Baltimore/ We'll Sweep Out the Ashes in the Morning/ The New Soft Shoe/ Return of the Grievous Angel/ In My Hour of Darkness/ Ooh Las Vegas/ I Can't Dance/ Sleepless Nights/ Love Hurts/ Brass Buttons/ Hickory Wind/ Brand New Heartache/ The Angels Rejoiced Last Night

(3 CDs) WARNER BROTHERS/ RHINO R2 74669

Nick Drake:

Fame is Like a Fruit Tree

'Nick Drake's songs are whispered poems. Their profound charm, composed in hues where humour and emotion vaguely conflict, is out of this world.'

Herve Muller, *Best-France*, 1972

Chapter Seven

One of These Things First

He was born Nicholas Rodney Drake on 19 June 1948, at the Dufferin Hospital in Rangoon, Burma. His father, Rodney, had emigrated from England to Burma to take up a senior position with the Bombay–Burma Trading Corporation, then one of the world's leading exporters of teak, and had married Mary (Molly) Lloyd in 1937.

To describe the Drakes as privileged may be an understatement. These were the days when a white Westerner was waited on hand and foot by a coterie of native servants. Rodney and Molly had stayed in Rangoon until the Japanese invasion of 1942, from where they had been evacuated to Lahore, in Pakistan. Here, two years later, Nick's elder sister, Gabrielle – later a successful actress – had been born.

The Drakes returned to Rangoon upon its liberation, and stayed here until 1950, when Rodney was appointed manager of his company's office in Bombay – a position he held but for a few months before uprooting his family and the children's Burmese nanny to England, where he was taken on by the Wolseley Engineering Company, in Birmingham. England was recovering from the hardships of the war, rationing was still in force, but for Rodney Drake there was no compromise: for years, he had been accustomed to luxury and he put down roots at Far Leys, a large Edwardian mansion-style house on the edge of Tanworth-in-Arden, a sleepy village in the Warwickshire hills, south of Birmingham and some 12 miles from Stratford-upon-Avon.

On the face of it, Nick's was a happy childhood. He attended the local primary school, next to the church, but only until March 1953. Then he was dispatched to join sister Gabrielle at Hurst House, a pre-prep school at Henley-in-Arden. Though this was within very easy travelling distance from Far Leys, the children boarded. It was an establishment that, if contemporary reports are anything to go by, was not far removed from the Dickensian discipline of Wackford Squeers – save that those preaching the maxim, 'Spare the rod and spoil the child', were mostly no-nonsense spinsters. No small wonder then that the child grew up to be a mixed-up young man, and that he counted the minutes to the weekends and school holidays when he could come home to his mother – at this stage in his life he was very definitely a mother's boy, though this was a trait which would cause him great psychological problems in the future. In adulthood, Nick's parents would have absolutely no idea how to relate to him, being more concerned with their social standing and reputation than they were about him. Yet as will be seen, in an impossible-to-live with, impossible-to-live-without situation, while Nick would find his mother's over-cosseting oppressive, he would still keep returning home and letting her selfishly control him.

In April 1957, two months before his ninth birthday, as per family tradition (Gabrielle had already been enrolled at the Wycombe Abbey School for Girls), Nick was dispatched to the Eagle House Preparatory School, situated in the grounds of Wellington College, Sandhurst, in Berkshire. Over a hundred miles from his home, there was now no question of his coming home on weekends. During the next four years he fared well with his lessons, and as he entered his teens in the then boys-only establishment, he developed into a very tall, strapping sportsman who excelled at athletics and rugby. He was also a member of the chapel choir, though he does not appear to have been interested in music just yet.

In December 1961, having passed his Common Entrance exam, Nick left Eagle House and returned to Far Leys for the Christmas holidays. Three weeks later, he followed in his father's and grandfather's footsteps – and those of celebrated alumni John Betjeman, Siegfried Sassoon, Francis Chichester and master-spy Anthony Blunt – by enrolling at Marlborough College, in Wiltshire. 'An institution where the sensitive experienced a horrific disassociation with reality that sometimes never fades away,' was how he would denounce the establishment some years later.

Disliking his surroundings did not prevent Nick from doing well at Marlborough. Towards the end of his stay here he captained the rugby team, became a prefect, then head boy. He set the school record for the 100 yards sprint, going on to take the title in the Wiltshire Athletics Championships. He trod the boards as an actor, and took up music, excelling at the saxophone, clarinet and piano. In December 1964, asked to play in the end of term concert, he raised eyebrows when he eschewed the usual festive fare for a piano version of Bukka White's 'Parchman Farm Blues'. Years later, this ode to racial brutality within the infamous US state penitentiary would be performed by Gram Parsons and covered by Jeff Buckley.

When the Beatles arrived on the scene, Nick was immediately smitten and asked his parents to buy him a guitar for his birthday. The Drakes complied, rather hoping that this might be a passing phase: in their classical world (by now, Far Leys had its own music room and both Molly and Rodney were composing songs), guitars were very definitely not on the agenda. Nick had learned to play his other instruments with extraordinary speed and dexterity, and he did so again, eventually buying himself a good quality acoustic guitar. Within a week he had mastered the basic chords, and after just three months he had perfected the elaborate finger-picking (he never used a pick) technique that in years to come even some of the finest rock guitarists would attempt, but fail, to emulate.

It was the Beatles, and not the cheap guitar the Drakes had bought Nick, that would prove a passing phase as he turned his attention to Bob Dylan, Bert Jansch and Zoot Money – with a dash of John Coltrane, Django Reinhardt and Odetta thrown in for good measure. In common with Gram Parsons, his favourite Odetta song was 'All the Pretty Little Horses', which he is known to have sung at some stage, but it seems he did not commit to tape. Girls, it appears, were not on his curriculum and never really would be. After a hard day's study or a sweaty session on the rugby field or athletics track, Nick preferred under-age drinking at the local pub with his equally posh pals – at least one of whom is known to have been amorously involved with him, though where relationships were concerned, he kept the details to himself at the time. Despite what has been written, according to his French lover, Michel (of whom more later), Nick confessed that he had never had problems coming to terms with his sexuality. 'Of course women *interested* me,' he told Michel, 'but never in that way, never in a sexual sense!'

It was, perhaps, inevitable that Nick should form his own group. The Perfumed Gardeners (so-named after the erotic tome) comprised his best friend Simon Crocker on drums, Johnny Glempster and Randall Keynes on guitars, and Nick on just about everything, including vocals. Like many introverted stars – notably Morrissey, Freddie Mercury and French icon, Barbara, of whom more later – once Nick stepped on to a podium, certainly in his formulative years when there were musicians on stage with him offering moral support, his shyness magically disappeared. In a way, he was a combination of all three, his character a something of a juxtaposition of Morrissey's acerbic wit, Freddie's imperious and clipped colonial accent, and Barbara's mystique. A great fan of troubadours Barbara, Jacques Brel, Georges Brassens and Boris Vian, one might have expected his repertoire to consist of *chansons* adapted into English. In fact, The

Perfumed Gardeners' repertoire was as way out of their individual musical niches as could be imagined. Nick may have loved to entertain a promenade audience with Beethoven's *Moonlight Sonata* and the occasional Scott Joplin rag if he was feeling in a lively mood, but with his group a typical evening's entertainment would include 'set-pieces' such as The Supremes' 'You Can't Hurry Love' and the Rolling Stones' 'Not Fade Away'. The fact that there were few complaints from the audience amused him. In a BBC television documentary of 1998 (*Picture This*), Gabrielle Drake would read a letter which Nick had sent to his parents, and closed, 'The fact the ninety per cent of all Marlburians are musical ignorami is certainly helpful at times!'

Although at first Nick did well academically at Marlborough, his increasing involvement with music led to him doing badly in his A-levels. Hoping for three grade As in English, History and Latin Translation – and having jumped the gun by not waiting for the results and already applying for a place to read English at Fitzwilliam College, Cambridge – he was shocked to learn that he had been given an E, a D, and a Fail respectively.

In 1965, the height of the Swinging Sixties – sometimes staying with friends, or with Gabrielle – Nick and his pals discovered the nocturnal delights of Soho. These excursions were more fun, however, during term time when they would sneak out of Marlborough after dinner, and return before breakfast – exhausted, and running the risk of getting caught and being expelled. Though they could easily afford the fare, they hitched rides there and back for the sheer thrill of it all, and mixed with the cream of the permissive society.

Of the music hot spots, Flamingo and the Marquee were Nick's favourites. This was the time when the Beatles, Stones, Yardbirds, Kinks and the Spencer Davis Group were crowding the nation's airwaves and dominating the pop charts, though the contemporary artists who inspired Nick most of all were Georgie Fame, the now forgotten Graham Bond Organisation and Chris Farlowe. Some have said that Nick inadvertently emulated Farlowe with his breathy, stilted style – and Fame with his jazzy approach, though fans would argue that the only person Nick Drake emulated was himself, and that he did this inordinately well.

What *did* have a massive, lasting effect on Nick, in August 1965, was his introduction to France and its culture, a sojourn that brought out his existentialist qualities and transformed him into the enigma he is now widely recognised as. Hitch-hiking with a friend, David Wright, the pair spent some time in Paris before travelling via Avignon to the Côte d'Azur. 'The music scene in France is pathetic,' observed another friend, Colin Betts (of whom more later), in his memoir of the time, though Betts clearly was not looking and listening in the right places. The so-called *yé-yé* period of French popular music that had given the country the likes of Johnny Hallyday, Sylvie Vartan, Petula Clarke, Richard Anthony and Claude Francois was drawing to a close. Though these stars would endure far longer than their British counterparts, the new sensations were the *chansonniers*: Jacques Brel, George Brassens, Mouloudji, Barbara, Jean Ferrat and Léo Ferré. Then there were the *grandes interprètes*: Juliette Gréco, Catherine Sauvage, Pia Colombo and other very talented women who invariably walked on to the stage wearing their hearts on their sleeves. Nick fell in love with these artists, learned their more popular songs despite his limited French, and later borrowed from their stylised techniques to add depth to his own work. Nick also discovered the Scots troubadour, Donovan, while in France. Having ignored his 'Catch the Wind' a few years earlier, the French had taken his 'Mellow Yellow' to the top of their hit parade, with its snatch of verse in their own language. Nick also admired Donovan's guitar work and tried to copy his unusual method of tuning by listening to the record on the jukebox every time he entered a bistro.

To experience the same level of discomfort suffered by his bohemian heroes, Nick slept in tawdry backstreet hotels with sagging beds, cracked bidets, and used the communal lavatory on the landing. He spent hours wandering around the streets of St-Germain-des-Prés, where existentialists Gréco and Ferré had learned their craft and earned meagre livings performing in the Gauloises-clouded bars and clubs. He visited the Écluse, at 15 Quai des Grands Augustins on the Left Bank. Here, Barbara (Monique Serf, 1930–97) had performed as artist-in-residence for five years before becoming France's most important singer after Edith Piaf. Initially, she had sung cover versions of Brel and Brassens, gradually gaining the confidence to compose herself. Nick bought her album, *Barbara Chante Barbara*, then topping the French charts having just been awarded the Grand Prix du Disque. One of its songs, 'Nantes', told of the death of her errant father and sold a million copies. Nick loved this, but was equally impressed by the immense privacy coupled with the darkly semi-comic intensity of 'A Mourir Pour Mourir', the theme being that death is only significant if one expires while young and beautiful. James Dean had famously pronounced that he wanted to die young and make a beautiful corpse, and Barbara's song similarly translated, 'To die for dying's sake, I choose a tender age . . . to go for going's sake, I don't want to wait! Better to die beautiful than faded and decked out in lace!' Albeit reading the text from a book of Barbara poems, Nick frequently sang this in France – on park benches, in bars and cafés, and even at the Écluse. Ironically, Barbara would die on the 23rd anniversary of Nick's death.

Nick also sought out the haunts associated with Jean-Paul Sartre and Simone de Beauvoir, and retraced the footsteps of the novelist Albert Camus, another troubled genius who had died young, in a car crash. He visited places associated with the Boris Vian, whose 'Le Deserteur' he would sing for his friends – siding with the *poét-chansonnier* in this beautiful song, an open letter to the president from the soldier about to be shot for deserting because he has seen so many of his loved ones die in the Algerian War. He visited the graves of Piaf, Oscar Wilde and Colette in the city's Père Lachaise cemetery.

Nick's greatest inspiration in France was Arthur Rimbaud (1854–91), the doomed, beautiful boy-genius poet who, when the same age as Nick was now, had shocked society by embarking on a very public, frequently violent affair with the much less attractive Paul Verlaine, 10 years his senior and married. A precursor of symbolism, as a way of expressing his dissatisfaction with the world about him, Rimbaud had coloured his works with dreams, childhood experiences and mysticism – as would happen with Barbara and Nick. Also like Rimbaud, Nick would form attachments to men older and more stable than he was. Like him he would take rejection from an older man – deliberate or inadvertent – badly, and virtually give up on his work because of it.

Nick's stay in France seems to have encouraged him to knuckle down to some serious study. When he left Marlborough in July 1966, not only did he have better grades in the three A-levels he had flunked before, he had been elevated to captaincy of his house. However, they were still not good enough to get him into Fitzwilliam and the snobbish Drakes were firmly against him applying to a second-choice university. They wanted him to stay on at school for another year and sit further scholarship exams, and hopefully get better grades this time. But Marlborough, Nick declared, was out of the question. He loathed the place! Against Rodney and Molly's wishes, he made enquiries about enrolling at Bantock's Tutorial School, a 'cramming' college in Birmingham.

Nick was still heavily into rock and Britpop and 'flipping his lid' over Bob Dylan's *Blonde on Blonde* album, but he could not get France out of his mind. As he would not be starting at Fitzwilliam until the autumn of 1967, he decided to spend as much of his gap year as was possible in Europe. He had recently passed his driving test and, borrowing Molly Drake's Morris Minor – almost as much an existentialist status symbol for British tourists on a budget as the Citroën Diane was for the French – and buying a tent from Milletts, he and three pals set off for France.

For several weeks, the quartet drifted from one provincial campsite to the next, eating at cheap cafés, with Nick entertaining whoever wanted to listen with his campfire ditties – spur-of-the-moment arrangements of Dylan, with the odd Brel or Barbara *chanson* or folk song thrown in for good measure. A ready supply of bottled beer and marijuana put paid to any nerves he might have had back then. Nick had recently read Ernest Hemingway's *The Sun Also Rises*, and seen the film with Errol Flynn and Tyrone Power, two of his movie favourites who had also burned the candle at both ends. The story tells of a love-triangle set against the bloody spectacle of the bullring. The friends took in the various Hemingway locations – the arena at Nîmes, the topless beaches of San Tropez, the Bar American in Paris' Place de l'Opéra.

Returning to England, Nick spent less time with his parents than before. An opulent rural retreat, no matter how tranquil and picturesque, could not compete with the sizzle of London or Paris, and by January 1967 he was back in France, though not of his own volition this time. Nick was in London when his A-level results arrived at Far Leys, and his father had opened the envelope: there was now no need for Nick to go to Bantock's because he had been accepted at Fitzwilliam, but with a proviso. He would have to make his own arrangements to catch up with all the lectures he had missed at Marlborough on account of his 'gallivanting' up and down the country instead of studying.

Rodney Drake's cheque book solved the problem. Using one of his connections, he secured Nick a six-months stint at the Aix-en-Provence University's prestigious – and very costly – faculty for exchange students wishing to improve their conversational skills. To learn more about the French way of life, students would lodge *en famille* within the town – with the family in question being asked to make weekly reports back to the faculty regarding the students' behaviour, drugs and anti-social behaviour being as much of a problem back then as today. Nick was having none of this and put up with being 'spied' on for a week before using his own money to rent a flat in the Cours Sextius area of the town with a friend called Jeremy Mason, whose family lived nearby. Whether Mason was the young man with whom he was allegedly involved at the time is not known. The pair missed more lectures than they attended, were a familiar sight in the town centre, easily identified by Nick's great height and a pronounced stoop, even at 19, busking for pocket money for such 'luxuries' as Disques Bleus cigarettes. He strummed his guitar and sang the *chanson* of the moment – with a marked accent that the locals found intriguing and sexy – in his gentle, whispered baritone while Mason went around with the cap. My godfather, the singer-songwriter Roger Normand, recalled a young man fitting Nick's description – hunched shoulders, legs that went on for ever, long hair and a plaintive voice with an English accent – sitting on a bench in the market square singing, 'Viens Sur la Montagne' – the French version of 'Go Tell it on the Mountains' – to a bunch of giggly schoolgirls.

That there were amorous encounters in Provence probably goes without saying in this so-called 'Summer of Love' when youngsters' fancies were invariably aided and abetted by a seemingly limitless diet of sex and pot. Nick may have leaned more strongly towards members of his own sex, but he certainly appears to have given one young woman an inkling that he had fallen for her – though this could easily have been wishful thinking on her part.

In 1997, a Miami-born singer-songwriter named Robin Frederick posted an essay on the *Nick Drake Internet Files* detailing how, as an 18-year-old hopeful, she had met Nick while appearing at the Club Tartare and how, afterwards, they had enjoyed a jamming session in Nick's room. In an article sub-headed *Truly, Madly, Deeply*, Frederick later told *Mojo* magazine in February 1998. 'Falling in love with Nick was a no-brainer, and I promptly did, not that I ever let on, mind you. He was extraordinarily attractive and that, plus his natural quietness, made it easy to weave a web of fantasies about him.'

For years, Frederick has dined out on her brief Nick Drake 'adventure', though what makes her story credible is that she did not claim she had sex with him, which she could have done, as it all happened so many years ago that no one would have been any the wiser. All she admits to is playing him her 'Been Smokin' Too Long', which he memorised and taped. Many years later it would turn up among some of his effects found at Tanworth. Frederick *does* say how she fell for the handsome Englishman, but that she had been too insecure at the time to properly express her feelings and that when Nick had made the first move by asking her to meet him in a café the next evening, he had failed to show up.

Robin Frederick has always claimed that her song, 'Sandy Grey', recalled her fury over being stood up by Nick Drake. This may, however, be one of the many myths that have sprung up concerning his 'lost' years – that period between his virtually anonymous death and the rediscovery of his work decades later, when it seemed only inevitable that so many should step forward and recount impossible-to-prove anecdotes concerning the life of the young singer. Such bohemian romanticism, certainly in the way Nick lived and conducted himself while wandering around Provence, inspired him to take a leaf out of Barbara's book and begin writing for himself. Among his early compositions were 'Birds Flew By', 'Princess of the Sand' and 'Time of No Reply', with its unmistakable Continental ambience, a beautiful evocation of endless hazy summer days.

Some of these songs, along with covers of other singer-songwriter's works, were taped in an Aix-en-Provence kitchen, either by Nick himself or the lover/friend he was with, on the battery-operated tape recorder he carried around with him much of the time. These included Bob Dylan's 'Tomorrow is Such a Long Time' that he had heard Elvis Presley sing, Bert Jansch's 'Strolling Down the Highway', and Nick's own 'Strange Meeting II' and 'They're Leaving Me Behind'. For years, Nick's family always maintained that they held the copyright for this material, refusing its commercial release, and giving many people the impression that the Aix tapes had never existed in the first place. Legally, of course, performance copyright would belong to whoever recorded it – the friend or lover – whether it was Nick's voice or not, though if Nick had supplied the tape and recorded it himself, then copyright would have belonged to him, or latterly his estate. In the liner notes for the 2007 release, *Nick Drake: Family Tree*, containing or purporting to contain these Aix-en-Provence recordings, Robin Frederick cites that the tapes were made by a friend called James, possibly a lover, who remembered exactly what happened during the kitchen sessions, and claimed that *he* personally had persuaded Nick to record the material, but conveniently forgets where he had met Nick for the first time. 'Because this session was prearranged and therefore not spontaneous meant that he was a bit too sober for his own liking when playing,' James says. And yet another source, quoted elsewhere, is certain that a girlfriend taped the songs when Nick was drunk! All that *is* certain is that we shall probably never know the truth.

Family Tree was Gabrielle's idea. Rodney Drake's way of coping with his son's death was to run off an endless supply of Tanworth tapes, which he and Molly had handed out like sweets – their way of thanking those dedicated fans who had made the pilgrimage to Far Leys. As a result of their generosity, the market was flooded with poor quality bootleg CDs, and Gabrielle felt that her brother deserved better than this. To celebrate the release, she and Joe Boyd gave an interview for KUSF Radio, in October 2007, an enterprise which was sponsored by PAWS, an organisation which raised money for the pets of AIDS victims. 'He wanted to be part of this world of commercial music,' Boyd told the host of

Nick's reluctance to give live performances, 'but his nature was not cut out for that.' Asked to choose his favourite Nick Drake song, he plumped for 'Three Hours', the one that he said highlighted Nick's guitar playing more than any other. Gabrielle chose 'Saturday Sun' and 'Mayfair' which, she said, was a humorous song, and few people associated Nick Drake with humour.

Although Nick told his French lover, Michel, that he was completely at ease with his sexuality, this was several years down the track and he may not have been quite so open while in Aix-en-Provence, when the talk among his friends often centred around who was sleeping with whom, and when he was pursued, according to them, by so many girls. Possibly on account of this suppressed homosexuality, Nick seems to have already begun his descent into the profound melancholy that, though an influence on his work, would contribute to his premature, agonising downfall. Some of the friends who accompanied him on his travels testified to a sudden change in his behaviour to Patrick Humphries, for his biography (*Nick Drake*, Bloomsbury, 1997). One was sure that he had returned 'more drug-orientated' from his travels in the spring of 1967, another that he had taken LSD – having first taken the precaution of blocking off the entrance to his hotel balcony, having heard the rumour that 'trippers' often believed they could fly. How much of this was true is of course open to question: as has already been explained, until Nick's posthumous 'comeback' many years after his death, when everyone who had known him had their own personal Nick Drake anecdote to share and no doubt embellish, he had not exactly been at the forefront of everyone's minds.

Exactly *why* Nick opted to visit Morocco is not known, though almost certainly it would have had something to do with the country's relaxed laws on drugs and – in the last few months that homosexuality was against the law in Britain – quite possibly its openly thriving rent-boy trade. Celebrity gays such as Joe Orton had recently been astonished to find gay sex on offer for a few coins, a pack of cigarettes, or even a chocolate bar. Neither do we know exactly which of his posh college pals accompanied Nick on this trip, and who augmented his entourage en route: accounts vary, with many seemingly hopping on to the bandwagon in a '15 minutes of fame' attempt to convince us that they were there, experiencing and witnessing the artistic development of a man who, largely forgotten for many years, would one day become a household name. Indeed, it is frequently impossible to ascertain who borrowed whose anecdotes, enlarged on them, or invented new ones to become a part of the Nick Drake legend.

In 2007, Colin Betts, a man perhaps best described as a Rolling Stones camp follower-beatnik-busker published an account of his experiences, lived out in a haze of pot smoke, between the London of 1963 and, by way of his trip to Morocco, the Paris student riots of May 1968. An aficionado of Beat Generation icons Ginsberg and Kerouac – the latter whose writing style he attempts to emulate, Betts kept a diary so on the face of it one would expect his story to be fairly accurate. Robin Frederick later said that it must have been, because so many of Betts' anecdotes tied in with her own recollections of Nick at the time. It could be argued, of course, that in waiting 40 years to self-publish *Frozenlight: True Tales of the Sixties* by way of the Internet and not by the conventional method, Betts was tempted to 'embellish' what he had written back then and make Nick a more central character of his work than originally intended. To all intents and purposes, during the summer of 1967 Nick was but one of hundreds of buskers who plied their trade in the streets and parks around Aix, yet Betts elevates him to being the most famous person there. In retrospect he was, but no one knew this at the time.

Betts, 18 at the time, claims that he first encountered Nick and three male friends, driving a battered Ford Cortina on to the Tangiers–Algeciras ferry, before heading for the sundeck, where he joined them. Here, he had marvelled at Nick's guitar-playing, part-inspired by his having listened to Oum Kalthoum while in Morocco. In fact, Nick's style was as far removed from that of the great Egyptian singer's musicians as was possible. Betts also says early on in his narrative that Nick was a Gemini, like himself – which begs the somewhat cynical question, were birthdays the first item on their agenda, or did Betts add this later? It is this, if anything, which casts a shadow over his subsequent story, curiously written throughout in the present tense, of how Nick persuaded Betts not to head for Paris, as intended, but to join their company for the drive through Spain and stay with him in Aix-en-Provence. 'Those pretty little rich girls will just love two good-looking six-foot-three-inch guitar-pickers who can really hold a tune,' he cockily observes.

In Aix, Nick introduced Betts to Robin Frederick and, according to his new friend, learned several Piaf songs including 'Non, Je ne Regrette Rien' and 'Milord' – the latter the story of the prostitute who picks up the Leslie Howard toff, which one could not possibly imagine him singing in the street, or even getting away with, if he did, without attracting ridicule. Neither would he have sung 'Hymne à l'Amour' – this was only four years after Piaf's death, and absolutely no one was permitted to sing her most revered song in France at the time. The story becomes increasingly far-fetched: Nick and Betts busking together, then retreating into the shrubbery to pop 'Blue Cheer' acid pills. Then Nick's 'swaying hug that ends in wet eyes' at their farewell, six weeks later. Reading other accounts of the period, collected by Patrick Humphries and Trevor Dann, it just does not all add up.

It was in Morocco that Nick wrote what many believe to have been his first song, 'Strange Meeting II – which of course begs the question, was there ever a 'Strange Meeting I?' There was, but not from the pen of Nick Drake. War-hero poet Wilfred Owen (1893–1918), in common with Nick, achieved lasting fame only after his death. Also like Nick, he spent his happiest years in France, where homosexuality had always been more readily accepted than in Britain, and in an age when gay men had invariably been denounced as effete and lily-livered, Owen had been awarded the Military Cross for bravery on the battlefield, only to be killed in action a few days before the Armistice was signed.

Nick's song is a take on Owen's 'Strange Meeting', wherein he substitutes the encounter between the young enemy soldiers, one who has killed the other, with a 'boy-meets-girl' scenario – effectively recognised, if one reads Joe Orton, as a 'boy-meets-boy adventure', for in the tradition of many gay public schoolboys addressing each other as 'she', it is just as likely that Nick's 'princess of the sand' was actually a young French-Arab boy.

The other song composed by Nick at around this time, heavily influenced by some of the French music he was listening to back then, was 'They're Leaving Me Behind', which for its slanted delivery leans heavily on Marie Laforet (b.1939), an immensely popular folk singer who had first sung 'Viens sur la montagne', the song Nick had busked around the streets of Aix-en-Provence. Laforêt's big hits during the spring of 1967 were 'Manchester et Liverpool', and 'Marie douceur, Marie colère' – her own adaptation of the Rolling Stone 'Paint it Black' which was more popular in France and Morocco than the original. Nick blatantly copies the slightly hesitant Laforêt vocal slant in 'They're Leaving Me Behind', and portentously takes an inadvertent peek into the future by pronouncing the line, 'Success can be gained, but at too great a cost.'

The Rolling Stones themselves were in Tangiers at the time, accompanied by an entourage that included Marianne Faithfull and Anita Pallenberg. One evening, so the story goes, they visited a restaurant where Nick was busking. According to the friend who spoke to Patrick Humphries, they were 'more than polite'. Later, during the trip to North Africa, Nick and his friends, their finances running low, are said to have been actually be *mistaken* for the Stones when their car came off the road near Meknès, and ended up with a near-written-off driver's side. The driver was (again there are doubts as to his identity) said to have taken the ruse a step further: repairing the car free of charge, in exchange for a shot of himself and the 'Stones', admiring his handiwork, which would be framed and displayed in his garage. Suffice it to say, the photograph has never surfaced.

In the autumn of 1967, Nick entered Fitzwilliam, a move that coincided with the Wilson government's decriminalisation of homosexuality, which may or may not have had any effect on Nick. All of his relationships this far had been discreet, and none is thought to have been serious – as with Gram Parsons and Jeff Buckley, affairs of the heart were always secondary to the music, and as such untenable. Nick certainly appreciated Cambridge's relaxed atmosphere and the fact that, unlike Marlborough, his peers were not forever breathing down his neck. What he disliked was Fitzwilliam itself – for while the other Cambridge colleges mostly dated back to the Middle Ages, this one, a sprawling concrete and glass monstrosity on the outskirts of the town, had only been founded the previous year.

If Nick had dreamed of settling down to a Wildean sojourn among the lofty ancient spires and ghosts of long-dead academics, he would be disappointed. Some years later, one of his well-heeled friends, Victoria Ormsby-Gore, recalled dropping in on him here with her sister, Alice, a notorious heroin addict among London's society set. 'He was profoundly disappointed by it,' she told the *Sunday Telegraph*'s Mick Brown in 1997. 'He had this wonderful vision of going to Cambridge – the dreaming spires, the wonderful erudite people. We went up to visit and he was in this grim red-brick building, sitting in this tiny, motel-like bedroom. He was completely crushed. He just sat there saying, "It's so awful!"'

When in a creative mood, Nick would find himself wandering around at night, alone, exploring the other more historical colleges. He particularly liked King's, imbibing the ambience left behind by the man some claim he believed to have been his alter-ego: the similarly doomed, sexually confused young poet, Rupert Brooke (1887–1915). Brooke had been wooed by students of both sexes while at Cambridge; John Maynard Keynes and Lytton Strachey had famously scrapped for the privilege of bedding him. Like Nick, Brooke had been a realist, his work equally embracing *la joie de vivre*, homoeroticism, and impending death. Also like Nick, he suffered from depression and died in his mid-twenties.

Unable to afford a car – though his parents would buy him one a few months later – Nick got hold of a second-hand motorcycle that he drove at break-neck speeds around Cambridge, his long hair whipping about his face. With a staggering capacity for 'holding his ale', he trawled the local pubs, chain-smoked French cigarettes, and scribbled his best lines while under the influence of drink – or marijuana, which appears to have been readily available at Fitzwilliam. What he did not take too seriously were his studies, largely on account of those friends who crowded into his room each evening to hear him perform his latest composition.

The covers of other people's songs were starting to take a backseat and Nick's friends, among them the flautist-saxophonist Iain Cameron, recalled how at these gatherings they tried to convince him that he had the makings of a successful singer-songwriter. Speaking to the sadly defunct *Pynk Moon* fanzine, Cameron remembered Nick enthralling everyone with 'River Man', singling out, 'The beauty of the invention, the meaning coming in and out of focus, the technical accomplishment, the timbres and sonorities. It was as if I had finally found something which until that point I had only come across various hints and suggestions might exist.' Cameron had jammed with Nick and another musician pal, Paul Wheeler, and added that if Nick was cool and aloof, then the real communication had occurred when they had been playing together.

Nick's musical sphere now embraced up-and-coming American singer-songwriters such as Tim Buckley, Leonard Cohen, Laura Nyro and Randy Newman, though the songs he was composing still leaned unmistakably towards the Continental. While in France, he learned that he had a female near-contemporary: Gribouille (1941–68), a Lyons-born *chanteuse*, discovered by Jean Cocteau towards the end of his life. Extremely talented, with a deep, velvety voice, Gribouille (Marie-France Gaité) had had her finger firmly pressed on the self-destruct button for some time, and had for a while been sectioned in an institution. She was just 27 when she took her own life in January 1968, and Nick incorporated shades of her biggest hit, 'Matthias', into his 'Hazey Jane II'.

During numerous trips back to Far Leys during the winter of 1967–8, Nick recorded the so-called *Tanworth Tape*. This comprises some 20 covers and original compositions of varying quality, taped in his bedroom. The tape has never been released commercially in its entirety, but there have been so many bootlegs over the years containing extracts that it is possible to have almost a complete collection of Nick Drake 'rarities', which are important in that they offer an invaluable insight into the mind of the Rimbaud-fixated teenager *before* disillusion beckoned.

Nick's choices for an imaginary 'retrospective' are both eclectic and surprising. 'Get Together', the Youngbloods' theme for the National Council for Christians and Jews, was then in Gram Parsons' repertoire. There is Bert Jansch's 'Strolling Down the Highway', which was covered by Gram and Jeff Buckley, and Bob Dylan's very striking 'Tomorrow is a Long Time', also covered by Jeff and, more famously, Elvis Presley. There is Dave Van Ronk's 'If You Leave Me'. Three more compositions – 'Here Come the Blues, Blues Run the Game' and 'Milk and Honey' – are from the pen of the little-known American blues singer, Jackson C. Frank. Rimbaud's influence is at its most potent in Nick's own 'Day is Done', 'Way to Blue' and 'Blossom', which French songstress Françoise Hardy would later add to her repertoire, but never sing. Here, an obviously drunk Nick sings it slightly off-key, his voice slanting into nowhere at the end of each line. Then there are 'Rain', 'Come into the Garden' and 'Birds Flew By' – a maudlin ode to suppressed homosexuality in which he pronounces, 'A list of broken hearts comes from the need to play so many parts.' Then there are the traditional songs: 'Winter is Gone', Black Mountain Blues', 'Paddling in Rushmere', 'Cocaine Blues', 'Kimbie', 'My Baby So Sweet' and 'All My Trials' – a simplistic, extremely effective and moving duet with Gabrielle.

In 2007, most of these songs were issued on the collection, *Family Tree*, with extensive liner notes by Gabrielle Drake, several previously unseen photographs of Nick with his family, but rather a lot of unnecessary 'padding'. While one thrills to Nick on clarinet and two friends (aka The Family Trio) playing Mozart's *Kegelstatt Trio*, one cannot help but thinking that Molly's Drake's corny, 'Anna Neagle' warbling of two of her own compositions was added at the expense of several missing items from Nick's very early repertoire, which would have been much more appreciated by many fans.

Nick's best friend at Cambridge was Robert Kirby, a young musician who attended Caius College who, it would appear, auditioned (and failed) with him for the Cambridge Footlights. It was he who began recording Nick, obviously aware of his potential, on to a stereo tape recorder early in 1968. These tapes (they included 'River Man' and 'Mayfair', of which more later) were not as raw as one might have expected: Nick was possessed of an absolute clarity of diction, and at 19 had developed perfect pitch. With virtually no retakes, Kirby was able to work on these and fashion the most startling arrangements for woodwind and strings, so that Nick could perform them in a neo-baroque setting on campuses around Cambridge. These early audiences were small, but never less than enthusiastic.

On 22 December 1967, Nick appeared at the Roundhouse, near Chalk Farm. The evening was part of a 12-day festival aimed at promoting world peace, organised by 23-year-old Ashley Hutchings, the bassist with Steeleye Span, and topping the bill was Country Joe MacDonald & the Fish, famed for their protests against the Vietnam war and making their British debut. Nick's booking here is known to have been courtesy of a man known only as 'James' – whether this was James Fraser, a music scholar friend from Caius College, or the James who had supposedly been present when the tapes had been made in Aix – indeed, whether they were one and the same man, is not clear.

This was an important evening at a fairly prestigious venue. Among those who had passed through the former turntable engine shed's portals were Led Zeppelin, Jimi Hendrix, Jefferson Airplane, the Rolling Stones and The Doors, and the place served as a mecca for record company executives and talent scouts. Nick took the stage at two in the morning and was allotted just 10 minutes, but the three songs he performed went down well. Confessing that he had not taken the songs themselves in, Ashley Hutchings told *Pynk Moon*, 'The thing that struck me first was his demeanour and his charisma. It was Nick the person, the figure on stage which really registered.' It was Hutchings who subsequently urged his manager, Joe Boyd, to consider taking Nick on.

Joe Boyd was a handsome, loquacious entrepreneur, six years Nick's senior, who hailed from Boston, Massachusetts. Besides working with Fairport Convention, Pink Floyd and Cream, he had helped put together the 1965 Newport Folk Festival, for which he had famously engaged Bob Dylan. In 1966, Boyd had formed his own production company, Witchseason (so named after Donovan's 'Season of the Witch', from his *Sunshine Superman* album), then based in London's Charlotte Street. Boyd had produced best-selling albums for Eric Clapton and The Incredible String Band, among others. The small witch-on-a-broomstick logo appeared on the company's album covers and publicity material. Boyd's speciality, a rarity in those days, was to offer his artists the complete package: record, publishing deal and publicity.

There is no record of Boyd auditioning Nick, so he must have taken Hutchings at his word. One week after the Roundhouse show, Nick called in at Witchseason's front office to drop off an open-reel demo-tape featuring four of the songs he had recorded at Tanworth: 'River Man', inspired by his daily walk across the Cam between his lodgings and Fitzwilliam College, the delightful 'I Was Made to Love Magic', 'Time of No Reply', and the haunting 'Time Has Told Me'.

Knocked sideways by Nick's spellbinding talent, Boyd immediately signed him to make an album – not for Polydor, who recorded Fairport Convention, but for Island, one of the country's top independent labels. Island was founded in Jamaica in 1959 by British-born Chris Blackwell, who had spent much of his childhood here: he recorded mainly British West Indies artists. The company had relocated to the UK in 1962, and would remain the world's largest independent record label until 1989, when Blackwell sold it to PolyGram for $272 million. Among Island's leading lights had been, for a brief spell, Bob Marley and 'My Boy Lollipop' singer, Millie Small. Their first white contractees had been The Spencer Davis Group, in 1965, since which time they had signed Jethro Tull and Free. Fairport Convention and Mott the Hoople would also eventually swell their ranks.

That Nick developed a crush on the man who became his mentor seems more than likely. Boyd may not have known this – at least one reviewer referred to him as Nick's 'record company sugar daddy' – and may well have enjoyed being placed upon a pedestal by this cute-looking young man who outwardly appeared as timid and unassuming as Boyd was extroverted and outspoken. Whether this interest was reciprocated is not known, but thought to have been unlikely given Boyd's prominent position. In retrospect, he certainly coaxed more out of Nick's precocious talent than any other producer might have had the patience to do, bearing in mind that he would prove anything but easy to work with – and this of course is all that really matters.

Chapter Eight
A Way to Find the Sun

Though appreciative of the attention he had received, Nick was initially displeased with the package offered by Island. Joe Boyd would personally produce the album, but he would also act as Nick's manager, adviser, record producer, agent and music publisher. Such a deal would be rare nowadays, with the client suspicious that he or she might be in risk of exploitation, with no one to fall back on should one or other of the aforementioned disciplines fail them. The actual recording of the album would be supervised by Island's in-house engineer, John Wood, and Witchseason's sister company, Warlock, would handle the copyrighting. Wood hired the bassist, Danny Thompson, who had just founded The Pentangle with John Renbourn and Nick's favourite guitarist, Bert Jansch. What made Thompson extra-special so far as Nick was concerned was that he had played for one of his idols, Tim Buckley, during his recent British tour. Strangely, though the two are heard on the same songs, they never actually got around to playing together in the studio – Thompson's bass parts would be overdubbed only after Nick had completed the vocals.

Nick's songs would be arranged by Richard Hewson, who had worked on the Beatles' *Long And Winding Road* album and, more recently, on Mary Hopkin's chart-topping 'Those Were the Days'. This was the one part of the deal that Nick objected strongly to, demanding that he be allowed to use Robert Kirby – who no one at Island had heard of. Nick must have held some sway over Boyd, for the request was granted and the much more experienced Hewson asked to stand down.

Twenty-four years later, Joe Boyd would still be singing his protégé's praises: 'Of all the albums I ever made, the two I produced by Nick are the ones I'm most proud of,' he told *Record Collector* in 1992. 'Nothing he ever did was less than striking, and he had the gift of writing melodies of incredible beauty.' In the same feature, Robert Kirby described Nick's songs as, 'A series of extremely vivid, complete observations, like epigamic proverbs.'

Kirby was one of the few people in England capable of getting Nick to open up and relax. The two attended parties, got drunk together, swam and punted. Kirby has also spoken of Nick's sardonic humour – of how Nick would coerce him into accompanying him on trips to the local cemetery, not just to scare him, but to have Kirby listen to his latest composition there.

Speaking in a Swedish interview of 1990, Kirby dismissed the theory of the elusive, mysterious sage, saying, 'People think that if Nick spoke, the words he said would somehow be like the words of Mohammed or Jesus Christ, that everything would have a meaning. But he'd say, "Terrible weather we're having today!", just like everyone else, or, "God, I fancy a hamburger!"'

For many, though, Nick Drake would erroneously be regarded as some kind of neo-Gothic figure, a harbinger of poetic doom, the precursor to Morrissey and Leonard Cohen, who spent the better part of his life hiding in one of several bolt holes, feeling miserable and sorry for himself. Thirty years later, despite much renewed evidence to the contrary, a typical 'character assessment' would appear in the *Guardian*:

> *Look at Nick Drake . . . hunched over his acoustic guitar, half-lost in his hair, unable to commit to the camera, he wants to be alone. Just because he makes tormented, elegant folk music, it doesn't mean he should communicate with the rest of the human race.*

The album was recorded at the Sound Techniques studio in Chelsea, and given the title *Five Leaves Left* – an 'in-joke' among pot-smokers in that the message ONLY FIVE LEAVES LEFT was printed inside packs of Rizla cigarette papers when the contents were about to run out. Nick juxtaposed this with his fascination for doomed literary icons. O. Henry (William Sydney Porter, 1862–1910), one of the masters of the American vignette whose style of composition was not unlike Nick's – with both, it is obligatory to carefully analyse the complicated phraseology and on occasion even make a guess at what they are getting at – had penned *The Last Leaf*, included in his 1904 collection, *Cabbages and Kings*. This tells of a young Greenwich Village artist, dying of pneumonia and watching the leaves dropping off the ivy outside her window. 'Three days ago there were almost a hundred,' she tells her doctor. 'There are only five left now . . . when the last one falls, I must go too.'

The fact that O. Henry was, like Oscar Wilde, gay and also a victim of 'self-circumstance' – he spent time in prison for embezzlement – also appealed to

Nick. A photograph taken at the time depicts him standing under an archway, from which ivy trails. Fans and critics, reading too much into this, have suggested that Nick was telling them something, seeing as *he* only had five years to live. This is of course wishful thinking, ridiculously added to the 'doom-and-gloom' legend.

Most of the 10 songs had been around for some time in one form or another, performed by Nick in France or on the college circuit. But if Joe Boyd was expecting the tracks to be laid down in a couple of sessions, he had not reckoned on his protégé's niggling perfectionism. Nick's quest for this, a trait he would have in common with Jeff Buckley, bordered on the paranoid – plus his time was limited because he was cramming for his finals.

The songs were recorded over a staggering two-months period, beginning in July 1968, something of the norm nowadays, but then very unusual. This proved a nightmare for Joe Boyd: upon Nick's insistence he had hired 15 classical musicians, led by principal violinist David McCallum, father of the *Man From U.N.C.L.E* actor. Boyd and John Wood were accustomed to recording the vocals with a minimum of accompaniment, then overdubbing the orchestra at a later date. Nick was having none of this. Barbara and Brel were famed for recording songs and sometimes whole albums in single takes, the theory being that when an artist is on stage before an audience, they only get one chance to get it right. Nick insisted upon following their example – once he and Robert Kirby had run each musician through their solo part – and at most there would be just two takes of two songs, followed by a six-week hiatus which saw Nick disappearing to goodness knows where to recharge his batteries, to spend the £10 weekly allowance which Island were paying him as part of advanced royalties and work out the next arrangement in his head so that this could be passed on to Kirby.

Not all of the recorded songs ended up on *Five Leaves Left*. 'Clothes of Sand' and *Joey* were dismissed by Nick, who may have been afraid of would-be fans working out their true meaning – male prostitution in the first song, where the 'she' is actually a he, and the second song almost certainly a homage to Joe Orton, murdered by his lover the previous August. In it, Nick has the dead icon returning to his grave to see the flowers left there by an admirer, and laments, 'She wouldn't be there if it could be that you were.' Amazingly, he also rejected 'Time of No Reply' and 'I Was Made to Love Magic' – 35 years later, Nick's voice would be removed from the latter, and his simple guitar arrangement replaced by Robert Kirby's gorgeous new arrangement for orchestra.

Five Leaves Left defies description for it sheer beauty. It is years ahead of its time, and has never dated. One only has to close one's eyes to marvel at the scene that Nick paints, not infrequently bringing the listener to the point of tears. Byronesque and parochial, he evokes cream teas served on verdant lawns in endless, strife-free English summers. His delivery is impeccable – the gentle, honey-toned husky voice (as with all the *chansonniers*, maintained by a generous intake of French cigarettes), sometimes little more than a raised whisper, yet undeniably thrilling and sending shivers down the spine. This intimate, ethereal effect was achieved quite simply, applying the same technique that had been used to record Marilyn Monroe: engineer John Wood positioned four microphones in a semicircle, positioned Nick on a stool in the middle, then added a fifth microphone farther away to pick up the musicians.

Nick sounds so much the hardened professional, it is hard to believe that he was barely 20 when he cut his first album. Diction-wise, he is almost the male equivalent of Marianne Faithfull, before her voice cracked: refined, fragile, poignant, wistful and longing, as she had been on classic folksy albums like *North Country Maid*. Added to this is his innovative guitar work, with its unusual, inimitable tunings.

Opening the proceedings is 'Time Has Told Me', a soulful piece which, despite the country feel brought about by Richard (Fairport Convention) Thompson's electric guitar, is heavily steeped in the *chanson* tradition into which Nick had been inducted during his first trip to France. It sets us off on a pleasant excursion into the realm of lost and unrequited love, fantasy, drugs benders, loneliness and death – the perfect musical cocktail of the classic *chansonnier*. The song is a gentle attack against those who expect one to conform to the so-called 'norm', feigning heterosexuality when the opposite is clearly evident. After telling the object of his affection that he is a 'rare find', Nick continues, 'So I'll leave the ways that are making me be what I really don't want to be.' Yet he concludes, optimistically, having persuaded his lover to stay by his side so that they might hopefully stick it out, 'For someday our ocean will find its shore.'

'River Man' was arranged by Harry Robinson (1932–96), a Scots composer for Hammer Films whose band had appeared regularly on television's *Oh Boy!*. He had also fronted Lord Rockingham's XI, an outfit specialising in novelty songs: their 'Hoots Mon' had topped the charts in 1958. Nick's blues-style number, its stanzas expertly linked by Robinson's lush orchestrations, seems to have been part-inspired by Jacques Brel's 'L'éclusier (The Lock-Keeper), played to death on the French radio the previous summer. No one knows for sure who the central figure of Betty was – she could have been anyone, a distant relative, a friend of the Drakes, alternatively someone Nick made up. It is also more than likely that the River Man himself is Charon, the mythical creature who ferried the dead across the Styx to Hades, which rather suggests that, whoever Betty was, she was not alive when she arrived here!

On the other hand, the Jeremy and Jacomo in 'Three Hours' (allegedly how long it took to travel from Cambridge to London in those days) are believed to be the same person – Jeremy Mason, Nick's friend from Marlborough. Mason (quoted in several sources, most recently in Trevor Dann's *Darker Than the Darkest Sea*) has confessed that the song is about him, and grandiosely suggested that Giacomo was Casanova's first name. A more likely explanation is that Nick was Italianising the name of James, the lover thought to have been in Aix-en-Provence. The master-slave element of this lengthy piece, with its complex rhythm, also highlights the fact that, so far as is known, Nick was invariably, though not always physically, the submissive partner when it came to relationships.

More shimmering strings introduce 'Way to Blue' (Nick's original choice of title for the album, until he changed his mind), which juxtaposes his experimentation with drugs and his fondness for playing the blues. In 'Day is Done', allegory determines that we should be unsure whether Nick is referring to love lost because of impatience, or whether he is directly referring to premature ejaculation after a swift and fumbled act of love when he pronounces, 'Newspaper blown across the court . . . Lost much sooner than you would have thought!' 'Cello Song', with its stunning solo on this instrument by Claire Lowther, is both lovely and maudlin, a *symphonie-en-miniature* dealing with the grief-troubled mind of the man who waits to die so that he can rejoin the one he has tragically lost. 'The Thoughts of Mary Jane', read over a Percy Grainger-style pastoral lament, is not about an actual person, but what goes on inside a pot-smoker's mind – 'Mary-Jane' being a popular euphemism for marijuana!

'Man in a Shed' is a volte-face of the division of the classes, and evokes Edith Piaf's 'De l'autre coté de la rue', the story of the poor girl who from the window of her tawdry apartment watches and envies the wealthy prostitute across the street – until she realises that this girl has everything she wants except love. In this instance Nick, the scion of an upper middle-class home, tries to imagine what it must be like to live humbly, to suffer the disappointment of rejection by the rich woman in the big house nearby. Again, the lines, 'So leave your house, come into my shed . . . Please stop my world from raining through my head', have double meaning – the singer's desire to end loneliness, and his admission to being on some sort of hallucinogenic trip. It is a fine piece, but one that could have been improved upon: for a more powerful voice, the heavy blues-in-the-night backing might have worked well, but here it drowns and deflects from Nick's melodic tones.

To say, as many have, that 'Fruit Tree' was Nick's 'death-wish' song is both untrue and ridiculous. One of his finest works, it certainly *is* in praise of posthumous fame, but he had absolutely no way of knowing, when he wrote and recorded it, of the portentous way in which it would be later perceived. As such, he adopts the rather bleak stance applied to Wilfred Owen, Rupert Brooke and others who expired well before their time and the achievement of celebrity status, that it is *only* when one is dead and safe within the earth, that those left behind appreciate one's worth. The song would reach a mass audience many years later when played over the segment of television's *Heartbeat*, where the Nick Berry character loses his young wife.

'Saturday Sun', on the other hand, is a lyrically disappointing close to what has been a beautiful experience. A failed excursion into the world of gospel-jazz-muzak, it might have passed muster without the awful drums and vibraphone. Again the theme is double-edged, Nick's take on Hubert Gregg's wartime ditty, 'Bad Times Are Just Around the Corner'. He reminds us that it may all be very well to enjoy a brief spell of clement weather, or the good things in life – but that it will never last!

Nick borrowed the classical ensemble from *Five Leaves Left* to accompany him on 10 June 1969 when he appeared at the (misnamed) Oxford May Ball, a society event where evening dress – including feather boas for the ladies – was compulsory. The performance, way down a busy programme headed by bluesman John Mayall, was more or less a repetition of the songs he had been singing to the same people for over a year, save that they had now been gift-wrapped in luscious orchestrations and given the official seal of approval by a top record company. The programme notes even boasted that Nick's forthcoming album had been 'hailed by the press as the record of the year', which was untrue.

Thrilled by the prospect of releasing his first album, while contemporaries usually started off with a 45 rpm 7-inch single, Nick accepted a request to tape four songs for Radio One's *The John Peel Show*. Appearing on radio, he declared, would be fine because he would not have to face an audience of strangers. The session took place at the BBC's Maida Vale Studios during the afternoon of 5 August, and was broadcast the following evening. With just his guitar for accompaniment, Nick sang 'River Man', 'Cello Song' and 'Three Hours' from *Five Leaves Left*, along with 'Time of No Reply' – which he had recorded for the album but asked Joe Boyd not to use. The session ended with a brief instrumental of Martini's *Plaisir d'Amour*. Contrary to popular belief, the tape still exists and lies in a BBC vault.

Later that year, using the *Peel Show* material as an 'audition', a BBC committee met to determine whether Nick Drake's name should be added to their exhaustive list of B-Category entertainers, which they commissioned as 'fillers' for other variety programmes. The subsequent report, published on 14 October, listed him as a 'contemporary singer-guitarist' and observed of his style, 'Good for its kind, but of limited appeal. Voice moody and rather down, but a little uninspiring. Not a general appeal contribution.' The audition sheet may have had the word PASSED stamped across it in large letters, but from Nick's point of view it had been a pyrrhic victory. Even the coda, 'At last, something that holds one's interest from the start,' cut no ice with him. He was invited to do a second *Peel Show*, and offered a 10-minute slot on *Top Gear* but promptly turned them down, swearing that he would never set foot in a radio studio again.

Five Leaves Left was released on 1 September 1969. A pink-label album – coming just two months after New York's Stonewall Riots had gone a long way towards eliminating gay emancipation – would later be regarded by Nick's gay fans as his coy way of informing him that he was one of them. This was more a coincidence than an actual fact. Island had chosen *him*, rather than the other way around. The sleeve, like its successors, was thought provoking, and subsequently the subject of discussion among fans and critics. As would happen when dissecting his songs for hidden meanings, many would attempt to work out what kind of mental state Nick had been in when each photograph had been taken – and invariably get it wrong because a shot would turn up of him, grinning and looking radiantly happy, mere seconds after he had been photographed looking like he had the weight of the world on his shoulders. An 'unlucky' viridian green, the front of the sleeve reveals a three-quarter shot of Nick, by photographer Keith Morris, gazing at nothing in particular through the window of a derelict Wimbledon garret. Behind him, in this Kafka-esque setting, is another half-open window, beneath which is a table scattered with debris and dead leaves. The back of the sleeve has a study of Nick, very tall and slender, his thumbs customarily tucked into his belt – seemingly in a world of his own as a middle-aged man dashes by on some unexplained mission.

The whole thing was clarified upon the release of the CD, in 1987 – we see that Nick has moved a little further down Lindsey Street (near Smithfield Market) to lean against a lamp post close to where the man, tab-end in mouth, is buying a copy of the *Evening Standard* to catch up on the Budget report. Thirty years after Nick's death, Island's *Way to Blue* compilation would contain the contact prints from the Lindsey Street shoot: an assortment of factory workers, hurrying past Nick on their way the Tube station. For the *Made to Love Magic* collection of rarities, Nick would be seen standing next to the newspaper kiosk, again oblivious to his surroundings. The overall theme of these pictures is that, while these 'Ordinary Joes' are wrapped up in their humdrum existence, Nick could not really care less!

Over the years, there has been considerable speculation that Nick carried a torch for Keith Morris, who tragically drowned in 2005, while on a diving expedition in the English Channel. There is some evidence to support this in the photograph mentioned above, where Nick gazes through the window, quite clearly sporting an erection. Island Records have always maintained that this was merely a crease formed in his tight jeans, but at the time it caused enough concern for them to consider trimming the picture so that Nick would only be seen from the waist-up – which would have meant Morris removing the table, and the symbolic leaves, which are level with his crotch. In view of this, Island elected to leave the photograph untouched. Island records added to Nick's mystique – on the assumption that the general public believed that all poets were elusive, poverty-stricken or consumptive – by issuing a press release, part of which read:

> *Nick Drake is tall and lean and lives somewhere in Cambridge, somewhere close to the university where he is reading English. He does not have a telephone, and tends to disappear for days at a time when he is writing. But, above all, he makes music!*

The music press, however, was divided in its opinions about the album. These were the closing months of the decade. Journalists were much more interested in recalling those rock icons who had fallen by the wayside during the Swinging Sixties, and attempting to predict which ones would still be around in 10 years' time, than they were in paying too much interest to newcomers.

Melody Maker may have described *Five Leaves Left* as 'poetic', but it went out of its way to single out Nick's accompanists, and not him: 'Listen to the record because of the great playing by Danny Thompson, Paul Harris and

Richard Thompson . . . *then* you'll find out about the singer and his songs.' The anonymous reviewer in the *New Musical Express* offered a largely dismissive, 'I'm sorry I can't be more enthusiastic, because he obviously has a not inconsiderable amount of talent, but there is not nearly enough variety on this debut LP to make it entertaining.' Ouch! *Five Leaves Left* sold a modest 5,000 copies by the end of the year – though since Nick's death it has sold several million.

Nick was so confident, at this stage in his life, that he would make the big time that he dropped out of Cambridge, ready to take on whatever his professional life threw at him. Many have speculated that, had he finished his studies and graduated, he might still be alive today. We shall never know, save that had he not thrown in the towel, albeit at tremendous personal cost, the music world would have been that much poorer. Nick's decision to abandon his studies did not bode well for his parents, who now resented having gone to the expense of sending him to a costly public school, all for nothing. Many years later, Rodney Drake told Chris Brazier, who interviewed the Drakes for an amateur film tribute, 'I remember trying to persuade him not to leave, by saying that if he could get a degree, he would have a safety net. His reply was that a safety net was the one thing he *didn't* want.'

To escape the rows and the badgering, Nick moved to London, where he crashed for a while at Gabrielle's flat before moving into one of his own that he shared with a musician lover who had dropped out of Cambridge with him. This arrangement did not work out. Nick much preferred his own space and company, and a few weeks later rented a bedsit in a rambling Victorian house in Hampstead, which he claimed better suited his bohemian leanings. Off and on he would keep coming back to this place, though from now on he would rarely settle anywhere for long – drifting from one friend's home to the next, even taking a lease on another flat at a secret location so that he could hide from the world while composing, if he thought life was getting him down.

Nick's peers at Island realised that they had probably bought into a white elephant, when he refused to promote *Five Leaves Left* in the conventional way – before the promo video – by hitting the tour circuit. He was terrified, he said, of performing alone now that the musicians he had recorded with had moved on to other projects. Under duress, he gave way to compromise: he would appear *only* as a support act, sitting down for his entire set, as he had when entertaining friends from an intimate corner of his college room. This of course was the traditional stance of the *chansonnier*: Jacques Brel, Georges Brassens and the

The 'Waycross Waif', just starting out on that ole bumpy road to success!

So real!!!!

This charming man . . .

'Je n'en connais pas la fin . . .'

British troubadour Jake Thackray often sang perched on a stool, hunched over their guitar in the centre of an uncluttered stage. Nick's choice of stage garb was similarly orthodox: black jacket and trousers, usually with a white, open-neck shirt underneath.

Though he did not fit into any particular category – he was certainly *never* a rock/pop star – Nick was promoted as a folk singer and marketed in the same way as Paul Simon and Cat Stevens. On 24 September 1969, he supported Fairport Convention on a seven-day tour that opened at London's Royal Festival Hall. This was the group's first major show since the car crash, four months earlier, which had claimed the lives of their drummer, Martin Lamble, and Richard Thompson's girlfriend. The promoters considered Nick such a risk on account of his crippling stage fright that they omitted his name from the playbills in case he failed to show up. Two weeks later, he played his first authentic folk date, as part of the Upper Room Folk Club showcase, in Middlesex. He also made the mistake of allowing someone to talk him into playing some very rough and rowdy working men's clubs, such as the Haworth, in Hull – and the Magpie, in Sheffield – not the ideal environment (as I learned to my chagrin, three years after Nick!) if one is sensitive to the demands of hard-edged audiences who only like to hear songs they know – and who *always* put bingo first!

Like Morrissey's later solo ventures, Nick's recitals invariably ended prematurely and saw him sloping off into the wings – nothing to do with stage invasions, as would be the case of his Mancunian near-counterpart, but on account of his shattered nerves, though he always managed a timid smile and gracious nod of appreciation. If he *did* complete a 12-song set and there were cries for more, he never returned for a curtain call. And like the French *chansonniers*, he *never* spoke between songs.

There was an additional problem concerning promotion. Nick considered himself – like Sinatra, Peggy Lee and his European favourites – entirely an album person, and as such was virulently against record companies 'ripping off' fans by issuing singles taken from these. Had there been singles, of course, and more personal appearances, he would have become widely known during his lifetime, and the debilitating depression of his latter years might have been avoided. As such, the more success beckoned, the more Nick refused to be seen in public – and the more despondent he became.

One venue which Nick actually loved playing was Les Cousins, the basement club in London's Greek Street, and the only place he truly felt at ease. Rimbaud and Verlaine had lived near here in 1872, towards the end of their tempestuous relationship. Nick favoured Les Cousins, founded in April 1965, because the auditorium was relatively small and uncompromising: artists often got up for an impromptu 'turn', and the audience was always eager to give newcomers a chance. Off and on over the next couple of years, Nick would play here 53 times. It was here too that he met the young Frenchman who became his lover. His name was Michel Bidault, and unlike Nick's other lovers was younger than him, though only by two years. More than three decades on, Michel spoke of him with great fondness:

> *It was my first trip to London, and to this day I've no idea what made me go into that club. The first thing that struck me about Nick was those incredibly long legs and enormous feet. His songs didn't make much sense to me at the time, but he had a pleasant singing voice, not unlike that of Serge Gainsbourg. After he finished, I complimented him on this – we got chatting, the next evening we went for a drink together. My English wasn't very good then, and as his French was little better, much of the time we communicated by giggling a lot. I stayed at his flat for a few days, and not long afterwards he stayed with me in my tiny apartment in Paris, above the restaurant where I worked as a chef. In the years that I knew him he rarely spoke about his career. It was as if there were two Nick Drakes – the manic-depressive you read about in the press, which certainly was not in evidence when he was with me, and the fun-loving guy that I knew, who only picked up his guitar when there were people around who truly appreciated him.*

Early in 1970, Nick undertook around 20 concerts, between regular spots at Les Cousins, each taking its toll on his fragile nerves. In January he supported Genesis at Ewell College, Surrey. On 24 February he opened for folk singers John and Beverley Martin at London's Queen Elizabeth Hall. He began with 'Hazey Jane I' and ended his set with 'Hazey Jane II' – somewhere between, 'Fruit Tree' received the biggest applause. Between 16 and 30 March he supported ex-Fairport Convention singer Sandy Denny (a tragic figure who died four years after Nick, as a result of a fall) and her new band, Fotheringay, at Birmingham, Leicester, Manchester, Bristol and the Royal Festival Hall, London. John Martyn was with him for the latter show and was astonished how terrified he was of giving live performances, and how uncomfortable he looked on stage, particularly during the over-long pauses between songs when he was re-tuning his guitar – though Gabrielle Drake, also in the audience that evening, told a different story to the *Brytermusic* website in 1997:

> *I only saw Nick perform twice on stage, and my impression was rather that, unlike most performers who reach out to the audience and make themselves available to be loved or hated, Nick made no compromise with his audience. He was simply there. He existed in his songs, and his audience had to come to him and participate in his own intense isolation. Such was the force of his presence, on both the occasions I saw him, the audiences, slightly bemused by themselves, fell under his spell.*

On 25 June, a few days after an unbilled spot on a Leeds rock festival headlined by Free, Nick played Ewell College again, this time supporting Ralph McTell – so far as is known, apart from an impromptu recital in Paris in 1974, the last time he forced himself to walk the path to Calvary by facing an audience. Neither was it a complete performance, for halfway through 'Fruit Tree', he mumbled an apology before walking off. Slotted into this schedule of extraneous suffering for the sake of one's art was a hurriedly assembled session for the BBC. Against his better judgement, Nick had decided to give them another chance. Taped at Broadcasting House on 23 March, the clutch of (unknown) songs were broadcast on *Night Ride*, Radio Two's link-up show with Radio One, on 13 April. A few evenings later, some of this was relayed by José Arthur on his acclaimed *Pop-Club*, for France-Inter.

Probably wishing to nurture the 'elusive poet' image fabricated by Island's publicist, but also to offer himself breathing space from 'media pestering', Nick deliberately made himself difficult to pin down during the winter of 1970–1. The music press, who badly wanted to know more about him – the gatefold cover for *Five Leaves Left* had contained no sleeve notes whatsoever – and who now found themselves relying on hearsay 'biographical' details from unreliable sources, accused him of orchestrating his own mystique. They were probably not wrong. Though introverted to the point of being regarded by some acquaintances as psychologically dull, Nick is known to have used his shyness to his advantage. Because he had lately begun copying the *chansonniers* by almost always wearing black, and on account of his undernourished appearance, some detractors accused him of being downright morbid. Adding to the mystery was the fact that there were no visible lovers, female or male.

Danny Thompson, who played bass on *Five Leaves Left*, somewhat ungallantly told biographer Patrick Humphries of the time he had invited Nick to stay with him, in an attempt to 'sort him out': 'I thought all he needs is a bloody good bacon and chip butty and a good kick up the arse and couple of good shags and he'll be all right.'

With Nick's fascination for doomed writers and poets, not to mention the wealth of 'evidence' contained within his songs, it is surprising that only one man – Michel Bidault – has come forward and confessed to having had an affair with him. However, there seems to be no reason to believe that he was anything but gay. With a man so astonishingly good-looking, women would have been incapable of preventing themselves from boasting that they had slept with him. On the other hand, as most of the men he *was* involved with professionally and personally have since married, *these* are hardly likely to come forward now. Nick's very starchy upbringing – the fact that his parents were later so obviously embarrassed by his drug-taking and depression, without the added 'humiliation' of a family scandal – would have taught him to be discreet. Also, there was the fear factor, as Michel explained:

> *I don't think Nick actually told his parents that he was gay. In those days you didn't do that sort of thing. But they knew, I'm sure of that, because he was always going off with some guy or another and inviting him back to the house – no girls were ever taken back to Far Leys. His mother, he said, was all right with it so long as he never brought the subject up but his father, he said, could be a nasty old bastard at times. To his way of thinking, all that Nick needed was a stint in the army and a haircut, and maybe a good hiding to knock the pouffiness out of him. Nick said that his father abused him all the time – and I'm talking mental abuse, though he said that he had knocked him around as a child. I suppose all that stuff stopped when Nick grew up. But the mental abuse he had to put up with from that man – the names he used to call him in front of people. Today you'd call him homophobic, but to people like Nick's parents in those days, homosexuality was an affliction. He would say really crude things – like wishing he'd wiped it on his shirt tails, or that when Nick was born, the midwife threw the wrong stuff away. Nick was a very big guy, and much stronger than you would think, yet he was terrified of standing up to him. The way he'd been brought up, you respected your parents, even if they did treat you like shit. Rather than fight back, Nick would just shrink into the shadows, or get away for a while.*

Paul Barrera also refers to an episode in his mini-biography (*Nick Drake: No Reply*, Agenda, 1997) where Joe Boyd allegedly tried to fix Nick up with a 'Cockney friend', the tone of the piece suggestive that this might have been more than just an attempt to cheer him up. 'Joe felt that this chap was particularly therapeutic for Nick,' Barrera observes. 'He would ignore Nick's lack of response to questions and force tea and food on him. He just generally jollied him along. Nick responded with smiles. He did not have to converse – the man made Nick's mind up for him.'

This 'Cockney friend' almost certainly seems to have been 'Dave', the 'East End villain' referred to, once he had effected a change of name, by Trevor Dann (*Darker Than the Deepest Sea*) – a married man and drug dealer who lived in Holland Park, and who according to Dann 'could supply mandrax, nembutal, LSD, hash oil, in fact any uppers or downers, barbiturates or hallucigens his musician friends requested'. Michel Bidault mentioned a similar character in our interviews:

> *Nick got himself involved with this very shady character, a thug who he thought might have once been involved with the Krays. This man was absolutely crazy about him – he offered to buy him a car and set him up in his own little flat. Nick said that though he had been tempted, he had turned the man down because he hadn't wanted his parents to find out he'd become a gangster's moll! But he did allow his manager to fix him up with a place, and I've always wondered what that was all about.*

The place Michel was referring to was a ground floor flat at 112 Haverstock Hill, in London's Belsize Park, not far from the Chalk Farm Tube station. Boyd was paying the rent and telephone bills, and still paying Nick his weekly stipend as per his Witchseason contract – additionally, he was getting a monthly allowance from his parents. Here, Nick began writing material for his next album, keeping even his closest friends at bay – the ones who had been accustomed to dropping in on him, as he had them, now were seen by appointment only. Only occasionally did he emerge from this self-enforced solitude, to visit Boyd's office at Witchseason, or for the occasional engagement at Bunjie's, on Litchfield Street, at the Troubadour in Earl's Court, and at his old stamping ground, Les Cousins, probably the only venue where he ever felt truly comfortable performing live.

Nick already had a number of new songs in his portfolio, and in the lead-up to the release of *Five Leaves Left* had decided to concentrate on polishing these up rather than 'wasting time' on press interviews. He had heard from Michel how, in France, Jacques Brel was doing the same thing: having retired from public recitals at 38, Brel now spent much of his time in the studio, or writing new material. The difference between the two, of course, was that Brel was a massive star who could afford to sit back. Nick was a novice, albeit a novice with immense talent, but except for his small fan base and those about him, few knew who he was.

Nick had decided to call his new album *Bryter Layter* – title courtesy of a television weatherman from the North of England, whom the platinum-toned Nick had criticised for not speaking properly. This would once more be a 'family' affair, with Joe Boyd producing, and Robert Kirby handling the arrangements.

Chapter Nine
Rider on the Wheel

Eventually, the new songs were completed to Nick's finicky satisfaction, and he emerged from his cocoon to begin working on the arrangements with Robert Kirby. Fairport Convention were rehearsing in an unlikely location: The Angel, near Bishop's Stortford, a former public house which they had converted into a studio. Accompanying him once more were Richard Thompson, along with the group's bassist, Dave Pegg, and their drummer, Dave Mattacks. There was the added bonus of ex-Velvet Underground member John Cale, who had just finished working with Nico, their former singer, on her groundbreaking *Marble Index* album.

Shortly after winding up *Bryter Layter*, Nick collapsed at a friend's home with agonising back pains. He was rushed into hospital, where doctors diagnosed kidney stones. Joe Boyd took him to Paris to recuperate. As a surprise he and the musician-producer Tony Cox (who would subsequently produce two of her albums, including the million-selling *Message Personnel*) had arranged for Nick to meet one of his idols, Françoise Hardy – like Barbara and Juliette Gréco – the *coqueluche* or darling of the gay community. He had hoped to meet these two as well, but Barbara was notoriously reclusive, and Gréco was touring. According to Michel Bidault, Nick also wanted to meet Marie Laforêt because he wanted to them to sing 'Viens sur la Montagne' together – and Anne Vanderlove, who had a hit that year with 'Ballade en Novembre', another song he performed in Provence.

As a teenager, Nick had raved over Hardy's hits such as 'Tous les Garçons et les Filles', and 'All Over the World', but most especially 'Comment te Dire Adieu', a Vera Lynn song ('It Hurts to Say Goodbye'), which Serge Gainsbourg had adapted into French in 1968. The meeting took place in her Paris apartment, on the Ile de la Cité, near Notre-Dame, and appears to have been successful, despite Nick's alleged terror of talking to her, and her own admittance that Nick selected a chair in a corner of her sitting room, as far away from her as possible! Later in the week, she and her singer partner, Jacques Dutronc, asked him to dine with them at the Tour d'Argent, the exclusive restaurant halfway up the Eiffel Tower. The next evening, leaving Dutronc at home, Hardy accompanied Nick and Michel to the restaurant near avenue Montaigne where Michel worked – and which he subsequently bought. Hardy later told the French press how she had been 'smitten by Nick's frailty, charm and perfect English manners'. She also gave him her personal telephone number and asked him to stay in touch because, she said, she was interested in recording one of his songs.

Bryter Layter was released on 1 November 1970. The purple cover had a photograph by Nigel Weymouth: Nick sitting on an antique chair with his enormous thick-soled blue suede loafers off, hunched over his guitar, his dark hair reaching to his shoulders. On the reverse was a shot by Keith Morris: Nick leaning against a motorway flyover, indolently watching the night-time traffic. More Morris pictures would turn up in the 1987 CD booklet: a head-and-shoulders shot of Nick looking angelic and wholesome as he poses against a backdrop of climbing roses; one of him looking unkempt and rakish (and it has to be said, effeminate) as he wanders across a patch of wasteland bordering an industrial stretch of the Thames; a third from the photo shoot at Hampstead Heath where, photographed from behind, he stands with his book and guitar. The album is generally regarded as Nick's best. Critics have cited any number of influences, including Leonard Cohen, Tim Buckley and even Serge Gainsbourg, but it is essentially Nick Drake, with just a few of the nuances he had picked up on his trips to France.

As *Five Leaves Left* had been a rural outing conceived in Tanworth and Cambridge, so *Bryter Layter* is mostly metropolitan – just seven songs and three instrumentals, including the title track – evoking Nick's renewed surroundings since leaving home. This is most obvious in 'At the Chime of a City Clock', his take on Edith Piaf's 'La Ville Inconnue', which Michel had introduced him to. Whereas Piaf had used the harmonica to extol the gnawing feeling of solitude – finding oneself stuck in a strange town, where all one wants to do is sleep and forget – Nick utilises the jazzy, delectable tones of Ray Warleigh's alto sax. One almost wishes to see this sound-tracked over an old Steve Cochran gangster *film noir*, for here, in the Big Smoke (aka Soho), one is either weird, lonely, or just another face in the crowd – though there are benefits to be had here, such as 'Sonny Boy, with smokes for sale'.

Chronologically, 'Hazey Jane II' comes before 'Hazey Jane I'. To a jaunty brass arrangement by Robert Kirby, and with *drums* appearing for the first time on a Nick Drake song, the theme is sexual confusion – Nick's own, maybe, during adolescence, when he was trying to work out on which side of the fence he belonged. As with Betty in 'River Man', no one has ever been to work out who Jane was, if indeed she was an actual person, or just some oblique reference that Nick was making to drugs, as had happened with 'The Thoughts of Mary Jane'. As if to explain to the listener what he is not really explaining at all, Nick concludes of the typical *chansonnier*'s frequent lack of communication, except for his or her work, 'If songs were lines in a conversation, the situation would be fine.' Baffling, maybe, but brilliant most definitely!

In 'One of These Things First', a late-night set-piece whose jazzy ambience is enhanced by Paul Harris' fine piano work, Nick pleads the shortcomings which caused him to lose a lover – albeit pleasantly and totally without regret – as he reels off a list of the things that he might have been, or even *should* have been, if only he had known how. In 'Fly', almost an 'Olde English' madrigal with John Cale on the viola and harpsichord, Nick puts on a brave face, upping his voice almost an octave to beg his lover to give him a second chance, though ultimately he feels he may be too late.

'Poor Boy', which has Nick playing an *electric* guitar and alternating between the third and first person, is on the other hand, another saga of self-deprecation within which Nick's doleful mood is contradicted by the presence of a gospel chorus provided by soul singers Doris Troy and Pat Arnold – and is woefully out of place here. Island were hoping to put out a single from the album, on both sides of the Atlantic, and anticipated that it would be this song, almost in emulation of the same title that Elvis Presley had performed in his debut movie, *Love Me Tender*, back in 1956. With its wailing, fake American-sounding backing for what was a quintessentially *English* singer, this is so *not* Nick Drake, and would become one of those tracks, with the advent of the compact disc, which would have many fans reaching for the skip button.

The final song on the album, 'Northern Sky', figures among Nick's best. The *New Musical Express*, not renowned for offering too many compliments where Nick was concerned, later described it as, 'The greatest English love song of modern times.' John Cale excels himself here on piano, organ, and the celeste – an instrument comprising metal plates struck by hammers played from a keyboard. Dark and mesmorisingly atmospheric, it encapsulates windswept landscapes and storm-tossed seas, and is as Byronesque as anything Nick ever created, very definitely a tone poem from the pen of an unsung hero-genius. Despite what they would say about him in the not-too-distant future, work such as this does *not* come from the mind of a manic-depressive. 'I never felt magic as crazy as this,' he tells the love he has found at last, the one who is here to brighten his Northern sky – the one he chillingly and fatalistically cannot help asking, 'Would you love me till I'm dead?' A masterpiece!

The music press was more enthusiastic about this one than its predecessor. The *Record Mirror* obviously carried a torch for this new-kid-on-the-block. Calling him 'a beautiful guitarist', who added, 'Nick isn't the world's top singer, but he's written fantastic numbers that suit strings marvellously. Definitely one of the prettiest – and *that* counts! – and most impressive albums I've heard.' The journalist Kris Kirk told me, 'The music was beautiful, the man even more so. He was gorgeous. One flash of those eyes and he would have had the straightest man in the world grovelling at his feet. After he died, people pretended that they cared about him, but most of them didn't give a shit about looking after him. That was Nick Drake's greatest tragedy.' *Melody Maker* tended to prefer sitting on the fence. 'This is a particularly difficult album to come to terms with,' observed Andrew Means. 'The reaction it produces depends very much on the mood of the listener. It's late night coffee 'n' chat music.'

Bryter Layter sold around 10,000 copies, twice as many as *Five Leaves Left*. Island had recently released two compilation albums (*Nice Enough To Eat* and *Bumpers*) of their biggest names, enabling two of Nick's songs to reach a much wider audience. Fans had heard these and wanted more. Nick may have been half-willing to promote any of his songs, so long as *he* was doing the choosing, but when Island told him that they planned to release 'Poor Boy' as a single, and that he would be expected to promote it on – horror of horrors! – *Top of the Pops*, he hit the roof. The response was a resounding 'No', backed by a few well-aimed expletives at the BBC producer who approached him. Similarly, he rejected a second *John Peel Show* session, and also an appearance on BBC2's *Disco 2*, a precursor of the channel's acclaimed *The Old Grey Whistle Test*. The BBC now informed him that, unless he 'woke up his ideas' he would not be gracing the airwaves in the foreseeable future.

Under duress, on 8 March 1971, Nick agreed to give what would be his only press interview, for the now defunct *Sounds* – the piece appeared in the 13 March issue. The journalist was Jerry Gilbert, who certainly seems to have had a struggle on his hands getting Nick to open up. 'Nick Drake is a shy, introverted folk singer who is not known to speak unless it is absolutely necessary,' he observed. 'But Nick is not the kind of folk singer who will drift into your friendly neighbourhood folk club. In fact, if you've seen him perform, the chances are that he was on the bill of a sell-out Festival Hall concert.'

After interviewing Nick at some great length – though the published interview was relatively short, so what else they talked about is not known – Gilbert got him to confess why he had been so obviously hung up about the venues he had been performing in:

> *I think the problem was with the material, which I wrote rather for records than for performing. There were only two or three concerts that felt right, and there was something wrong with all the others. I did play Cousins, and one or two folk clubs in the North, but the gigs just sort of petered out.*

And was it true, Gilbert wanted to know, that Nick had only done the concerts under the same duress that he was now submitting to this interview? Nick elaborated, not even caring that he was slagging off his record company:

> *I was under some obligation to them, but it wasn't the end of the world when I stopped. If I was enjoying the gigs it would have made much more sense.*

As for the songs, Nick agreed with Gilbert's observation that Robert Kirby's arrangements were as good as the songs themselves, and spoke of his concerns for the future:

> *I had something in mind when I wrote the songs, knowing that they weren't just for me . . . But I'm not altogether clear about this album. I haven't got to terms with the whole presentation. I think there will be another album and I have some material for it, but I'll be looking around now to see if this album leads anywhere naturally [i.e. without making personal appearances]. For the next one I had the idea of just doing something with John Wood, the engineer at Sound Techniques.*

Finally, would there be any live appearances to promote the album? Nick was very sure that there would not, certainly not with the way Island and Witchseason had handled things so far:

> *I don't think that would help, unless they were done in the right way. I'm just not very sure at the moment. It's hard to tell what will turn up. If I could find making music a fairly natural connection with something else, then I might move on to something else.*

And that was it – Nick Drake's *only* press interview!

Gilbert later intimated to Patrick Humphries that interviewing Nick, in a flat in Swiss Cottage, had been a nightmare: Nick had fidgeted, and constantly toyed with his long hair. He had been incapable of looking his interviewer in the eye and had been totally void of charisma, responding to most of his questions with a muttered yes or no. 'It was almost as if he was denying his existence,' Gilbert concluded.

Jerry Gilbert could not have been more wrong when issuing the latter statement, or more offensive to Nick's memory. Difficult and withdrawn Nick certainly may have been. So many have testified to this over the last 30-odd years. But everyone – and there have been *no* exceptions, who ever crossed his path has described him as being *potently* charismatic.

Neither had Nick's work been overlooked by other performers. Millie Small recorded a cover-version of 'Mayfair' for her *Time Will Tell* album, and this was also released as a single. Nana Mouskouri and the Italian *chanteuse* Milva included several Nick Drake songs in their concert repertoire. Reginald Dwight, employed as a session singer and fresh from cutting his new album as Elton John, made a job of 'Saturday Sun', 'Time Has Told Me', 'When Day is Done' and 'Way to Blue'. These were recorded in July 1970 as part of the now legendary, mega-rare (a copy, one of ten in existence, sold for £2,500 in December 2007) *Warlock Sampler* album which also contained covers of songs by John and Beverley Martin, Mike Heron of the Incredible String Band, and Ed Carter of the Beach Boys' band.

At around this time, Nick also hired himself out as a session musician, though no one had the foresight to document exactly whose recordings he played on. Along with a folk singer named Vivien Fowler, he was also commissioned to appear on a now very elusive educational record, *Interplay One*, for Longman. His very distinctive guitar playing may be heard on three songs: the traditional hillbilly favourite, 'I Wish I Was a Single Girl Again', 'With My Swag On My Shoulder', and 'Full Fathom Five', previously revived by Marianne Faithfull on her *North Country Maid* album which he so admired.

Nick is said to have been extremely distressed when, at around this time, his mentor Joe Boyd upped sticks and returned to Los Angeles to work for Warner Brothers Music. For some time, it would appear, there had been dissension in the Witchseason camp, and the crunch came when Richard Thompson, generally regarded as the group's leading light, left Fairport Convention.

Boyd threw a sweetener in Nick's direction – inserting a clause into

Witchseason's sale contract which stated that Island would be compelled to release any Nick Drake album, whether they approved of it or not, and *prohibited* them from ever deleting the two albums he had made. Even so, this and Boyd's departure weighed heavily on the young man's shoulders, for he was terrified that Boyd's successor would only demand much more of him than he could possibly give.

Boyd's 'desertion' of Nick quite obviously set in motion the beginning of the end. He was about to enter the studio to cut his third album, *Pink Moon*, but being deserted by his anchor in his greatest hour of need pushed him deeper into depression. Not only had he lost the only man in the world he believed he could truly trust, he had lost a manager, record and music producer, agent and confidant which, from his fragile way of looking at things, brought him to the chilling conclusion that, so far as his career was concerned, the only direction from now on would be downhill. Indeed, his sudden deterioration in the wake of Boyd's departure suggests that Nick *must* have been in love with the handsome American, though whether Boyd realised this is a matter of conjecture. Nick lost a stone in weight, seemed to stoop more than usual, and was frequently seen in public dishevelled and unshaven. Michel recalled:

> *Nick was head-over-heels in love with his American manager – frightened to tell this man how he really felt, in case it all blew up in his face. He was also in love with one of his musicians – and that one was reciprocated. He did spend much of his time stoned, but all this stuff about him looking dirty and living in squalor. That was bullshit. Maybe he'd go a few days without a shave, but that only made him look cuter that ever!*

With Boyd gone, Nick left London for a while and in late September 1971 accepted an invitation from Paul Wheeler, his friend from Cambridge, to spend a few days with him and his wife at Titenhurst Park, near Ascot. This was the country home of John Lennon and Yoko Ono, currently in America: Wheeler was the Lennons' personal assistant. Nick later told Michel Bidault that he had had the 'great fortune to tinkle the ivories' on the grand piano used by Lennon for *Imagine*. Other than this, he had spent much of his time wandering about the house, smoking pot and marvelling at the wealth of Beatles memorabilia.

From Ascot, Nick returned to the only safe haven he knew – Far Leys, which turned out to be a big mistake. He had friends in the capital, good friends, who though linked to the then notoriously self-destructive society-pop-rock business would have proved much better equipped to steer him through his rapidly approaching breakdown.

Despite what has been said – mostly by people searching for their own five minutes of fame, linked as they suddenly and unexpectedly found themselves to his posthumous glory, without which they themselves would have been assigned to obscurity – Nick was *not* mentally ill. He was distressed over Boyd's departure, despondent because his records were not selling as well as those of his Island contemporaries – a combination of bad management and near non-existent publicity. Even his refusal to give live performances was not entirely his fault. Boyd and the other Witchseason executives had been well aware of his fragility and terrible stage fright and should have found him work at the smaller venues he had always felt comfortable with – having him on the bill at the Festival Hall and then to book him in rowdy working men's clubs had been nothing short of sheer stupidity.

Effectively, Nick's performance anxiety led to the same form of depression the great poets had suffered as the result of writer's block. Rimbaud and Verlaine had coped by guzzling vast quantities of absinthe. Jean Cocteau had turned to opium. Nick's closest friends believed that what he really needed was counselling, to help him overcome his stage fright. Maria Callas and Eartha Kitt had thus been cured of their demons: others had submitted to tranquillisers, administered by a doctor before curtain-up.

Then there were those who believed that the antidote to Nick's misery would have been better coming from an older, more forceful but caring lover – but that he was so withdrawn, he would never allow anyone near him. Few if any of Nick's friends knew about Michel, who in any case was too far away – and Nick was not in any fit state to travel far from home. According to Michel, there was such a person: 'A singer, just separated from his wife. He was in London, right under Nick's nose. Nick moved in with him for a little while, but it never worked out.'

So far as Nick's parents were concerned, ignorance prevailed, or so they liked to let us later believe. Though he claimed never to have come out to them, they appear to have known that he was gay. Similarly aware that Joe Boyd's absence was at the root of their son's problems, they called Boyd in Los Angeles, which suggests that they may also have suspected more than a professional relationship between the two men. What, if any, advice Boyd offered them is not known, but certain that this was the proper thing to do, the Drakes took Nick to St Thomas's Hospital, in London, to have him assessed by a psychiatrist. That he agreed to this displays not just a singular weakness, but just how much he placed his trust in people who, far from being concerned for his welfare, were acting in their own interests. As Michel said, 'It was more a case of thinking, "What will the neighbours say if he kicks off at home and all this gets out?" They were always having a go at him for having long hair and not having a proper job. And now they jumped to the obvious blinkered conclusion that poor Nick must be nuts.'

Whether this psychiatrist was told of Nick's fondness for smoking pot is not known – his jittery mannerisms should have suggested that he was on *something*, though addicts are of course adept at hiding such things. Whatever, the psychiatrist prescribed him the antidepressants that would inevitably lead to tragedy.

One friend who offered some support was Chris Blackwell of Island, the nearest Nick would get to having a manager. Though not obliged to do so, Blackwell had kept Nick on a weekly retainer in the hope of coaxing him back into the studio. He now loaned him the use of his villa in Algeciras, in Southern Spain. Whether he actually did enjoy two weeks of 'sun, sea and sex', as has been suggested, aided by an unlimited supply of cannabis, is very likely. He certainly returned to London refreshed and sufficiently recovered to record the new album. He also ruffled a few feathers – especially Robert Kirby's – by announcing that this would be his most personal album so far, and as such *he* alone would be doing the arranging and accompanying.

Pink Moon was completed in just two midnight taping sessions and a piano over-dubbing session for the title-track (as opposed to the several months that it had taken to complete its predecessors), which has led to suggestions that Nick was at such a low ebb, he simply wanted to get it over and done with. This was nonsense: Nick had had enough of being let down by friends, and felt more comfortable with only himself to rely upon. Also, much has been made of his behaviour in the studio – claims that by now, he was so shy and withdrawn that he played and sang with his back to the technicians. Again, he was following the *chansonnier* tradition. Entertainers on the Continent had been doing this since the turn of the century – and it was much less to do with tetchiness and timidity than a desire to achieve maximum concentration.

Similarly, because the album turned out to be the last record released during Nick's lifetime, critics and fans alike (as with Jeff Buckley's posthumous *Sketches For My Sweetheart For the Drunk*) have searched its contents for 'clues' of impending doom and suicide. These *are* here, but no more so than in his other two albums. As Nick had followed in the tradition of the existentialist poets, so it was expected that every aspect of the human condition should be explored within his work. And in any case, Nick had not predetermined that this should be his swansong.

'Pink Moon', with its delicious, bluesy overall approach, is a beautiful concept, woefully too short, but it is neither bleak nor despairing. Nick's voice is bright and fresh, breezy throughout and its usual perfect pitch. This is the Nick Drake album where one pours a good vintage, dims the light, and enjoys!

The title-track opens the proceedings, and is cynically portentous only in that it refers to the ancient superstition that the 'pink moon' occurring during an eclipse was regarded as an unlucky omen forecasting sudden death – a curse which never differentiated between the classes. Nick adopts the stance of the medieval seer as, half an octave higher than usual, he pronounces, 'Zaw it written and I zaw it say . . . Pink moon gonna get ye all!' Those gay fans who wrongly believed that Nick had chosen pink labels for his albums in clandestine support of the post-Stonewall revolution now believed that, with the advent of gay-friendly androgynous glam-rock, the song contained a hidden message that the gay community's time had come at last. This may be true: almost the entire album centres around the joys and pains of gay love.

'Place to Be', which Nick had wanted to be on *Five Leaves Left*, is a mature piece for a man of just 23, telling of how old age enables one to take stock of one's life, albeit that doing so brings with it a certain foreboding. 'Now I'm deeper than the darkest sea,' Nick confesses of his *cafardeux* state, brought about by a desperate desire to love. The song also has Nick borrowing from the Beatles. Not only is the opening line almost a word-for-word repetition of the first line of 'Help!' ('When I was young, younger than before'), each verse may be sung to the same tune as the Beatles' hit.

'Road', by way of contrast, sees Nick optimistically proclaiming, 'I can take a road that'll see me through' – that may allude to coming to terms with sexuality or drugs, whichever way one wishes to interpret it. 'Which Will' is an allegory of sorts wherein he equates lovers with the stars, asking one lover in particular – almost certainly the musician referred to by Michel, who spurned him – that *he* must now make a choice. 'Horn', an intricate instrumental that Nick plays with just two fingers, seems out of place here (as many had believed of *Bryter Layter*, claiming that it had served no purpose to perpetuate the Nick Drake legend), and is over no sooner than it has begun, lasting just 76 seconds.

'In Things Behind the Sun' (written in 1968, and included in his programme at the Festival Hall), Nick lashes out at the hypocrisy of the record industry, and maybe at Joe Boyd especially – the fact that if one took time getting to know some of these people whose 'charms are hired', one would never wish to offer them time of day: 'Look around . . . you'll find the ground is not so far away from where you are.'

In 'Know', a piece containing just four lines, Nick mocks the brevity of love, certainly so far as his own experiences are concerned, by assuring the object of his affection that, though he loves him, he does not care! 'Parasite' (which Nick had performed during his 1970 tour) is a perfect companion-piece to 'At the Chime of the City Clock'. Nick, the archetypal black sheep descends the stairs en route to catch the Northern Line to Chalk Farm. Embarking on a spree of restrained self-deprecation, he stares at his shoes, listens to idle gossip, and blames class on his despair as the train hurtles him towards his destination. 'Falling so far on a silver spoon,' he opines, though somehow we get the impression that he is merely feeling sorry for himself, and may even be gleaning sardonic pleasure from his misery.

'Free Ride' has been mistakenly described as a pun on the surname of Sophia Ryde, a one-time girlfriend of Nick's, though only in the platonic sense. Nothing of the kind, it is another unveiled attack on record-company bureaucracy which sees Nick urging the rich fat cat who treats his clients badly – 'All of the pictures that you keep on the wall . . . Counting the cattle as they go by the door' – to give *him* another chance. If *this* was not levelled at Joe Boyd, Nick's adherents have since demanded, then who *was* it aimed at?

In 'Harvest Breed', a number even shorter than 'Horn', Nick laments a lack of love and friendship, and almost certainly is not thinking about death, as wishful-thinking critics have suggested. The inspiration for the song comes from Marie Laforêt's 1963 hit, 'Les Vendanges de l'Amour', one of the first French *chansons* he had heard while at Marlborough. This tells the story of the 'singletons' who, having experienced a winter of unhappiness and tears, set off in search of amorous adventure now that the grape-harvesting season has begun. In 'From the Morning', the same theme allows the album to end on a sexually ambiguous but optimistic note – the fact that in the French language, 'day' is a masculine noun, while 'night' is feminine. Here, Nick loves both with equal fervour and conviction: he enjoys watching the dawn rise, but also awaits one of those endless summer nights when love is in the air. All in all, another concept masterpiece!

Pink Moon was released on 25 February 1972. Having attracted criticism after the sleeve of *Bryter Layter*, not least of all from Nick himself, Island opted not to have a photograph of him on the sleeve of this one. They therefore commissioned a painting by Gabrielle Drake's artist friend, Michael Trevithick, a Dali-esque work depicting sea shells, a clown's face, a yellow (for friendship) tulip, a cup, leaves, and a flaming rocket headed towards a moon made of cheese!

Island commissioned Keith Morris to supply photographs for the interior of the gate-fold. He and Nick spent the afternoon on Hampstead Heath, though in the only study used from this session, Nick looks uncomfortable, tense and scowling before a backdrop of leafless branches. Another shot of him, where he sits staring into space while hunched on a park bench (later used for a posthumous retrospective) captures perfectly the spiritlessness of the young neurasthenic. Gabrielle Drake, who never missed out on the opportunity to tell journalists that her brother had been born 'with a skin too few', was quoted (*Record Collector*, February 1992) as saying of this shot, 'Everyone, no matter how bad they are feeling, will try to pose when they're having their photograph taken. But here, all Nick's desire to pose has gone. He's not even aware of the camera.'

Equally thought provoking was the Keith Morris photograph from this session, later used on the reverse of the CD release of *Pink Moon*: Nick, his back to the camera, sloping off towards the river. His trousers are too long while his jacket sleeves are way too short, and he seems oblivious of the golden retriever which has just turned the corner – and which itself looks unsure whether to greet or bite him.

Pink Moon sold around 20,000 copies – comparatively few in those days, though today this would be sufficient to get it into the charts. It was up against stiff competition: Cat Stevens, Roxy Music and Sparks all released high-profile albums at this time. And of course, this was the age of glam-rock. Even so, Nick was lucky to have done so well, for not only did Island inject a substantial part of their resources into re-releasing albums by Fairport Convention, Sandy Denny and Jethro Tull, the press officer, David Sandison, used up the *whole* of *Pink Moon*'s publicity budget to place a curious advertisement in *Melody Maker*, which to some might have been tantamount to assigning Nick to the scrap-heap. One might also be excused for thinking that, as Nick had slagged off his record company in the *Sounds* interview *and* in two of his songs, now it was payback time.

The piece was headed, NICK DRAKE'S NEW ALBUM: THE FIRST WE HEARD OF IT WAS WHEN IT WAS FINISHED! This alluded to Island's disbelief of Nick's claim that this album would only have the most basic accompaniment. When he had taken the tapes away, they had expected him to work through them with Robert Kirby, as had happened before. Instead, he had returned to Witchseason a few days later, and without uttering a single word he had left them, untouched, on the secretary's desk! In the *Melody Maker* advertisement feature, David Sandison included an uncalled-for, very unflattering review of Nick's performance at the Queen Elizabeth Hall, when he had opened for John and Beverley Martin:

> *He came on with his guitar, sat on a stool, looked at the floor and sang a series of muffled songs punctuated by mumbled thanks for the scattering of bewildered applause from the audience who didn't know who the hell he was, nor cared too much. At the end of his last song, his guitar still holding the notes of the song, he got up, glanced up, then walked off, his shoulders hunched as if to protect him from the embarrassment of actually having to meet people.*

Sandison then offered the backhanded compliment as to why Island had gone to the trouble and expense of releasing *Pink Moon*:

> *The chances of Nick actually playing in public are more than remote. So why, when there are people prepared to do anything for a recording contract or a Queen Elizabeth Hall date, are we releasing this new Nick Drake album, and the next one (if he wants to do one)? Because we believe that Nick Drake is a great talent. His first two albums haven't sold a shit, but if we carry on releasing them, maybe one day someone in authority will stop to listen to them properly and agree with us, and maybe a lot more people will get to hear Nick Drake's incredible songs and guitar playing. And maybe they'll buy a lot of his albums, and fulfil our faith in Nick's promise. Then. Then we'll have done our job.*

The subsequent reviews, what few there were, were half-hearted and mocking. *Sounds*' Jerry Gilbert, the recipient of Nick's only interview, accused Island of neglecting one of their brightest stars, yet could not resist the dig, 'Nick Drake remains the greatest silent enigma of our time. Maybe it's time Mr Drake stopped acting so mysteriously and started getting something properly organised for himself.' *Time Out* observed, 'Nick Drake is likely to remain in the shadows – the private troubadour of those who have been fortunate enough to catch an earful of his exquisite 3am introversions.' *ZigZag*'s Connor McKnight was more supportive: 'Nick Drake is an artist who never fakes. It is impossible to avoid the searing sensibility behind the record . . . it's simply one musician's view of life at the time, and you can't ask for more than that.' Mark Plummer of *Melody Maker*, while unappreciative of Island's unpleasant press release, nevertheless opted to sit on the fence:

> *His music is so personal and shyly presented, both lyrically and in his confirmed guitar and piano playing, that it neither does nor doesn't come over. Drake is a fairly mysterious person. No one appears to know where he lives, what he does apart from writing songs, and there isn't even a chance to see him on stage to get closer to his insides. It could be that Nick doesn't exist at all.*

After *Pink Moon*'s release, bullied by his father and nagged to distraction by his overbearing mother, Nick slumped into his deepest depression so far. He was booked for an appearance on Bob Harris' *Sound of the Seventies* radio programme – a 15-minute slot where he was invited to sing whatever he chose, and not necessarily any of the songs from the new album. This was scheduled to be taped on 23 March 1973 and broadcast on 17 April. Harris turned up at Broadcasting House, but Nick did not and the BBC – who felt he had been warned once too often – added his name to their 'unreliables' list, which in those days meant a total ban from appearing on any of their programmes 'unless under exceptional circumstances'.

Nick's fairly heavy but still controlled intake of marijuana had been replaced by prescribed antidepressants. Friends rallied around him when they could: if he was not staying with them in London, they travelled up to Warwickshire and the Drakes put them up at Far Leys. Some have said how he would drop in on them unannounced, not say more than a dozen words in two hours, then leave without bidding goodbye. Others talked – long after his death when it became 'fashionable' to dwell on negative aspects of his last two years – of finding him in various states of abject distress, once crouched against the wall in the foetal position.

Being launched on the US market hindered rather than helped Nick's recovery. In April 1972, his first two albums were combined for a retrospective and released – many thought with deliberate insensitivity – on the Asylum label. The sleeve featured the reverse of *Five Leaves Left*. 'The beauty of Drake's voice is its own justification. May it become familiar to us all,' observed *Rolling Stone* who went on to applaud the compilation as 'beautiful and decadent . . . a triumph of eclecticism . . . a hypnotic spell of opiated languor.'

In America, *Pink Moon* was sent out to the press with a publicity sheet so glaringly over-the-top in praise of Nick's talents that many, believing him too good to be true, refused to review it. An exception was Texas Rolling Stones' fan Jim Conley, who included a glowing tribute to Nick in his feature celebrating the Stones' *Exit On Main Street* album. Having praised Nick's 'throaty, shaggy and captivating' voice, Conley observed in the 18 June edition of *The Abilene Reporter*,

> *Frankly, I didn't think Nick Drake was going to be 'another Cat Stevens' or would have 'the kind of album Donovan might have produced, if he'd been lucky'. But the record is here and everyone was almost right . . . He lifts some unpolished, simple lyrics into a private world which you are made to share through his convincing sincerity. Where Cat Stevens seems to make a bit of fun of his situation, Nick Drake voices the sorrowful incompleteness of a man who is struggling helplessly to be tender, like a drifter whose squinty, quick gaze is the facade of a scared-to-smite, too-often hurt sensitivity. Indeed, Drake – says his record company sugar daddy – is somewhat of a loner, a mystery man who avoids interviews. That's fine for his image, too. Maybe his next album jacket will give more than a negative as a substitute for a perceptive photo of his face . . . But whether or not he's as reclusive as his people say, I think he's where 1972's music is going, maybe where 1973's will be. At least I hope so, because it's a beautiful direction.*

Had Nick seen this review, he might *just* have been tempted to cross the Atlantic, for with such high-profile championing he really did stand a chance of making it big in America. He did not, and when Asylum tried to set up a brief promotional tour, the best they got was a cardboard cut-out of the singer which stood eerily on an empty podium each time the album was auditioned for sales reps and disc jockeys. 'Like the Sandman, Nick Drake doesn't really exist,' one of these told a bemused crowd, echoing the earlier *Melody Maker* advertisement feature for *Pink Moon*.

Chapter Ten

Hanging on a Star

Throughout the whole of 1973, Nick did virtually nothing to further his career. Holed up much of the time in his bedroom or the music room at Far Leys, he struggled as best he could – writing and composing intermittently, frequently in a daze on account of the medication we now know he should not have been taking. Most of his friends and acquaintances in the music industry had deserted him. Drugs, debauchery and booze they could deal with, but like Nick's parents, many of them confused clinical depression with actual insanity.

One who cared more than most was John Martyn, who wrote one of his most celebrated songs in honour of Nick, just to remind him how special he considered him, how important he *should* have been to the British music scene. *Solid Air* includes the statement, 'You've been getting too deep, you've been living on solid air . . . you've been missing your sleep.' Twelve years after Nick's death, Martyn would lash out at the very establishment in *Pynk Moon*, telling the biographer Brendan Quayle, 'Nick was a beautiful man, but walking on solid air, helpless in this dirty business . . . He was killed by the indecent, parasitic opportunism that pervades the music business.' Yet in November 2008, he told the *Sun*, 'I don't think anyone realised how troubled he was, how severe his mental illness was. Poor Nicky, none of us knew what to do about it. It's odd how huge he's become. And he's a gay icon now—he'd be appalled by that!' The latter part of his statement, coming from a man known to have had a crush on Nick and now very wrongly suggesting that Nick may have been homophobic, upset many of Nick's gay fans. Two months later, a victim of his drink and drugs excesses, which at the zenith of his addiction resulted in his having to have a leg amputated, Martyn would follow Nick to the grave.

Neither did Rodney and Molly Drake help by circulating the story in the first place that their son was on the verge of madness. Acting on the advice of another psychiatrist who prescribed Tryptizol – and, as Michel said, undoubtedly concerned that Nick's erratic behaviour might set society tongues wagging in Tanworth – they had Nick committed to Barnsley Hall, a psychiatric hospital in Bromsgrove. Here, against his will, he remained for over a month – not in a private room which the Drakes could easily have afforded, but in a 12-bed ward, surrounded by mostly middle-aged men who really were mentally ill, some of them screaming the place down from morning until night.

Why Nick submitted to such degradation remains incomprehensible, and is a sad testament to the fact that he, who had striven so hard to get away from these people, should now crumble to their whim. Years later, the Drakes claimed that their son had volunteered to the treatment at Barnsley Hall. This is untrue, for it has since emerged that he was told at the time that unless he admitted himself willingly, they would have him sectioned – which of course meant, back then, that if this happened there would be no guarantee of his ever being de-sectioned.

Thankfully, Nick did get out, and upon his recovery spent two weeks in Paris with Michel. The pair visited the familiar *chansonnier* locations, and the sojourn appears to have cleared his mind and allowed him to take stock of his life. As much as Nick loved his parents, he was starting to find their presence stifling, as indeed he did everyone else after so long. Their constant nagging was only aggravating his fragile state of health, as life at Far Leys grew increasingly oppressive. Nick had always been a loner, but solitude in London had always been a better option than stagnation in the middle of nowhere. In Paris he had seen *life*, and he wanted to do so again.

In June, bullied by his father who declared for the umpteenth time that all he really needed was a haircut and a decent job, Nick made an appointment with the Army Recruitment Centre, in Birmingham – the idea being that if accepted, he would enlist for two years, still find time to compose, but sort out his life once and for all. Yet again, Rodney Drake was confusing discipline with compassion, and his actions only confirmed that he had never really taken his son's career seriously. The interview was successful, but the Army withdrew their offer when someone – almost certainly Molly Drake, secretly opposing her husband – brought it to their attention that their new recruit had 'certain mental problems' which had not been discussed during his medical examination. Nick next applied for a job as a computer programmer with a company in Birmingham. He was accepted, and dispatched to London on a training course. Though an amiable man, he was unable to cope with a large open-plan office situation, and two weeks later was back at Far Leys.

In January 1974, Nick learned that Joe Boyd was back in London, and it was his former mentor who – inadvertently – threw him his last lifeline. Scarcely able to hold himself together, one could say that Nick humbled himself by going to see Boyd in the February. He had completed four new songs and wanted Boyd to hear them and his ideas for their arrangements. Boyd was sufficiently impressed, but may have been acting for old times' sake and out of pity when he recorded two of these at once: 'Rider on the Wheel' and 'Black-Eyed Dog'.

Boyd later claimed that Nick was in such a shocking state that the vocals had to be recorded separately from the music because he could no longer sing and play the guitar at the same time. Hearing the result, one finds this hard to believe – particularly with 'Rider on the Wheel', which Island were planning to release as a single – because Nick sounds so together. Similarly, one may never know if Nick really did take engineer John Wood aside, as Wood claimed in a *Record Collector* interview of 1992, and tell him, 'I can't think of words. I feel no emotion about anything. I don't want to laugh or cry. I'm numb, dead inside.'

'Rider on the Wheel' is a bouncy, light-hearted piece; only the occasional cracked phrase suggests that its interpreter may have been unwell. That Nick was by now truly suffering for his art is evident from the way he pronounces, 'Must keep up the show for the rider on the wheel.' In other words, he combines Fate with the precognitive dream – the fact that all will turn out well if one so wishes – which he felt had deserted him, but which now be believed could he addressed flippantly.

'Black Dog' was the term used by Sir Winston Churchill for his mood-swings and darkest depressions, though in 'Black-Eyed Dog' Nick is almost certainly *mocking* his demons as he sweeps into Libby Holman–Robert Johnson territory – meeting them head-on, whereas the infamous black torch singers had allowed themselves to be sucked into the murky quagmire of mental malady. The song *is* melancholy and, for those who have the urge to believe that Nick was at the extreme end of his tether, it is harrowing to listen to. However, taking into account the manner within which this most quintessential of English poets Americanises the lyric – 'Black-eyed dog ain't gonna claw't my door . . . grown old and I wanna go home' – it's indicative of how he is merely *emulating* these early blues artists, nothing more.

In June 2004, 'Black-Eyed Dog' would figure among *Mojo* magazine's *100 Most Miserable Songs*, drawn up on the occasion of 'arch-miserabilist' Morrissey's return to the limelight after seven years in the artistic-commercial wilderness. Nick came in at Number 18 in the 'Whinger Songwriters' section.

'Few have been as vulnerable to the beast as fragile, doomed Drake,' observed the editorial. Nick would have felt proud to be among such distinguished company: his 'weep and moan' companions included Bob Dylan, Elvis Presley, Leonard Cohen, Tim Buckley and Neil Diamond!

After recording the two songs, Nick stayed on in London. He had kept up the flat in Hampstead, which suggests that he was not so close to the breadline as many have claimed – though his parents could of course have been picking up the tab. Again, the pattern was the continuous dropping in on friends unannounced – and a failed attempt to get back with his musician lover who, like the Drakes, was hard put to discern between depression and insanity. Before leaving Far Leys, Nick had thrown an out-of-character tantrum and flushed his tablets down the toilet, declaring that he could cope better without them, but rather than send him for the specialist treatment Michel claims he asked for, his doctor had merely followed the Drakes' request to prescribe more. Unable to cope without these antidepressants that were only making his condition worse, Nick managed to write every now and then, and in July entered the Sound Techniques studio for the last time.

'Hanging on a Star' sees each line starting with an un-Drake-like falsetto wail, and makes one wonder how Joe Boyd – from Nick's way of thinking almost certainly the part-orchestrator of his misery – could have actually listened to him singing this in the studio without feeling acutely uncomfortable. 'Why leave me hanging on a star when you deem me so high?' he pleads, in this paean to neglect.

'Voice From the Mountain', which Nick had been singing off and on since 1969, was to have been the opening track on his fourth album and its resurrection clearly refutes the fact, as has been suggested these past three decades, that he was all washed up and waiting for the end. On the contrary, it displays the peace of mind acquired from his trip to Paris. His demons were caged, and the voice of a happier, more contented destiny now called from all quarters – from the mountains and the sky, from the ocean waves. 'A tune from the hillside, and a tune full of light,' he defiantly proclaims.

This optimism is reconfirmed with 'Tow the Line', which would be found at the end of the reel, 30 years after Nick's death, when Island were checking through one of their tapes for an anniversary retrospective of out-takes and rarities. What makes this song of paramount importance is that it had been recorded *after* 'Black-Eyed Dog' in the sequence of events leading up to the tragedy everyone close to Nick had supposedly anticipated. Like 'Voice From the Mountain', it more than suggests that he had *not* reached or surpassed the limit of his endurance.

Robert Kirby and John Wood later observed (*Mojo*, June 2004) that, in their opinion, 'Hanging on a Star' and 'Tow the Line' had been, 'A direct address that had all but deserted [Nick] in the latter two years of his life', and that the songs *were* about Joe Boyd. The former may have certainly been aimed at Boyd in a negative way, though Nick seems to have reserved his opinion of his ex-mentor by the time he composed 'Tow the Line', and it is gratifying to know that the very last song he recorded was so blatantly *positive*. Bearing in mind that his lyrics were always extremely personal, the evidence is so strong that he had every intention of doing whatever may have been necessary to get back on track. 'This day is the day that we rise or we fall,' he declares, 'and now that you're here, you can show me the way.'

'Tow the Line' expressed Nick's delight over having Joe Boyd back in his life, and that they would be doing another album together. Its lyric also leaves no doubt that he *was* in love with him, even though Boyd may not have felt the same way about him. Boyd's presence had boosted Nick's never rock-solid confidence, so much so that the new songs were recorded in a single evening, with no retakes, and again with just Nick and his guitar. And so long as Boyd stayed around, even if their friendship had absolutely no chance of progressing beyond the platonic, for Nick there would always be that small flicker of light at the end of the tunnel.

Shortly afterwards, against his better judgement, Nick returned to Tanworth. A side-effect of the Tryptizol, along with two other prescribed antidepressants, was a form of dyspraxia. Occasionally he would bump into things, and there were occasional bouts of absentmindedness. Some critics have unfavourably compared him with James Dean, largely because, like Dean, he was neurotic and frequently tetchy, though only on account of his quest for perfection within his work, and of course because, like Dean, his work was not truly appreciated until he was dead. In fact, at this stage of his life Nick was closer to Montgomery Clift, when the American actor had been in a similar depressive state in the wake of a 1956 car accident. Like Monty, Nick would wander off into the night wearing just his pyjamas, or less – or drive his mother's car for miles until he ran out of petrol, then call whoever happened to be nearest his location to come out and rescue him. The flame of hope appeared to be burning stronger early in October when Nick plucked up the courage to drive to France. Françoise Hardy, yet to record his work, had expressed interest in a cover-version of 'Time

Has Told Me'. Like her earlier *Comment te Dire Adieu*, this was to be adapted into French by the legendary Serge Gainsbourg.

The *chanteuse* was still living with her long-time partner, Jacques Dutronc (they would marry in 1981), and the previous year – three days before Nick's 25th birthday – had given birth to their son, Thomas, who would follow in his parents' footsteps and himself become a successful singer. The pair received Nick warmly, and for old times' sake once more dined at the Tour d'Argent. Nick had told his parents that he would be staying with friends on their barge moored near the Canal St Martin. He actually spent most of his time with Michel. The two went to see one of Nick's favourite films, *Elvira Madigan*, and Nick compromised by going to see *Jules et Jim*, starring Jeanne Moreau. Nick admired her song from the film, *Le Tourbillon*, and according to Michel attempted to sing it while they were alone – only to give up on account of the tongue-twisting lyrics. They also went to a Cora Vaucaire recital. Vaucaire had achieved international recognition in 1954 singing 'La Complaine de la Butte' in Jean Renoir's celebrated film, *French Cancan*, which tells the story of the birth of the Moulin Rouge. Her husband, Michel, had written the music to many Piaf songs, including 'Non, Je ne Regrette Rien'. On another evening, Michel persuaded him to get up and sing three songs at their favourite watering-hole, L'Écluse. The establishment had ceased functioning as a cabaret back in the January, but still opened most evenings as a wine bar, and the management encouraged patrons to get up and give a turn, so long as they did not drive the customers away! Nick sang 'Fruit Tree, Time Has Told Me' – and reading the words from a sheet of paper – 'À' Mourir Pour Mourir' – in what would be his very last public performance – as he had started out, before an appreciative audience of just 25.

From one of the many tiny stalls on the bank of the Seine opposite the Écluse, Nick bought a book which he gave to his mother. Albert Camus' *Le Mythe de Sisyphe* is a tough read, a grim work which champions the existentialist theory that death, doom and suicide should be regarded with equal importance to the more positive aspects of life. Sisyphus was the mythical king of Corinth, famed for his deceitfulness and greed: for his sins, the gods had ordered him to perpetually shoulder a huge rock up a hill, only for it to roll back down again when he reached the top and make him start again. He did not, however, buy the book, as has been ridiculously suggested, because he was thinking of ending it all, and neither was Sisyphus' story an analogy of Nick's own life, with its many setbacks, as wishful thinkers have assumed. As Michel Bidault explained,

This was Nick taking the piss. He wanted to give his mother something to think about. He said he found the theme appropriate for all the shit he had been forced to put up with since his breakdown, most of it from his family. In some ways, his life was like that of Sisyphus – all the obstacles in his way, banging his head against a brick wall much of the time. If only he'd thought more of his own welfare instead of worrying about his self-centred relatives – you know, how they were forever trying to convince him that he had failed them, when truthfully it was the other way around. I suppose I can see their point of view – they'd forked out a fortune for him to go to Cambridge, and in their eyes Nick had ended up little more than a glorified busker. But they should have tried to support his career instead of harping on every time they saw him how he should get a haircut and a real man's job, whatever that was supposed to mean. If Nick's parents had taken the time to understand him, instead of nagging him all the time, I'm sure things would have turned out differently than they did. In this respect I can't help thinking that they were at least partly responsible for his death.

From Paris, and apparently in good spirits, Nick drove down to Algeciras, in Spain, where he spent two weeks at Chris Blackwell's villa – Michel believes with the same 'old flame' he had stayed with before. The pair are thought to have also travelled to nearby Gibraltar. Then he made the grave mistake of returning to Far Leys, suitably refreshed it would appear – only to collide once more with his demons.

Nick's parents were worlds away from his enslaved sphere, and again he would have been better off staying among his friends in London. The trouble was, most of these were too wrapped up in their own problems or careers to do much more than leave him to his own devices – or maybe he himself managed to camouflage his inner torment so well that they merely assumed he was going through another bad patch. From the evidence that we have, Far Leys was little different from the institution where Nick had spent five of the most miserable weeks of his life. Despite the size of the house, Nick's quarters amounted to a 'monk's cell' bedroom equipped with a single bed barely big enough to contain his lofty frame, and cheap furniture which one visitor described as 'having come out of the Ark'. It was as if Nick had donned the proverbial hair shirt, and actually enjoyed wearing it.

Eyewitnesses have stated that, between June and late October 1974, Nick's state of mind showed a distinct improvement – that he was content with the way his new album was progressing. Michel recalled,

> *We met up in London the first week of November. I'd never seen him so miserable, though once we hit the town he was soon his giggly self. He'd promised to come out to his parents, but I don't think he ever got around to it. Or maybe they had worked it out for themselves. They were snooty, like butter wouldn't melt in their mouths. They nagged the hell out of him when he was at home. Nick was close to his mother, and told me she'd once had a nervous breakdown, therefore it was easier for her to understand what he was going through. He also said the old man could sometimes be a right royal pain in the arse, dictating like a sergeant major. Nick was quiet, but he loved a joke and he was never crotchety with me. Nor was he shy. I'd have friends around and he would walk in from the bathroom with just a towel wrapped around him. When we parted, that last time in London, he told me that he was eager to get the new album finished so that he could put down roots in Paris. Had he done that and got away from that overbearing mausoleum and its occupants, I'm sure that he would be sitting here with us right now. Then again, you wouldn't be doing your book . . .*

We do not know, of course, *exactly* what the relationship was like between Nick and his parents – how they treated him, how *he* treated them when he was at his lowest ebb – only what they chose to make public by speaking after his death. Were Rodney and Molly Drake as genuinely understanding of their son's condition, in these days of medical ignorance, as they claimed to have been? *Did* they nag and bully him during his last weeks, as Michel says, thinking this was only for his own good? Did Nick give them merry hell and make *their* lives near impossible with his tantrums? As they are now dead – Rodney in 1988, aged 80, Molly in 1993 aged 77 – it is unlikely that we shall ever know.

During the afternoon of 24 November 1974, Nick is known to have switched on the machine in the music room at Far Leys and taped several sketches for the new album. According to the story put out by his mother, over the last two weeks Nick had been suffering from insomnia, but that evening, feeling tired, he went to bed especially early after taking his prescribed dosage of Tryptizol, only to get up again a few hours later. He fixed himself a bowl of cornflakes and after eating these went up to his bedroom. The next day was Sunday, when he liked to have a lie-in. When Molly went in to wake him – around 12 noon, she claimed – she found him, wearing just his underpants, sprawled across his bed. Nick had passed away during the night. He was just 26.

*

The official cause of death was suicide, which few believed – then or since. The coroner's report has never been made available for public scrutiny, which in itself makes one suspicious. The doctor who signed the death certificate claimed that Nick had been dead 'for some hours' when he examined his body. Molly Drake used this information to draw the conclusion that her son had died around 6am on the morning of 25 November. The sequence of events, however, suggests that he died sooner – almost certainly before midnight.

At around 10pm after taking his Tryptizol, Nick had undressed, put on his dressing gown, and descended to the music room where he had listened to one of Bach's *Brandenberg Concertos*: the record was still on the deck the next morning. Subsequently he had gone up to his room, and got no further than removing his dressing gown before collapsing.

The fact that Molly Drake found Nick slumped *across* his bed and not in it strongly suggests that he had not deliberately intended to kill himself, otherwise he would have climbed into bed immediately after taking the Tryptizol, and not lingered for half an hour in the music room. As Molly had usually sat with Nick if he could not sleep, and looked on him every morning – neither of which she had done on this occasion – was the claim that he had got up for something to eat fabricated to salve a guilty conscience? Molly later told Chris Brazier, 'I was very tired that night. I was sleeping very heavily and I didn't hear one single thing at all.' Of course, she had nothing to feel guilty about. Additionally, neither Nick nor his parents are thought to have been aware that just one Tryptizol over the prescribed dose could prove fatal.

Upon the Drake's insistence, which itself sounds more than a little suspicious, there was no post-mortem, and the inquest did not take place until 18 December, by which time Nick had been cremated. The only evidence provided to the coroner came from the Drakes' doctor who professed that he had done little more on the morning of 25 November than certify Nick dead. The coroner's verdict – 'heart failure due to acute amitryptyline poisoning, self administered when suffering from a depressive illness' – has led to wild exaggerations over succeeding years as to the number of pills Nick may have taken, depending on which account one heeds, between two and 30. The Drakes' doctor claimed that the Tryptizol bottle had been full. Molly counteracted this by maintaining that she kept Nick's and her own medication under lock and key to prevent such an accident from happening, and only handed out his tablets when he required them. If so, the smaller amount would seem more likely. Some years ago, this author took three Tryptizol instead of one, and ended up in the coronary care unit.

Speculation has only increased since 1998 and the discovery, in a Cardiff University vault, of an amateur film tribute, *Way to Blue*, made by Chris Brazier in 1985, three years before Molly's death. In this she says, 'I knew that he'd taken Tryptizol from time to time as a sleeping pill, but I think he was having a bad night and he said, "Oh, what the hell!"'

Some of Nick's friends, including Michel Bidault, believe that there was a cover up, though not necessarily for malicious reasons. Michel told me,

> *Nick's parents were so stiff upper-lip. With them it was always a case of, 'What will the neighbours say?' They weren't criminals or anything like that. They were just genuinely ashamed that their son had some kind of secret life, and didn't want everyone knowing about it – the drugs, the boyfriends, etc. That's why none of Nick's friends, who knew him far better than his family, were summoned to the inquest. From his parents' point of view it was better to suffer the indignity of having a suicide in the family than have the world know that Nick had liked smoking cannabis and having sex with other men. Similarly, all that bullshit about the Camus book being found near his body. If you want my opinion, the old lady put it there herself. It was, after all, her book that Nick had only bought in the first place as a joke!*

In 1987, Nick's sister, Gabrielle, shocked many fans by telling Kris Kirk in an interview for *Melody Maker*, 'I prefer to think that Nick committed suicide, in the sense that I'd rather he died because he wanted to end it, than it to be the result of a tragic mistake.' Such an unforgivably *callous* statement, coming from his next of kin, who in any event had seen little of him towards the end, only helped cement Nick's reputation as the hopeless manic-depressive whose only goal in life had been death. Kirk himself declared the suicide verdict invalid, claiming that it was hard to imagine a man killing himself with antidepressants, which might not have worked, when the more reliable aspirins and barbiturates were close a hand. 'There was no suicide note,' Kirk told me in 1990. 'Not essential, I know. But how many suicides do you know where the victim hasn't left a note? I always thought it's a pity that the law in this country doesn't prevent relatives from inheriting in cases of suicide. Nick's family wouldn't have been in such a hurry to say he topped himself then, would they? What really sticks in my throat is that he suffered and struggled so hard to get his career off the ground, and it was his relatives who ended up with all the money he earned.'

That Nick's death *was* a tragic accident seems much, much more certain than suicide because, in the intervening years, so many people have come forward to say how *happy* he seemed during his last weeks. Furthermore, most of these people, who knew him better than his family since he dropped out of Cambridge, believe that if he had planned taking his life, he would not have done so at Far Leys – and agreed with Kris Kirk's theory regarding antidepressants because, like antibiotics, with the lack of medical evidence in those days, there was no guarantee that even a large quantity would do the job properly. Therefore the most likely explanation for his death is that, like myself, Nick had been so desperate to get a good night's sleep that he had doubled up on his dosage – and, alone in his room, there had been no one there to save him.

There were just two references to Nick's death in the British music press – one part-cynical as only the tabloids could be, the other genuinely heartfelt. Island Records' press officer David Sandison, writing for the January issue of *ZigZag*, was just as disrespectful now as he had been when penning the *Melody Maker* piece earlier. Hinting at the lack of obituaries, he observed, 'He released three albums in four years, and together they probably didn't cover the cost of one. What the hell do you want – front page in *The Times*?'

Sandison did attempt to come good in the end, albeit too late. Comparing Nick with the glam-rock phenomenon, he concluded, 'In a world full of bullshit, hype and glittery horrors with the talents of dead oxen and the integrity of starving rats, Nick Drake was one of the few entitled to be called unique.' One might add with equal cynicism that Island's forceful and insincere eulogising of Nick now that he was no longer with us – with dead stars invariably guaranteed to sell records – meant that, on account of his prolonged absence from the scene, Nick needed that extra plug.

Jerry Gilbert gained respect from Nick's family and friends when he headed his (albeit heavily trimmed) piece in *Sounds*, 'Nick Drake: Death of a Genius'. Gilbert also dispelled the suicide theory, observing, 'He had been ill – perhaps weary is a better expression – for some time, but at the time of his death his enthusiasm had never been so high, for at the time of his death he was totally immersed in the prospect of completing his fourth album.' Gilbert was supported by Robert Kirby, who was quoted as saying, 'Nick was ready for death all right. I think he'd had enough. There was no fight left in him. Yet I get a feeling that if he *was* going to commit suicide, he would have done it a long time ago.'

The Drakes placed a small announcement in the *Birmingham Post*, reporting his death and details of his funeral. This took place on 2 December 1974 at St Mary Magdalene's Church, in Tanworth. Around 60 people attended, a mixture of friends and locals. Many more *would* have been there, had the announcement been made in a national newspaper. Michel Bidault did not learn of his death until Christmas Eve, and it was he who contacted Françoise Hardy. 'A couple of pounds for a piece in *The Times*, and there would have been hundreds of people there,' he told me. Nick, the beautiful troubadour who had sung of and romanticised graves, and who had lived the life of an old-world bohemian poet, was not permitted to lie in the ground as per the edicts of 'Fruit Tree'. His parents had him cremated in Solihull, something he most definitely would not have wanted – though his ashes were interred (but not until 14 January 1975) in the plot that his parents had reserved for themselves, in the local churchyard beneath the spreading branches of a majestic oak.

The simple stone bears the inscription: NICK DRAKE 1948–1974: REMEMBERED WITH LOVE. On the reverse – some believe because so many photographs of Nick were taken with his back facing the camera, others that it was placed deliberately so, so that few would see it – is carved a second inscription: NOW WE RISE AND WE ARE EVERYWHERE, taken from his beautiful song, 'From the Morning'. There is also a brass commemorative plaque, commissioned by the Drakes, above one of the organ stops within the church.

Each year, in June and November, the faithful gather here to remember him. And with each passing year, their numbers only increase.

Chapter Eleven

À Mourir Pour Mourir

As if aware that their son would become a cult figure – or perhaps out extreme grief combined with unnecessary guilt over what had happened – the Drakes kept Nick's bedroom and music room exactly as he had left them, and hardly ever turned a diehard fan away. Admirers could sit in the orange armchair he had composed in, touch his clothes which still hung in the wardrobe, photograph the bed he had died upon. Against one wall was his old desk from Marlborough, never wiped clean of its coffee stains and joint burns. On shelves were his out-dated tape deck, headphones, French cigarettes and lighter; the volumes of Shakespeare, Blake and Rimbaud he had dipped into some evenings before going to sleep. On one wall was a Turner print – on another, the original artwork for *Pink Moon* that Michael Trevithick had given to Nick's parents after his death.

Joe Boyd had honoured Nick's memory by never allowing any of his albums to be deleted. Despite the fact that these had only sold spasmodically, Island released a Nick Drake retrospective in March 1979. *Fruit Tree* comprised a boxed set of his three albums, plus what were believed to have been his four last songs: 'Hanging on the Star', 'Voice From the Mountain', 'Black-Eyed Dog' and 'Rider on the Wheel'. Despite the lack of press coverage, the compilation sold well – around 10,000 copies, which today would have taken it into the charts. The music press was too occupied reflecting the decade and its numerous pop and rock casualties. Jimi Hendrix, Elvis Presley, Gram Parsons, Tim Buckley, Janis Joplin, Jim Morrison and the newly departed Sid Vicious headed the so-called 'A-List', while several rungs down the ladder of notoriety were Keith Moon, The New York Dolls' Billy Murcia – and Nick, who stood out because he had *not* been into hard drugs, drink and debauchery. He was championed by David Pepworth of the *New Musical Express*, a publication that had taken little notice of him during his lifetime. 'Most songwriters use their sadness,' Pepworth observed, 'but with Nick Drake it was the sadness that used him, and even music as rare and honest as this is never worth such a tragedy.'

Over the next few years, the records sold steadily as new fans flocked to Nick's banner. Then in 1985, his memory was given a massive boost when The Dream Academy entered the British charts with *Life in a Northern Town*, a song they dedicated to Nick. The first time Mike Read played this on Radio One, along with one of Nick's own recordings, the BBC switchboard was flooded with calls from listeners wanting to hear more. The Nick Drake phenomenon had begun! Island grasped the opportunity to placate this new wave of admirers – and of course make a tidy sum for themselves, deserved it must be said, for sticking with him over the years. In May 1985 they released the compilation, *Heaven is a Wild Flower* – title courtesy of a line from one of Nick's favourite poems, William Blake's *Auguries of Innocence*. Again he received support from the *New Musical Express*, whose Paul du Noyer remonstrated,

> *Rock has now a million morose young poets: bedsit brooders penning their pain, real or imagined, to angst-intensive refrains of frail pathos. What a bloody awful bunch. Yet by the law of averages, they were bound to spawn at least one genuine genius. They did. His name was Nick Drake.*

The term 'bedsit brooders' was an obvious reference to Morrissey, then at the peak of his success with The Smiths, and arguably the only British poet truly worthy of following in Nick's footsteps.

The *Heaven is a Wild Flower* compilation, inadvertently or not, caused a controversy that only helped boost sales. Its release coincided with Gabrielle Drake taking over from the late Noelle Gordon by heading the cast of Independent Television's cult but drossy early evening soap, *Crossroads*, set in a Birmingham motel (the locations were filmed in Tanworth). Island were accused of cashing in on this – on the face of it, not a bad thing. Interest in the 'morose young poet' escalated, and this time the record company set about assembling an album of mostly 'new' Nick Drake songs.

Time of No Reply was initially released as part of a four-album collection – with the three albums from the *Fruit Tree* box, which had been deleted two years previously – but in March 1987 it was issued separately, housed in a sleeve containing Keith Morris' portrait of Nick sitting under a tree with his book and guitar. It comprised various out-takes from the *Five Leaves Left* sessions, and three songs which Nick had recorded at Tanworth in 1968–9. These were 'Fly',

'Strange Meeting II', and Robin Frederick's 'Been Smoking Too Long', at that time the only non-Drake song to have been given a commercial release.

With the advent of the CD, Nick Drake bootlegs began flooding the market, the most curious – and collectable – being the so-called *Tanworth Tape*, which appeared in 1994. Here, we hear Nick pottering around in his room after returning from a pal's party, probably during the festive season of 1968. Not only did he record the songs listed in the Discography, he left the machine running while rambling on, sounding slightly inebriated and 'royal family posh', to whoever was with him, or maybe to himself, about driving, of all things:

> *When I leapt into the car to drive home after my merry abandon, I found the task extremely difficult. And it was extremely fortunate that there was nothing else on the road because, looking back at it, I seem to remember that I had a mental breakdown and I didn't realise at the time, I think I drove all the way home on the right-hand side of the road, which is something of course which comes from driving in France too much, which I've been doing recently. And in moments of stress, such as this journey home, one forgets so easily the lies, the truth and the pain . . .*

More to the point, Nick speaks about his insomnia, though in those days there was a positive side to his inability to sleep, as he had pronounced in *Northern Sky*:

> *I think there's something extraordinarily nice about seeing the dawn up before one goes to bed because there's something uncanny about it when it suddenly becomes light, because one connects darkness with going to bed . . . And when one is still up when it becomes light and it's a new day, you still haven't gone to sleep because the light equals sleep so easily, and when one is up and the new day begins, this is something you've achieved [because one has been taught to believe] everything should be black before one goes to bed!*

Fans might have ignored this release were it not for the fact that, with his never having given a radio interview, this is the *only* recording of Nick's speaking voice so far as has been established. With such high-polished tones, and given his privileged background, one might be excused for thinking him nothing short of an insufferable snob – which those closest to him, including Michel Bidault, have stringently denied:

Nick cursed and swore, broke wind, and poked fun at those around him as much as anyone else. He drove around in a clapped-out old car, and if he was short of cash he rolled his own cigarettes, usually with a liberal sprinkling of cannabis. He preferred the roughest bars in London and Paris, sometimes taking me to places that would scare the crap out of me. The way he spoke was just an accent, like yours and mine. It's how he'd been brought up.

In 1994, coinciding with the 20th anniversary of his death, Island released 'Way to Blue', promoted as an introduction to work for new fans who were starting from scratch. This featured a photograph by Julian Lloyd: captured against a woodland backdrop 'somewhere in Wales', he wears a multicoloured blanket, and extends one hand to reveal the magic mushrooms he has just picked. The album sold 50,000 copies that year, and introduced Nick to the United States. It was runner-up (to Marvin Gaye) in *Rolling Stone*'s Best Re-Issue Reader's Poll. The previous year, in Britain, *Five Leaves Left* had been voted Number 60 in *The Times*' Pop-Rock Albums of All Time poll: not a high position, but still beating Pink Floyd's *The Wall* and Michael Jackson's *Thriller*.

In 1995, fragments of Nick's work which he had taped over the years – right up to the afternoon of his death – but never got around to developing properly, were handed over by his parents to a young singer-songwriter called Scott Appel. These included 'Bird Flew By, Blossom', 'Our Season' and re-workings of 'Pink Moon' and 'Place to Be', and they were subsequently released on an album, *Nine of Swords*. Appel (1955–2003) exonerates himself well with this very personal material, but Nick Drake he very definitely is not.

In January 1999, the *Guardian* published the results of the poll they had conducted to find Britain's Top 100 Alternative Albums. Nick topped this with *Bryter Layter* – with *Five Leaves Left* and *Pink Moon* coming in at Numbers 5 and 80 respectively. The newspaper's Friday supplement had his photograph on its cover, captioned, 'Our Great Overlooked Genius'. The editorial observed of this 'brittle stick of a man',

Juxtaposing a peculiarly urban, subterranean, psychiatric darkness with gentle rivers, summer picnics and sunny meadows, Bryter Layter – stately, precious, tragic – leaves a trail of mysteries in its wake and a recurring icy sensation in the bones of everyone who hears it. Next time someone tells you that white boys can't sing the blues, lend them a copy.

In the spring of 2000, Volkswagen used just 30 seconds of 'Pink Moon' to promote their new convertible and suddenly, a singer whom almost no one in the UK had heard of, save his diehard fans, was catapulted into the limelight. The commercial, a regular feature between films in 7,000 cinemas nationwide, was extended to the television networks. It shows four college students embarking on a moonlight drive to the ethereal accompaniment of Nick and his guitar. The British press were somewhat cynical. 'Volkswagen appears to be aiming its new Cabriolet at the lucrative manic-depressive market,' wrote *The Times*' Mark Inglefield. 'I suppose the association with Mr Drake's music – great if you like the gloom – will mean the cars never leave the garage forecourts.' Even so, the commercial almost single-handedly led to a massive Nick Drake revival.

In Britain, Island was inundated with calls from American entrepreneurs wanting to book Nick for interviews and chat-show appearances – when the sad truth emerged, *Pink Moon* was released as a single and quickly made its way into the Billboard 100. Similarly, Nick's three studio albums and the 'Way to Blue' compilation went into sales overdrive, selling more copies in the week of their release than they had in the previous three decades. That same year his music turned up in *Young Americans*, a drama series set in a university especially reserved for the well-heeled. Later, he was heard in the Nicole Kidman film, *Practical Magic*. On and on it goes. At the time of writing, Nick's voice could be heard singing 'Day once dawned, and it was beautiful', while children were quaffing a well-known cough remedy!

There have been several radio/television retrospectives, some good, others hardly worthy of mention. Brad Pitt declared himself such a fervent admirer – having played two of Nick's songs at his wedding to Jennifer Aniston a few years earlier – that he insisted upon narrating *The Nick Drake Story* for BBC Radio 2. BBC2 aired a 40-minute documentary: *A Stranger Among Us: Searching For Nick Drake*, directed by Tim Clements. Any visual retrospective of an artist with no known filmed footage was always going to be problematic, and this one told us nothing that we did not already know. The film opens shakily, with a car driving the narrow road to Tanworth before shifting to Glastonbury, where passers-by are shown a photograph of Nick, and mostly do not recognise him – the nod to the celebrations in London in June 1998 for what would have been Nick's 50th birthday. This runs into an extended and frequently unnecessary conversation between several of Nick's acquaintances and friends: Keith Morris, Joe Boyd, Island publicist Garrell Redfearn, Lady Victoria Waymouth, Jeremy Mason, Simon Crocker and finally, Gabrielle Drake. One asks oneself frequently here if, with friends like these, Nick needed enemies. Almost all of them, with the exception of Nick's sister, had little to say that is not negative. Nick was generally regarded as 'abrupt and dismissive', 'fanciable to both sexes', and of course completely paranoid and eternally depressed. Redfearn in particular was the most offensive, calling Nick's lyrics 'adolescent', and declaring that his flat in Hampstead had been no more than a squat. Therefore, it was left to would-be or possible lover Keith Morris to refute the image of the shabby, Howard Hughes-type recluse, with smelly clothes and uncut fingernails, saying, 'I resent this picture of the tormented artist . . . in a romantic sense, perhaps. But let's not forget, the whole thing went out of hand. He died.'

Recalling their first joint assignment, the *Five Leaves Left* photoshoot, Morris goes on, 'We were like virgins together,' and adds of Nick's serious expression that it was not 'cool' to smile in the late sixties. Adding to the farce, director Tim Clements brings in an alternative Mr and Mrs Drake, equally snooty as the originals and wearily claiming that they are always being mistaken for Nick's parents by fans – impossible, of course, for the fans know all there is to know about their hero. Thank goodness then for Gabrielle, who reads aloud some of her brother's very moving letters.

A more interesting curiosity was *Way to Blue*, discovered at Cardiff University in 1998. Shot and narrated in 1984 by way of a 10th anniversary tribute by a student-fan named Chris Brazier, who one suspects may now be dead – he has never been traced – this recounts Nick's story in just 26 minutes, one for each year of his life. Of amateurish quality, it opens with the title-song and the familiar Keith Morris pictures from Nick's albums before moving on to the Drakes' hitherto unseen family album. There are some howlers, such as Brazier's comment on *Five Leaves Left*, 'It's the kind of record Keats might have made if *he'd* been a rock singer.' There is an interview with Nick's parents, and a fleeting tour of his bedroom and music room. In very poor taste is Brazier's impersonation of Nick – the image from the *Bryter Layter* sleeve where he sits on a stool, hunched over his guitar with his shoes in front of him. And if this image is insufficiently upsetting for Nick's fans, Brazier mimes badly to 'Know', fading from view and leaving just the shoes behind when he reaches the line, 'Know, I'm not there'.

More polished, but so darkly haunting and atmospheric in parts one is almost convinced that one is watching a late-sixties Hammer production, is *A Skin Too Few: The Days of Nick Drake*, made by Dutch director Jeroen Berkvens and released in 2000. That Berkvens was a diehard Drake fan goes without saying:

it took him over five years to raise money for the production, which was eventually financed by the Humanist Broadcasting Foundation. Way too short at just 48 minutes, it opens with an aerial view of Tanworth, then divides into segments: Burma, Far Leys, London and Cambridge. Berkvens somewhat sickly reconstructs Nick's bedroom, with its budget furniture and the crumpled sheets on the bed where he is supposed to have died, and his room at Cambridge, but interviews all the usual people, who share the same anecdotes but without the negativity of the earlier BBC film. Gabrielle looks slightly ghoulish, sitting in the half-light in her brother's 'room' – the view from its window changing with each new season – but reads his letters beautifully. 'I always said that Nick was born with a skin too few,' she says – hence the film's title. We see a Nick look-alike arriving at Cambridge, and what appears to be him in London – until the black-coated figure with the familiar white shoes turns out to be Joe Boyd, who in the 1960s uncannily did resemble Nick. Then the whole thing ends on a moving note – the *real* Nick, a little blond boy aged two, playing on the beach with Gabrielle and his parents, and again being tended by his Burmese nanny, in two fragments of colour home movies . . . while he sings 'Northern Sky'.

Something of an anticlimax, after all the hype it received, was *Nick Drake: Family Tree*, released in 2007. Though very nicely packaged, there was little new here for the diehard fan. The Tanworth songs, which had been around for years, were more or less all collected together at last, as were those Nick had recorded in Aix, along with four songs recorded by Robert Kirby while he and Nick had been at Cambridge. Interesting, too, was a rare recording of Nick playing the clarinet in Mozart's *Kegelstatt Trio*, with Molly Drake's sister on viola and her husband on piano. But did we really need the neo-Anna Neagle warblings of Molly herself, inviting us to 'Come into the Garden'. Probably what makes this release rather special (and worth the slightly higher purchase price) are the very extensive liner notes. These include a moving tribute by Gabrielle, in the form of an unsent letter, and an essay by Robin Frederick, detailing as much as she can of Nick's time in Aix-en-Provence. Other essays come from Robert Kirby, and childhood pal Andrew Hicks. There are also some very stunning, never-before-seen photographs from the Drake family album: Nick as a striking-looking teenager, Nick photographed with his father, the Drake family at Far Leys during the 1950s, then at Christmas. And again, one might argue surplus to requirements, a portrait of Molly – and one of Rodney sitting on a boat, looking just as pompous and preening as Michel Bidault had described him.

Before this release, however, and the crowning glory thus far, has to be *Made to Love Magic*, a stunning compilation of out-takes and rarities, along with alternative arrangements of Nick's more familiar songs, released in 2004 to commemorate the 30th anniversary of his death. *Why* Nick was dissatisfied with Richard Herson's original arrangement of the title-track, refusing to allow its release, is baffling. When this had been reissued earlier in the year, with an even more stunning score by Robert Kirby, it had enabled Nick to enter the British singles charts for the first time. It is quite possibly Nick's finest song (in my opinion, sharing the honour with 'Northern Sky'), and serves as the perfect epitaph. Nick Drake *was* made to love magic, and the magic he made so definitively makes us regret the sad, unalterable fact that he's no longer with us to continue casting his spell.

Nick's work has survived and never dated like some contemporaries because, he strictly adhered to the *chansonnier* tradition – eschewing the 'moon-rhymes-with-June' couplets of his contemporaries for sensible, well-thought-out phraseology and meaningful lyrics, all this perfumed with old world romanticism. His music sounds so very fresh. Anyone listening to him for the first time today would swear that some of his songs could not possibly have been recorded 40 years ago. Also, thanks to Joe Boyd's deal when selling Witchseason, they will always be there for new fans to discover.

Nick Drake remains an enigma not just because he died so young, but because of the sheer brilliance of his musicianship – the fact that, for over 30 years even some of the world's finest guitarists have failed to fathom the secret of his unusual tunings and pickings – the fact that singer-songwriters with but a fraction of his talent still try to copy his uniquely English, pastoral essays and *always* fail most majestically to get it right.

'Nick Drake departed the world without fanfare,' Vit Wagner concluded in a glowing tribute for the *Toronto Star* in August 2000, 'but the quiet music he left behind persistently demands a hearing.' At his best, like Gram Parsons and Jeff Buckley, Nick Drake makes the listener weep because he was, above all, a man who observed in others, in himself, and in the world about him, things which others failed to see. Hearing him now makes one wish to step back in time, if only to give him a great big hug and reassure him, as those closest to him failed to do, 'Don't worry! Everything's going to be just fine!'

Nick Drake Discography

The following represents the entire known output of Nick Drake. All songs, unless otherwise stated, are written-composed by him. Re-issues have not been included.

The Aix-en-Provence 'Kitchen' Tape
Michael, Row the Boat Ashore

The Tanworth Tape (Winter 1967–8)
A Season/ Come Into the Garden/ Bird Flew By/Blossom/ Get Together (Miller)/ *Been Smoking Too Long* (Frederick)/ *Don't Think Twice, It's Alright* (Dylan)/ *Sweet Sugar Blues* (Trad)/ *Blues Run the Game* (Frank)/ *Winter is Gone* (Trad)/ *All My Trials* (Trad, sung with Gabrielle Drake)/ *Counting Blues* (Jansch)/ *Summertime* (Gershwin)/ *Black Mountain Blues* (Trad)/ *If You Leave Me* (Trad)/ *Time Piece/ Paddling in Rushmere* (Trad)/ *Sketch/ My Baby So Sweet* (Trad)/ *Rain/ Green Eyes.* Recorded at Far Leys, released on various bootlegs and official CDs, but never as a complete set. The tape also includes what is believed to be the only example of Nick speaking as he voices his opinions on the dawn, driving on the wrong side of the road, truth and pain.

Nick Drake: The Peel Session (August 1969)
River Man/Cello Song/ Three Hours/Time of No Reply/ Plaisir d'Amour (Martini). On 5 August 1969, Nick auditioned for the BBC's B-Category List by way of a guest slot on the popular *John Peel Show*. Because he was subsequently blacklisted for failing to turn up for a radio session with Bob Harris, this one was not repeated. The tape lies in a BBC vault and has never been released commercially.

Five Leaves Left (September 1969)
Time Has Told Me/ River Man/ Three Hours/ Way to Blue/ Day is Done/ Cello Song/ The Thoughts of Mary Jane/ Man in a Shed/ Fruit Tree/ Saturday Sun
(LP) ISLAND ILPS 9105 (CD, 3/87) ISLAND CID 9195

Bryter Layter (November 1970)
Introduction (instr)/ *Hazey Jane II/ At the Chime of a City Clock/ One of These Things First/ Hazey Jane I/ Bryter Layter* (instr)/*Fly/ Poor Boy* (with Pat Arnold and Doris Troy)/ *Northern Sky/ Sunday* (instr)
(LP) ISLAND ILPS 9134
(CD, May 1987) ISLAND CID 9134

Pink Moon (February 1972)
Pink Moon/ Place to Be/ Road/ Which Will/ Horn/ In Things Behind the Sun/ Know/ Parasite/ Free Ride/ Harvest Breed/ From the Morning
(LP) ISLAND ILPS 9184
(CD, April 1990) ISLAND IMCD 94

Fruit Tree: The Complete Recorded Works (March 1979)
Boxed set containing *Five Leaves Left, Bryter Layter* and *Pink Moon*, to which have been added Nick's final songs of 1974: *Rider on the Wheel/ Black-Eyed Dog/ Hanging on a Star/ Voice From the Mountain*
(LPs) ISLAND NDSP 100
(CDs, December 1991) HANNIBAL HNCD 5402 *
The CD box also includes the album, *Time of No Reply*. See item

Fruit Tree Sampler (March 1979)
Introduction/ Hazey Jane II/ Time Has Told Me/ Fruit Tree/ Rider On the Wheel
(LP) ISLAND RSS 7
Promotion only.

Heaven is a Wild Flower (May 1985)
Fruit Tree/ The Thoughts Of Mary Jane/ Northern Sky/ River Man/ At the Chime of a City Clock/ Introduction (instr)*/ Hazey Jane I/ Hazey Jane II/ Pink Moon/ Road/ Which Will/ Things Behind the Sun/ Time Has Told Me*
(LP) ISLAND ILPS 9826
(CD) ISLAND IMCD 91

Time of No Reply (March 1987)
*Time of No Reply/ I Was Made To Love Magic/ Joey**/ Clothes of Sand*/ Man in a Shed/ Mayfair/ Fly/ Thoughts of Mary Jane/ Been Smoking Too Long/ Strange Meeting II/ Rider On the Wheel/ Black-Eyed Dog/ Hanging On a Star/ Voice From the Mountain*
An album of out-takes and alternative versions of songs recorded between October 1968 and February 1974. Officially released in some parts of the world at the end of 1986, the track listing is identical to the fourth disc of the *Fruit Tree* boxed set.
(LP) HANNIBAL HNBL 1318
(CD, March 1987) HANNIBAL HNCD 1318

Way to Blue: An Introduction to Nick Drake (May 1994)
Cello Song/ Hazey Jane I/ Way to Blue/ Things Behind the Sun/ River Man/ Poor Boy/ Time of No Reply/ From the Morning/ One Of These Things First/ Northern Sky/ Which Will/ Hazey Jane II/ Time Has Told Me/ Pink Moon/ Black-Eyed Dog/ Fruit Tree
(CD) ISLAND IMCD 196

Made to Love Magic (June 2004)
An album of out-takes and re-orchestrated rarities
Rider On the Wheel (July 1974)/ *I Was Made To Love Magic* (re-orchestrated 1968)/ *River Man* (March 1968)/ *Joey* (November 1968)/ *The Thoughts Of Mary Jane* (December 1968)/ *Mayfair* (March 1968)/ *Hanging On a Star* (alternate version)/ *Three Hours* (March 1969, with Kwaakhu Baah)/ *Clothes Of Sand* (November 1968)/ *Voice From the Mountain* (July 1974)/ *Time Of No Reply* (March 1968)/ *Black-Eyed Dog* (July 1974)/ *Tow the Line* (July 1974)
(CD) ISLAND CID 8141

Nick Drake: A Treasury (September 2004)
Introduction/ Hazey Jane II/ River Man/ Cello Song/ Hazey Jane I/ Pink Moon/ Poor Boy/ I Was Made To Love Magic/ Place to Be/ Northern Sky/ Road/ Fruit Tree/ Black-Eyed Dog/ Way to Blue/ From the Morning/ Plaisir d'Amour (Martini)
(CD) ISLAND CID 8149

Maximum Nick Drake (November 2004)
Subtitled 'The Unauthorised Biography', Nick's story, written by Keith Rodway and narrated by Sian Jones. No music here, but an important release in that it contains two examples of 19-year-old Nick speaking into his tape recorder at Tanworth.
(CD) CHROME DREAMS ABCD 187

Nick Drake: Family Tree (November 2007)
An album of rarities taped at Tanworth-in-Arden, Aix-en-Provence and Cambridge.
Come into the Garden/ They're Leaving Me Behind/ Time Piece/ Poor Mum (sung by Molly Drake)/ *Winter Is Come/ All My Trials* (sung with Gabrielle Drake)/ *Mozart's Kegelstatt for clarinet, viola and piano* (performed by Nick Drake on clarinet, Nancy McDowall on viola, Chris McDowall on piano)/ *Strolling Down the Highway/ Paddling In Rushmere/ Cocaine Blues/ Blossom/ Been Smoking Too Long/ Black Mountain Blues/ Tomorrow Is A Long Time/ If You Leave Me/ Tomorrow Is A Long Time/ Here Come the Blues/ Sketch 1/ Blues Run the Game/ My Baby So Sweet/ Milk and Honey/ Kimbie/ Bird Flew By/ Rain/ Strange Meeting II/ Day Is Done/ Way to Blue/ Do You Ever Remember* (sung by Molly Drake)
(CD) ISLAND 1734041

Jeff Buckley
Hymne à l'amour

'Jeff Buckley is gone but, like all other great artists who were cut down in their prime, his music will long outlive his tragically short life.'

Sydney Herald obituary, June 1997

Chaper Twelve

Father, Do You Owe Me?

His childhood was no less mixed up than that of Gram Parsons. His father was Tim Buckley: singer-songwriter extraordinaire, hellraiser, megalomaniac, drug addict and serial adulterer. Born in Washington DC in February 1947, Tim had moved to New York with his parents, then to Anaheim, in Southern California's Orange County. At the Buona Vista High School he had met 18-year-old Mary Guibert, as unassuming and quiet as Tim had been brash and rebellious. Theirs had been a classic case of opposites attracting. In October 1965, upon learning that Mary was pregnant, Tim had married her – yet no sooner had the rice settled than he had begun cheating on her. The pregnancy appears to have been a false alarm – either that, or Mary miscarried at the end of December. Whatever, by the spring of 1966 she was expecting again, and Tim reacted to this news by packing his bags.

Critics have always debated the Buckley voice: some considered it inspirational, while others have dismissed is as just a tuneless cod-opera row. Much of his own inspiration came from the avant-garde American mezzo-soprano, Cathy Berberian (1925–83), who besides interpreting the classics tackled pop songs, most famously the Beatles' *Help*, which with its unprecedented octave changes single-handedly lost her many fans. Tim's debut album, *Tim Buckley*, may only have sold a meagre 20,000 copies, but promoting it ensured him plenty of groupies. He was a sucker for a pretty face, and rarely resisted the same pretty face twice. Among his many mistresses was Linda Eastman, who later married Paul McCartney.

While Tim relocated to Topanga Canyon with his latest girlfriend, in August 1966 Mary moved back in with her parents. A few weeks later, Tim contacted her and demanded a divorce – this would be finalised in August 1967 – and on 16 November her son, Jeffrey Scott, was born in Anaheim's Martin Luther King Hospital. The name, Jeffrey, was in honour of a former boyfriend, the Scott after a teenage family friend who had recently died in a car accident. For several years, however, he would be addressed only as Scotty.

Tim Buckley took a swipe at his wife and new son on his next album, *Goodbye And Hello*, released in 1967. *I Never Asked To Be Your Mountain*, which he sings woefully off-key, contains the lines, 'The Flying Pisces sails for time, And tells me of my child', then goes on to suggest that Pisces (Mary, a reference to her by her birth sign) feels only resentment towards him when she tells their son, 'Your scoundrel father flies with a dancer called a queen', concluding that it was Mary's fault that he left her in the first place.

For Scotty, the next 15 years would see him uprooted more times than he cared to remember, making few friends along the way and learning to trust almost no one. Like Nick Drake, on account of his erratic upbringing, throughout his life he would form little cliques of intimates, confiding some exclusive to each but always ensuring they never met to pool their anecdotal resources to form a more complete picture of the complex young man he became.

Mary, adamant that she did not want to be supported by Tim, reverted to her maiden name and moved from one job to the next. Firstly, she found them a small apartment in Anaheim, and took a clerical job with a bank. This did not work out: fired for taking too much time off sick, Mary returned to live with her parents. When this arrangement also failed, she and Scotty headed for Hollywood. Here, early in 1968, she began working for a telephone company and found a new man: Dan Gordon, who also happened to be Tim's best friend. It was probably Gordon who persuaded Tim not to shirk his responsibilities to the family he had deserted: he began paying Mary a regular allowance, though this was only a paltry $80 a month.

The relationship with Dan Gordon proved short lived, and once again Mary and Scotty were taken in by the Guiberts. Mary enrolled with the local college, found part-time work, and began a stormy liaison with a 20-year-old footballer-turned garage mechanic named Ron Moorhead. After a lightning courtship, the pair married in December 1969 and Scotty was pageboy. Tim is believed to have attempted to prevent the wedding from taking place by asking Mary for a reconciliation. Later, he would unfairly blame his heroin addiction on her rejection of him. He himself remarried in April 1970. His new bride was Judy Sutcliffe, five years his senior, a widow with a seven-year-old son, Taylor, whom Tim legally adopted.

The following year, Ron Moorhead relocated his new family to Fullerton, north of Anaheim, where he started up his own repair shop. For a while there was dissension between Mary and Moorhead over how Scotty might turn out. Moorhead disapproved of the kindergarten teaching him the words to his first song – 'I'm a Little Teapot, Here's My Spout' – which, he claimed, would turn him into a sissy. Jeff would still be performing the ditty, complete with camp movements, 25 years later when goofing around on stage. Moorhead therefore encouraged him to listen to 'manly' music such as The Moody Blues and Cat Stevens – while Mary nurtured his sensitive side by introducing him to Barbra Streisand, Billie Holiday and Judy Garland. Scotty, however, had a mind of his own: though he loved all of these artists, over the next few years his favourite act would be the recently founded Kiss. Identified by their trademark face paint, outrageous stage outfits, and on-stage gimmicks of fire-eating and blood-spitting, these had for their part been inspired by The New York Dolls, who Jeff would dislike intensely – until learning, 15 years later, that *they* had inspired Morrissey, whom he would worship from afar for the rest of his life.

For Mary Guibert it was a case of history repeating itself when her second marriage fared little better than her first. In March 1972 she bore Ron Moorhead a son, Corey James, but soon afterwards Moorhead's business went under, and the couple separated early the next year when Mary discovered that her husband had a mistress. In their divorce settlement she was awarded their house, car and custody of both her children.

The next man in Mary's life was George Vandergrift, a married salesman with two children of his own. Having sold the house and decided that she wanted to go into the potted-plants business, Mary and Vandergrift bought a place together in Riverside, 40 miles north of Anaheim. Here, early in 1975, Vandergrift obtained his divorce, and the couple opened a garden centre at nearby Sunnymead.

Jeff hated Riverside. 'From womb to tomb, it's thug country,' he would tell *Raygun*'s Aidan Vaziri in August 1994. 'I'm afraid that I had any friends at all. It's misogyny, it's birth, death, work, it's misery. It's fucking hicks. And that's what I grew up with. I was rootless trailer trash!'

In April 1975, Mary read in the press that Tim Buckley was giving a concert at Huntingdon Beach, a coastal town some two hours' drive from Fullerton, where Jeff was staying with Ron Moorhead. Mary collected her son, and backstage after the show, Scotty – who apparently had always gone by the name Scotty Guibert – saw Tim for the first time, and learned that his real surname was Buckley.

Tim was with his new wife, Judy, but Mary readily agreed that father and son should spend some quality time together at the Buckleys' home in Santa Monica. Scotty stayed here for nine days, played with half-brother Taylor, did not see that much of Tim, but made his mind up when he returned to his mother – headstrong, even at just eight – that henceforth he wanted to be known as Scotty Buckley. He might not have been quite so fond of his father had he known that, much of the time, if his name came up in his conversation he was referred to as 'it'.

Whether Tim was planning to spend more time with his son, if for no other reason than to salve an uneasy conscience, will never be known. Tim's career had been on the skids, with record sales little short of pathetic, but of late it had appeared to have been on the up. His records were selling steadily, and he had recently appeared in an episode of *The Monkees* television show. On 28 June he performed before a capacity crowd at the Electric Ballroom, in Dallas. The following day, he and Judy returned to Los Angeles where they met up with an old UCLA friend named Richard Keeling.

Tim is known to have been blind drunk upon arriving at Keeling's house. Here, according to Keeling's subsequent confession and the police report, he drank some more, and Keeling 'dared' him to snort a line of cocaine, which was actually heroin. According to Judy's story, Tim's friends got him home and put him to bed, where she joined him a few hours later to watch television. Suddenly, Judy went on, Tim turned blue and his last words were, 'Bye-bye, baby!' It all sounds very far-fetched, and does not corroborate with the police report, which states that an ambulance was summoned, and Tim died en route to the Santa Monica Hospital.

Tim was just 28, and aside from the money assigned to trust funds for his sons, had died in debt. He also left nine albums which, perhaps on account of his more famous son, have since become classics. The newspaper obituaries declared that he had died of a heart attack, and failed to mention that he had another son besides Corey. The autopsy report reads 'death from acute heroin-morphine and ethanol intoxication'. Richard Keeling was arrested and, under California law, charged with first degree murder because he had supplied the drugs which had killed his friend. The charge was dropped when Keeling pleaded guilty to involuntary manslaughter. He served 120 days in prison. Tim was cremated at the Wiltshire Funeral home, but neither Mary nor Scotty were invited to the ceremony.

Scotty, meanwhile, got on with his life. 'How could I mourn someone I'd never even known?' he later said. He also forgot about changing his name for the moment, devoting most of his energy to despising his new 'stepfather'. The relationship between Mary and George Vandergrift was tempestuous, to say the least, and ended one evening when he flung a television set at her. Taking the children, Mary fled to Sunnymead and for two years – aside from the occasional trip back to Riverside to attempt a reunion with Vandergrift – the trio lived at the garden centre. Scotty was enrolled at a local school, where on account of his scrawny build he became focus of attention for the class bully – until he lost his rag one day and fought back. He was also becoming more and more interested in music, taking cello lessons at school and learning to play the mock-Les Paul guitar given to him by his grandparents for the Christmas of 1979. That he possessed an uncannily acute musical ear goes without saying. As an adult, he is known to have been able to pick up any musical instrument, even an unfamiliar one, and knock out a tune within minutes.

In July 1980, with the garden-centre business starting to flounder and cash in short supply, Mary sent her boys to Willits, a small town near San Francisco where Ron Moorhead lived with his new wife. Living with his favourite stepfather delighted Scotty, and it was probably Moorhead who let him in on the secret that he had actually been baptised Jeffrey. The boy shortened this to Jeff, enrolled *himself* at his next school as Jeff Buckley, and 'celebrated' this by attending his first heavy metal concert, head-lined by British rockers Def Leppard.

Jeff lived at Riverside for around a year, but as soon as he learned that his mother and George Vandergrift had split for good, and that she was heading back to her parents' place, he was on the next train to Orange County. However, if he was hoping to put down roots, Mary Guibert's complicated lifestyle assured him that he would have another think coming. Over the next year she, Jeff and Corey would move home at least five times, more often than not evicted following some spat with the landlord over rent or repairs.

Mary now had a job as a travelling sales representative with a wholesale horticultural supplier. This involved working long hours and Jeff was frequently relegated to the role of 'houseboy', which entailed cooking and cleaning, before and after school. Because of his frequent changes of abode, when he enrolled at the prestigious Loara High he gave his address as his grandparents' house in Anaheim.

In this rich kids' establishment, Jeff was one of the few who did not drive a car, and as such he was made to feel an outsider by his classmates. Some of the bigger boys mocked him, as had happened before, because he was not a 'regular guy' – the archetypal sporting jock. Jeff, however, no longer felt intimidated by such people because by now he had learned how to laugh at himself. At Loara High, Jeff joined the school's jazz orchestra. Mary had recently bought him an expensive Ovation Viper electric guitar which everyone envied, and with which he was a veritable wizard, emulating Kiss and Def Leppard. Jeff only had to hear a piece of music once or twice to know it by heart.

In April 1982, with three school friends (Jason Hamel, Robin Horry and Tim Marse) Jeff formed his first band, Mahre Buckram – an amalgamation of parts of their four surnames – which debuted at Anaheim's Woodstock Concert Theater in the September. None of these had heard of Tim Buckley, and Jeff was not enthusiastic about using his 'position' to gain favours. He later said that the *last* thing he had wanted to be at the time was a frontman, or even a singer, though his clowning around between numbers – impersonating Michael Jackson ('Michael's like a piece of costume jewellery that has no conceivable function!'), Yma Sumac ('She wasn't a Peruvian princess. She's Amy Camus from the Bronx and spells her name backwards!'), and Ella Fitzgerald, who he met after a concert with Count Basie – did get him noticed. Mahre Buckram played just four dates, mostly Genesis and Kiss covers, though there was the odd Buckley composition.

Until now, Jeff had not shown much interest in girls – or rather he had shied away from them, perhaps fearful of rejection on account of his being the butt of his classmates' jokes. At 16, however, though underweight he had matured from being a 'gawky kid' into a rather handsome young man. He would not grow beyond his current five feet seven inches, but he looked 'hip' with his new shag haircut – short and spiky on top, shoulder-length at the back. There were cries of 'faggot' from some sections of the audience – not that this bothered Jeff in the least. His is said to have been the classic case of 'big things come in small packages', and to advertise his 'wares', he took to wearing spray-on silver spandex trousers which left nothing to the imagination, and had females queuing at the stage door.

There was a reported incident when a jealous boyfriend stormed up to Jeff while he was smooching with his girl, and demanded to know what Jeff had that *he* obviously lacked. According to the story, Jeff unzipped his pants and exposed an impressive erection. Yet despite such flaunting, friends have affirmed that he was rarely interested in having sex at this time, save as a means of letting off a little pressure – that his music *always* came first. Again, he may have been fearful of travelling down the same road of self-destruction as his father, which was why, aside from a little pot, he never did drugs and rarely drank more than was good for him.

During his 1995 trip to France, Jeff would tell a press conference that he had been a late developer – losing his virginity at 17, but to a French-Algerian girl who had been so pretty, it had made the wait worthwhile. 'There had been others beforehand,' he added, 'but why should I want to screw anybody who couldn't pronounce the name Guibert properly? And she was the first girl I had the hots for who didn't smoke. Kissing the others was like sticking my tongue in an ashtray!'

Mary Guibert was so impressed by her son's talent – more so than she had ever been with Tim's – that when Mahre Buckram split, she vowed to support him every step of the way. She bought him his first amplifier, and encouraged him to drop the heavy metal repertoire and concentrate on writing his own material. For a little while Jeff played solo, backed by Tim Marse, but this partnership ended early in 1983 when Mary announced yet another change of address: she had been hired by another horticultural company. Instead of going with her, Jeff moved back to his grandparents in Anaheim, and it was from here that he graduated from high school.

In August 1984, Jeff relocated to Hollywood, where he had enrolled himself at the Musicians Institute, a top ranking, $4,000-a-year organisation situated in a seedy neighbourhood off Sunset Boulevard. Mary's new job had lasted but a few months and, as she was counting the pennies again, Jeff paid the fees himself by applying to the courts for an early release of the trust fund set up by Tim. He was scheduled to inherit $20,000 on his 19th birthday, but the court acquiesced to his request when he explained that he needed the money to complete his education.

Jeff and another student rented an apartment at 1810 Cherokee, an area rife with down and outs, drug addicts and Mexican gangs. In an unsuccessful attempt to make himself look older – and tougher – he had his shag haircut razored close to his scalp. This made him look more vulnerable than ever, but rather than pick on him as had happened at high school, the bigger students went out of their way to protect him– escorting him and his valuable Ovation Viper guitar to and from the Institute – their only 'condition' being that he allow them to play it every now and then.

The hours in class were long: eight hours of theory work and rehearsal, followed by jamming sessions most evenings. Jeff formed a band with two fellow students, playing guitar only, and would later swear that he had not sung a single note while at the Musicians Institute. Awarded a vocational diploma, he graduated in September 1985 and to make ends meet while searching for session work, took a job at the Institute as an electrician's apprentice. The extra cash helped him afford what he assumed would be a better apartment – at 7000 Hawthorn, where the gangs were even more fearful. Having seemingly inherited his mother's wanderlust, Jeff moved to Oakshire, in the Hollywood Hills and, dipping into his trust fund, he bought an old station wagon.

Not long afterwards Jeff teamed up with Michael Clouse, a thirty-something Boston-born New Yorker who ran a small studio in Glendale – one of the few people he had met in Hollywood who had heard of Tim Buckley. Clouse had acquired his music degree from the American College of Greece while playing basketball in Europe. In the early 1990s he would achieve some success as a television and movies music supervisor and songwriter, opening his own studio on New York's West 26th Street. For now, he took Jeff on as a partner and the pair founded X-Factor, a short-lived, poorly paid enterprise which allowed wannabes who would never get anywhere to invest money they could ill afford on demo-tapes. While here, Jeff made a demo of his own: *Whiteboy Music* was, he claimed, his personal tribute to legendary guitarist Jeff Beck.

At X-Factor, Michael Clouse was in charge of recording and mixing, while Jeff changed his guitar style a dozen times a day to accommodate whichever second-rater wished to pay for the privilege. Because the studio operated mostly during the evening, Jeff took a day job as factotum at the Magic Hotel, a 'budget' residence on Franklyn Avenue. Here he developed a passion for washing dishes and cleaning – his way, he said, of keeping himself at ground-level. Even when fame beckoned, if someone turned up backstage that he wanted to avoid, Jeff would disappear 'to do a little housework'. Some years later, he would sign a Paris hotel register, 'Miss Joan Crawford', drawing comparisons with his favourite movie star's mania for scrubbing out the bathroom and toilet each time she checked into a hotel.

At the Magic Hotel, Jeff became friends with Brooke Smith, one year his senior, and the actress who had just played Catherine Martin in *Silence of the Lambs*. Some years later she would star in television's *Six Feet Under*, and become a household name as Dr Erica Hahn in *Grey's Anatomy*. What made her 'extra special' in Jeff's eyes was that her birthday was 22 May – the same day as Morrissey's. It was Smith who introduced Jeff to several up-and-coming musicians, and over the next few months he played with some of these, including the saxophonist Al Kirk, with the AKB Band. This saw him making his first professional appearance, in a Bob Marley tribute concert at the Long Beach Arena.

Then in 1989, Jeff began working with Group Therapy, a heavy metal outfit that played some of the roughest joints in town. Group Therapy's 'show-stopper' was 'A Hot Date with a Buzz', a song about masturbation that their front-woman, Grimm, sang to a vibrator – which she subsequently passed to Jeff to use as a guitar-slide! By now he had grown his hair long, and looked effete with this and his trademark skin-tight white vest, yet not only did he manage *not* to be laughed at, he got away with boasting to the press, 'We're gonna be the next Led Zeppelin!'

This was pure bravado. Jeff was quickly becoming disillusioned with the rowdy Hollywood club scene, and had recently made a series of discoveries that would affect his life and career. When a friend loaned him a copy of Rimbaud's *Une Saison En Enfer*, like Nick Drake before him, he became hooked on it and the French boy-poet genius – a strange move for a heterosexual man. Self-published in 1873, Rimbaud's work – heavy on his emotional and physical struggle, exacerbated by his dependency on opium and absinthe – had coincided with Paul Verlaine's ending of their love affair in the most brutal fashion, by shooting him and being imprisoned for attempted murder. As such, *Une Saison En Enfer* represented Rimbaud's symbolic breaking with his flighty, irascible past. It had been savaged by the critics, resulting in Rimbaud burning all of his unpublished manuscripts and giving up on his brilliant career at the ripe old age of 19.

To a lesser degree, in February 1990 Jeff emulated Rimbaud by giving up *his* most prized possession aside from his guitar – he sold his station wagon to finance a trip to New York. One of the musicians he had studied with at the Institute lived in Harlem, and Jeff stayed with him for a while – until hearing that Brooke Smith was in town. The pair rented a small apartment in Manhattan, though it is believed their relationship never progressed beyond the platonic. Jeff paid his way by taking ad-hoc work and busking in subways.

Jeff's *big* discoveries in New York were Edith Piaf, and *qawwali* singer Nusrat Fateh Ali Khan, a gargantuan character whom he had seen in a concert in Central Park. He first became aware of Piaf by way of Michael Houldey's highly acclaimed television documentary, *I Regret Nothing!* and my own *Nights of Edith Piaf*, broadcast on NBC Radio. Jeff admired the great *chanteuse* for her tremendous courage during her life-long battles against ill-health and adversity

– for the way each tragic element of this life had been transcribed to her songs. Jeff would think nothing of slotting her 'La Vie en Rose, Non, Je ne Regrette Rien' and 'Padam, Padam' between songs by Genesis and Frank Zappa, a versatility unmatched by any contemporary. He was one of the few entertainers permitted to sing *and* mimic Piaf on a Parisian stage without attracting severe criticism – or worse still having objects thrown at him!

In June 1995, Jeff was interviewed by Jean-Daniel Beauvallet of France's top music magazine, *Les Inrockuptibles*. Citing Led Zeppelin, Miles Davis, Hank Williams, The Doors and Leonard Cohen as his earliest influences, he confessed that while these had inspired his musical sensibility, discovering Piaf had started off a process which he was certain would 'feed the soul' for the rest of his life:

> *With Piaf, nothing's phoney. Every emotion becomes epic because she plunged the depths and stared death in the face. There's such strength in that voice! It's like a flower trying to bore its way through a paving stone! I've always been drawn to personalities who invite tragedy to their table. For a little white Californian like me, though, being passionate about somebody like Piaf wasn't exactly the best way of fitting in without everyone assuming you were morbid – or gay!*

Nusrat (1948–97), the undisputed prince of Indian/Pakistani devotional (of Sufis, a mystical off-shoot of Islam) singers, found himself championed by Jeff because – though from completely different cultures – emotionally and in their upper range, their voices were remarkably similar. 'He was amazing, a fucking café-au-lait coloured Brando,' he told *Double Take*'s Josh Farrar in February 1996. When asked if he actually *owned* any Nusrat albums, Jeff once piped without boasting, 'So far I've only managed to find fifty!' Jeff met Nusrat in New York, and the two became friends. In January 1996 he interviewed him for *Interview* magazine, and proudly informed him that he had learned over a hundred *qawwali* songs by heart.

In 1997, Jeff would be asked to write the liner notes for Nusrat's latest album. This had a delayed release when Jeff died, and the irony is that on 16 August of that year, just three months after his death, Nusrat himself died suddenly in London of heart failure, brought on by liver failure, and the notes were used for a *Supreme Collection* tribute album:

> *I remember my senses fully froze in order to feel melody after melody crash upon each in waves of inspiration. I felt a rush of adrenalin in my chest – like I was on the edge of a cliff, wondering when I would jump, how the ocean would catch me.*

At that time in New York, however, there was little call for long-haired, baby-faced rockers performing *chansons* or wailing in Urdu! Lucky then for Jeff that Fate came to his rescue – courtesy of the late, very much unlamented father whose footsteps he had never wanted to follow in. Tim had toured England in the autumn of 1968 – his bassist had been Danny Thompson, shortly after Thompson had worked with Nick Drake – and one of his London concerts had been taped. Now, Tim's record company, Enigma, planned releasing this on a CD, providing that his estate – Tim's widow, Judy, and his sons – were in agreement.

The go-ahead was given, and Jeff chose the title *Dream Letter* for the album. In this song, Tim had poured out his guilt over the way he had neglected Mary and Jeff, and Jeff wanted the world to know what sort of man his father had really been. He was also irked by Tim's question in the song, 'Is he Mama's little boy?' which, though posed two decades earlier, was regarded by some Tim Buckley fans as their hero glimpsing into the future and predicting that Mary would end up spoiling her firstborn, which is exactly what happened. There is something Oedipal about some of the photographs taken at around this time, particularly of the ones where Jeff is seen sitting on his mother's knee.

At Enigma, Jeff was introduced to Herb Cohen, Tim's former manager who had taken in the pregnant Mary after Tim had walked out on her. From a distance, Cohen appears to have been keeping a watchful eye on Jeff's progress – Jeff claimed for no other reason than Cohen was seeing the dollar signs, should Jeff elect to hop on to the 'Tim Buckley gravy-train', as he called it. Cohen had latterly seen Group Therapy in Los Angeles, and now offered to finance a demo-tape. Jeff flew back there in the September, and temporarily moved in with his former band.

Like Nick Drake, Jeff often took his time writing and composing songs. He would jot down notes and arrangements in the exercise book he always carried around with him, forget about them, and move on to something else – then return to them weeks, sometimes months later, with a completely new approach. Tucked inside his portfolio when he entered the Eurosound Studios were four 'new' works which he taped under the collective title, *The Babylon Dungeon Sessions* – partly on account of the dismal recording conditions, partly in honour of Kenneth Anger, whose *Hollywood Babylon* books had lifted the lid off the film capital's more lurid scandals during the golden years of the studio system. 'Radio', an attack on the music business, seems to have disappeared, though the others would resurface. 'Unforgiven' was a lament for a lost love, almost certainly the French-Algerian girl to whom he's lost his virginity in New York. 'Strawberry Street' told of that show-business phenomenon, the casting-couch. And then there was '*Eternal Life*' . . .

Jeff always maintained that the first truly great song he composed centred around his thoughts about his own son, should he ever have one. Others close to him have said that it was about Tim in his 'twisted hell', which had seen him making some quite unforgivable remarks about the black and Jewish communities – on the face of it, this seems the more likely theory. 'Racist everyman, what have you done?' Jeff rants, before issuing the chilling statement, 'Man, you've made a killer of your unborn son. All I want to do is love everyone!'

Aside from the personnel at Enigma, few of Jeff's New York acquaintances knew who Tim Buckley was, and it was only now that Jeff began digging into the past of the father who had deserted him. He was reunited with Tim's widow, Judy, and her 27-year-old son, Taylor, for the first time in 15 years. He also met his paternal grandmother, Elaine, for the first time, along with Tim's sister, Kathleen. It was she who introduced Jeff to several of Tim's former musicians, and his closest confidante, a divorce lawyer named Danielle Sapriel.

For a little while, Jeff regarded Sapriel as some kind of surrogate mother, accepting her invitation to move into the spare room at her house. He did not appreciate, however, the lavish party she threw for his birthday in November 1990. Thinking she was acting in his interests, and unaware of the various family problems, Sapriel asked all the Buckleys she had in her address book to the bash – along with Ron Moorhead, Judy and half a dozen Guiberts who had loathed the ground Tim had walked on. Jeff later said that the atmosphere could have been sliced through with a knife, and that he hoped never to witness such a gathering again.

On 26 April 1991, Jeff found himself badgered into participating in *Greetings From Tim Buckley*, a tribute concert staged at St Anne's Cathedral, Brooklyn, as part of the *Arts at St Anne's* festival. The previous year, Jeff had seen Marianne Faithfull here. The event was organised by New York entrepreneur Hal Willner, the music co-ordinator for television's long-running *Saturday Night Live* – who had also produced Marianne's magnificent 1987 album, *Strange Weather*. Willner hired (on a no-fees basis, as this was a charity event) various local singers and musicians to perform Tim's 'best-known' songs, though effectively there were very few of these – Tim had never had a hit record.

Herb Cohen had boasted to Willner, a diehard Tim Buckley fan, that Jeff's singing voice was even better than his father's, but had seemingly omitted to tell him that he was also a gifted musician. As such, Willner brought in 37-year-old guitarist Gary Lucas, who 10 years earlier had played with Captain Beefheart's Magic Band. Since leaving Beefheart, Lucas had been employed as a copywriter with Columbia Records, and had latterly formed his own outfit, Gods & Monsters, with bassist Jared Nickerson and drummer Tony Lewis. The name came courtesy of a line from James Whale's *Bride of Frankenstein*, and would later be the title of the director's biopic, starring Ian McKellen and Brandon Fraser.

Until now, Jeff had never performed Tim's work, nor wanted to. Billed as Jeff Scott Buckley, he chose three songs: 'I Never Asked To Be Your Mountain', 'Once I Was' – another of Tim's laments for Mary which Jeff finished a cappella after busting a guitar string – and 'Sefronie, the King's Chain', a nihilist blanket of noise which lyrically makes little sense.

Jeff came on after the interval, wearing a black T-shirt and keeping his back to the audience for a few minutes while tuning his guitar. He had just washed his long, dark hair and allowed it to dry naturally without brushing it, just as Tim had done. When he turned around to face the spotlight and began singing in what *The New York Times* called 'a high-droning voice that echoed his father's keening timbre', there were loud gasps from the auditorium. Jeff *so* resembled his father that a few people actually believed for a moment or two that Tim, ever the practical joker, had faked his own death and returned to get his own back on the critics who had savaged him.

No one was more surprised than Jeff, who was later quoted (in David Browne's *Dream Brother*) as saying, 'My God, I stepped on stage and they backlit it, and it was like the fucking Second Coming!'

But, did Jeff actually *like* his father's music? Apparently not, if his statement to Matt Diehl (*Rolling Stone*, October 1994) was anything to go by:

> *Sometimes he sounds like the fucking Kingfish from Amos & Andy. 'I woke up this morning!' What the fuck is that? 'Every, every single day I've been loving you!' What kind of bullshit is that? 'Gonna look between your toes!' Fuck that shit! It's like you don't know if you're Tom Jones or Al Green, and the two mixed together don't really sound that great!*

Chapter Thirteen

I Used to Know a Little Square

The Tim Buckley tribute concert did nothing to temper Jeff's bitterness towards his father. A few years later he told the *Philadelphia Enquirer*, 'I sacrificed my anonymity for my father, whereas he sacrificed me for his fame.' As a result of the concert, however, just three days later doors started to open – not for Tim Buckley's son, but for Jeff Buckley in his own right. Gary Lucas, eager for Jeff to front Gods & Monsters, auditioned *The Babylon Dungeon Sessions* tape with Columbia.

Jeff, meanwhile, flew back to Los Angeles. Accompanying him to the airport was 23-year-old actress Rebecca Moore, a member of Fluxus, the underground, experimental arts movement originated in the 1950s by John Gale. This had been promoted as, 'An international network of artists, composers and designers blending different artistic media and disciplines.' These artists had included such luminaries at György Ligeti and Yoko Ono, though much of what they did was beyond the comprehension of most regular theatregoers, resulting in a great deal of adverse criticism. Rebecca had also been working as a volunteer for the St Anne's festival. Dark-haired, shy and pretty, she had met Jeff during rehearsals for the Tim tribute, and it had been love at first sight. During a trip to Paris he likened Rebecca to Juliette Gréco, claiming that as one had been the muse of the Existentialists, so Rebecca had been the 'muse of Fluxus'. He was, of course, being vastly overgenerous in his praise, for there was no comparison between an actress virtually no one had ever heard of, and the legendary French actress and *chanteuse* who had influenced an entire generation of *grandes interprètes*.

Jeff later confessed how, at the airport, he had sobbed like a child after kissing his new girlfriend goodbye in the rain. This parting resulted in him penning (with Gary Lucas) 'Grace', one of his most innovative songs – the plaintive which will be forever associated with his memory. 'She weeps on my arm, walking to the bright lights in sorrow,' he slants and pitches through three octaves. 'The rain is falling, and I believe my time has come.'

Separated from his lover, and with no positive news from Columbia, Jeff – usually the archetypal, chirpy little sparrow – lost it all and fell into a brief but profound period of depression. He and Rebecca spoke every day on the phone, but hearing her voice only made him feel worse. Fate intervened when Carla Azar, a musician friend, contacted him with an offer of work. Alan Parker's *The Commitments*, the hard-hitting, controversial film about a fictitious Irish rock band, was about to premiere in New York, and Azar needed an ambience band to play numbers from the production for the various cast receptions and parties. It was during this trip, briefly reunited with Rebecca, that Jeff and Gary Lucas wrote a curiosity called 'Mojo Pin' – the heroin addict's appellation for the hypodermic syringe.

'Grace' and 'Mojo Pin' were two of the songs taped by Jeff and Lucas in New York on 17 August 1991. On 10 November, the pair played the first of Jeff's four dates with Gods & Monsters. They also made their radio debut on New Jersey's WFMU: Jeff did the two songs, along with 'Bluebird Blues' and Joan Baez's big European hit, 'Adieu, Angelina' – sitting cross-legged on the floor like Nusrat Fateh Ali Khan, surrounded by joss sticks and lighted candles.

In the meantime, with Columbia having rejected the *Babylon Dungeon* tape, Gary Lucas arranged for this to be auditioned elsewhere. Tim Buckley's ghost was still hovering in the background: the best deal came from Imago. Hoping for 'chip-off-the-old-block' material, but not wishing to make too much of a commitment, Imago offered a paltry $10,000 advance, with the provision that if they disliked whatever Jeff and Lucas came up with, the pair would get to keep the cash but not be offered a further contract. They used this to polish up their act and prepare a showcase, for the benefit of Imago and any other interested parties – at St Anne's in Brooklyn, which Jeff had designated his 'lucky' venue.

Early in December, Jeff returned to Los Angeles to find that his apartment had been burgled. Among the items stolen was his prized Ovation guitar. He stayed here only long enough to pack his remaining belongings – the partings from Rebecca were getting to be too distressing for him to cope with many more, and a few days before Christmas he moved into her apartment in Manhattan's Lower East Side.

Taking a leaf out of Rimbaud's book – not out of necessity, for there was still plenty of money left from his trust fund – Jeff flung himself into what he interpreted to be the existence of the typical bohemian poet, a trait which would stay with him for the rest of his life. He and Rebecca ate at downtown greasy-spoon cafés, and his wardrobe came courtesy of the local charity shops. Rebecca nicknamed him 'Scratchy' – doubtless not without good cause, for many of the photographs taken at the time show him wearing ripped T-shirts and trousers and looking decidedly grungy – though on the other side of the coin he is known to have been extremely fastidious when it came to personal hygiene.

Jeff was well aware – though not conceitedly so – that as the vocalist with a group, he would be expected to take centre-stage and shoulder the brunt of their failure, should Gods & Monsters fall flat on their collective faces. For some reason, he felt uncomfortable working with Jared Nickerson and Tony Lewis, and asked Gary Lucas to replace them – either this, or he would walk. Lucas must have truly regarded Jeff as the key towards his artistic future: very much against his will he obeyed the command, though the move would cause friction between Jeff and himself. During the winter of 1991 and the spring of 1992, Jeff and Lucas recorded several songs at Lucas' home which, had Jeff lived, would never have seen the light of day. These, along with other numbers played in New York at the Knitting Factory, would be released on an album, *Songs For No One*, in 1992, and range from the passable ('Grace' and 'Harem Man') to dire (an 11-minutes-plus 'Hymne à l'Amour', arranged by Lucas and which would have had Edith Piaf spinning in her grave) to the sublime – Jeff's stunning solo version of Joe Hayes and Jack Rhodes 'Satisfied Mind', which could almost serve as his epitaph.

The re-formed Gods & Monsters debut concert took place on 13 March 1992 – an unlucky Friday. Jeff had adopted a new stage persona: that of the androgynous, lost boy with cropped hair, hedgehog-spiked on top, and a baggy shirt split to the waist, revealing his navel stud – and a somewhat scrawny frame which many felt he should have kept covered. *He* – for this was Jeff Buckley, certainly not Gods & Monsters – opened with a new song, 'Cruel', though much of the programme consisted of covers, now and in the future frequently superior to their originals and to an extent better delivered and received than Jeff's own material.

Jeff turned Van Morrison's 'Sweet Thing' into a chanson, but retained the original arrangements of the genuine *chansons* – Jacques Brel's 'Chanson Sans Paroles' and Edith Piaf's 'Hymne à l'Amour'. He filled what might have been awkward pauses with little 'monologues' – wisecracks, mimicking anything from

Jerry Lewis to a car alarm. And when he sang *Grace*, his voice rose a staggering four octaves during the final refrain. Such unfettered showing off led to Gary Lucas walking off the stage, ignored by Jeff who delivered a scorching rendition of Mahalia Jackson's 'Satisfied Mind', all but bringing the house down before a calmed-down Lucas returned to round off the evening with *Mojo Pin*.

Essentially, the St Anne's concert had been for the benefit of Imago's Kate Hyman, who now offered Jeff some career-building advice: if he really was intent on getting anywhere, then he should ditch Gods & Monsters – and Gary Lucas – and strike out on his own. This he did the very next day after reading a review of the concert in *The New York Times*. For while in singling him out as the focus of the evening, the musicians were denounced as, 'B-list celebrities as grey as yesterday's potatoes'.

Jeff's first appearance as an authentic solo act came courtesy of Rebecca Moore, currently appearing in a Fluxus production of *The Manson Family* at a backstreet New York theatre. Her co-star in this macabre opera about the Manson killings was Daniel Harnett, also a singer and whose band, Glim, were a regular attraction at a certain 'all-comers-welcome' café-concert bar in New York's East Village. Opened in 1990 by Irish immigrants Shane Doyle and silent partner Karl Geary, the Sin-É (pronounced *shin-ay*, Gaelic for 'that's it') stood at 122 St Mark's Place – an area rife with rent boys, prostitutes and drug addicts which had not prevented it from becoming *the* Irishman's watering-hole (the house speciality was its 'Rolling Rock' beer) and a popular hang-out for artists, writers and musicians. Like the Écluse in Paris, where Nick Drake had trod his first steps towards immortality, the Sin-É had no specific opening and closing times. On quiet nights, the shutters came down early. If there was a crowd in, which was always the case when Jeff was around, Doyle kept open until dawn. In an interview with *Interview*'s Ray Rogers in February 1994, Jeff would enthuse about this, his favourite New York neighbourhood, 'This is where I blossomed. This place turned out to be everything I knew it would be. It stinks like hell – a fucking majestic cesspool. Art is everywhere! Electricity is everywhere! It's very extreme. I'm not saying, "It's a great, wonderful dance!" But it makes sense to me!'

Unlike the Écluse in its heyday, at Sin-É there was initially no organised entertainment. Doyle auditioned the acts – usually, a couple of songs were sufficient to add their name to the waiting list, though if the act happened to be Marianne Faithfull, U2, or beat-poet Allen Ginsberg, they just walked in and got on with things. Doyle never provided a stage because there was no room – the auditorium measured just 900 square feet and seated some 60 customers if the tables were squashed together. Also, no one was ever paid! Doyle never applied for an entertainment licence because this would have proved too costly to keep the place going. He referred to his acts as 'indoor buskers' – after performing, they walked around with a 'Rolling Rock' beer jug collecting tips, which on good nights could amount to $200 or more.

On the negative side, the Sin-É was less intimate than its Parisian counterpart – the sound system was set up against a wall facing the street and subject to much of the traffic noise. Also, the delinquents roaming around outside would frequently hammer on the window and put the artists off their stride. This never happened when Jeff was appearing. Sin-É would become for him, on a much smaller scale of course, what the Paris Olympia had been for Piaf: time and time again he would return, even when he had moved up the artistic ladder.

Jeff first played the Sin-É on 3 April 1992, wearing thrift-shop clothes two sizes too big for him, and with the same second-hand guitar he had borrowed for the St Anne's concert. His repertoire, aside from a few personal compositions, was both electric and sophisticated: the heavy metal and Tim Buckley covers had been replaced by standards from the Piaf, Brel, Billie Holiday and Judy Garland songbooks. Jeff never defined whether he was straight, gay or bisexual – judging by later events in his life, one would assume his sexuality lay somewhere in between – he very definitely had a potent feminine side, and could have courted disaster by singing all the gay favourites: Judy's 'The Man That Got Away', Eartha Kitt's 1953 hit, 'Lilac Wine', and the female lyrics to Piaf's 'La Vie en Rose' to a frequently hard-bitten, possibly homophobic audience. However, as surviving tapes of his appearances show, the Sin-É crowd loved him no matter what he sang and – the males included – even shed a tear with him on the odd occasion.

Jeff was also a fan of the great *fado* singer, Amália Rodrigues, whose death two years after his would evoke three days of national mourning in her native Portugal, and the postponement of the country's general elections. Though he is not thought to have performed *fado* – declaring that the songs would have to be sung in Portuguese, which he could not master, even phonetically – Jeff borrowed from Amália in two ways. Firstly, he vastly elongated and embellished certain words and notes – it was not unusual for the shortest word to be dragged out to 20 syllables. Secondly, in the café-concerts, he followed in the *fadista* tradition of gleaning some titbit of gossip from a member of the audience, then singing something or throwing in a monologue relevant to the situation. This sometimes backfired on him, necessitating a hasty exit after the show to the kitchen to help with the washing up. Not every husband liked to find out, the Buckley way, that his wife was cheating on him, especially if she was sitting next to him in the auditorium!

Throughout the summer of 1992, Jeff was given a regular Monday evening spot at Sin-É, and became so popular that a crowd gathered whenever he was on, spilling out on to the street and making a welcome contribution to his beer jug. Other folk and rock greats had started out at such small establishments: the Loving Spoonful at the Night Owl, Bob Dylan at Folk City, Bruce Springsteen at Bottom Line. Word of Jeff's café-concert appearances soon spread, and he was offered regular work at Skep, Tilt, the Cornelia Street Café – and at Fez, a basement club (not unlike Les Cousins, in Soho) on Lafayette Street.

Here, Jeff's 'sparrow-like' appearance brought out the maternal instincts of the proprietor, variety agent Ellen Cavolina. Part of the uncontracted deal she made with Jeff – who was more than delighted with the $100 fee, even when performing for just a dozen people – was that he should never leave the place without having a good feed at the Time Café, Fez's upstairs restaurant. Most of the other cafés followed suit – not that Jeff ever put any weight on with all the free food he ate. In the liner notes for *Live At Sin-É*, the fabulous legacy album released six years after Jeff's death, Arista Records executive Mitchell Cohen observed of these café years, 'He was the Montgomery Clift of singer-songwriters, beautiful and bruised, struggling so hard you could feel it.' Jeff had also picked up one of Monty's less savoury habits (besides calling record company executives he disliked, 'interfering fuckfaces', a favourite Monty appellation) whenever one of his 'sponsors' forgot to feed him – wooing a diner with a song, then helping himself to something from their plate! Such was his cheeky charm, and the clientele's admiration, that there were never any complaints.

News of the 'scruffy-looking little punk' bringing the albeit tiny house down most evenings at one of the East Village cafés reached the ears of record company talent scouts, most notably Columbia's Steve Berkowitz. Though he had not heard Jeff sing, Berkowitz had read a press report for the Tim Buckley tribute concert. He now contacted Hal Willner, and the pair headed for Sin-É with the intention of negotiating a record deal – providing, of course, that Jeff lived up to his legend. Berkowitz was amazed. Much of Jeff's repertoire was half a century old, yet given the Buckley treatment sounded like it could have been composed yesterday. Jeff, however, was sceptical about discussing contracts and projected record sales. His idols – Piaf, Judy, Billie and Nusrat – had loathed commercialism and their primary aims in life had been to give memorable performances, though in the process of doing so they *had* sold records, in Piaf's case over 250 million. Jeff agreed in principle to *think* about a contract with Columbia, which had also been Piaf's label – most young men in his position would have snapped Berkowitz's hand off – and contacted his lawyer, George Stein, the man who had negotiated the Gods & Monsters deal with Imago. Stein and his business partner, Dave Lory, would represent Jeff for the rest of his life.

Within weeks, hailed as one of the hottest young talents in New York, Jeff found himself approached by executives from RCA, Imago and Arista who were surprised to see a smattering of celebrities among the Sin-É crowd: Marianne Faithfull, Kurt Cobain and Sinead O'Connor were just three who dropped by to see what all the fuss was about. George Stein took advantage of this, exaggerating his client's value, drafting a letter to 'all interested parties' stating that if anyone wanted his boy, it would cost them – a minimum $100,000 advance for a guaranteed three albums, complete control for Jeff over his choice of material, artwork and musicians, plus a non-negotiable 28 (as opposed to the more usual 25) per cent royalty on record and video sales. Suddenly, the record company bigwigs who had so fervently sung Jeff's praises were no longer quite so enthusiastic. Only Columbia believed him worthy of such a high investment. Agreeing to Stein's ambitious terms, they signed a contract with Jeff in October 1992.

With no date set for the recording of his debut album – Columbia had asked for more Buckley compositions which, he said, would take time – Jeff took a break from music to indulge in one of his fantasies: acting on the legitimate stage. Like the great married-to-their-public divas he championed so well, he was having a hard time forging a career while attempting to hold down a relationship. Rebecca Moore had introduced him to Fluxus and its stable of mostly trashy artists from all walks of life, whose forte involved emulating, and not always well, whichever branch of the arts they were supposed to represent.

Tim Buckley had appeared in several plays with the Los Angeles Theater Group, among them Edward Albee's *Zoo Story* and Jean-Paul Sartre's *No Evil*. There had been a movie cameo in *Why?*, starring O. J. Simpson, and at the time of his death Tim was being considered for a sizeable part in ex-Byrd Roger McGuinn's musical, *Gene Tryp*, based (hence the anagram) on Grieg's *Peer Gynt*. Maybe Jeff felt that he could do better than his father: he was certainly better looking, much less arrogant, and far more charismatic. Unfortunately, his debut performance for Fluxus, at New York's Anthology Film Archives Theater in 1992, was uninspired. Hoping that working with Rebecca might salvage what was left of their crumbling relationship, he allowed himself to be coerced on to the stage – wearing an undertaker's suit, fake acne, and playing a selection of instruments including a comb and a shower hose – leaving the Columbia executive sitting in the audience wondering what he had let himself in for!

The same executive attended another Buckley 'performance' later in the week – to witness Jeff screaming expletives at a potted plant while ironing his shirt with an electric guitar. Only slightly less ludicrous was his monologue, 'Miles of Death', delivered while playing the harmonium. Arguably his best role – indeed, the only sensible thing he did with Fluxus, and the one that saw some critics actually comparing him with the young Montgomery Clift, who had also played the role – was the central role in an off-beat production of Georg Büchner's *Woyzeck*. Written in 1837, this tells the story of a mentally retarded army private who kills his girlfriend in a fit of pique. The play ran for several weeks at the Atrium, a small fringe theatre in the East Village. Sadly, no photographs of the production have survived.

On 8 November 1992, Jeff entered a Times Square studio 'to throw a couple of tunes around'. Several items were taped – sketches for his debut album – but as usual he appears to have been dissatisfied with the end result. Over the next three months there were more performances at Sin-É and other cafés. Jeff refrained from telling George Stein about these because he was getting tired of record-company executives dropping in on him unannounced, asking awkward questions in the hope of poaching him from Columbia. Much of the time, these days, he would head for the kitchen straight after his show, to help out with the dishes and avoid anyone he thought looked 'official'.

Then in February 1993, Jeff spent several days in a studio on West 21st Street, where he taped five of his own songs, and around 30 covers. Among these was a stunning (*still* unreleased) arrangement of The Smiths' 'I Know It's Over'. Jeff reckoned that its opening line, 'Mama, I can feel the soil falling over my head', more or less summed up how he felt being trapped in a now loveless relationship with Rebecca Moore. Later, he would slightly amend this theme for 'What Will You Say?' in which he proclaims, 'Mother dear, the world's gone mad . . . my heart can't take this anymore!'

Jeff had been carrying a torch for Morrissey for years, ever since The Smiths' enigmatic frontman had penned 'Shakespear's Sister'. The song, an invitation to a cliff-top suicide, had as its inspiration an essay by Virginia Woolf: in Morrissey's case, the narrator is urged by the rocks below to, 'Throw your skinny body down', so that he and the singer he loved – widely reputed to have been Tim Buckley

– may be reunited in death. Jeff had since attended several Morrissey concerts since the group's split, though they are not thought to have met. The Mancunian singer so inspired Jeff that, several years later, he told a French reporter that if ever he did have a physical relationship with another man, he would like it to be with Morrissey.

One of Jeff's favourite books at this time was *Morrissey Shot*, a volume of photographs by the singer's closest friend, ex-Ludus front-woman Linder Sterling. This contains a large selection of mostly posed-for studies, as imperious as they are artistic, wildly homoerotic, and equalling anything to be found in the Kobal Collection. Jeff decided that he wanted something along the same lines (though the subsequent tome, *A Wished For Song*, would not appear in his lifetime), and from now on he would be accompanied on the professional trail by a young woman named Merri Cyr, who would prove, as with Morrissey, Valentino and Garbo, there was no such thing as a Jeff Buckley bad angle.

Like Linder Sterling, Merri Cyr was of the opinion that, though the world was rife with beautiful people, but a fraction of these were of any real interest *beyond* physical attraction – or 'fuckability', as Jeff put it. 'Jeff had a fantastic beauty, rare and originating on an energetic level,' she observes in her book on Buckley. 'It's got nothing to do with the meat of a body, and it's beyond talent. He was, on a creative level, totally open, beautiful.' Jeff had met Cyr a few months earlier when she had been commissioned to photograph him for a feature in *Paper* magazine. Her first task before being appointed his 'official' photographer, however – effecting his severance from Rebecca Moore – was to help Jeff to move into a new apartment at 233 East 12th Street, just a few minutes' walk from Sin-É. Here, free of the 'burden', which nevertheless had been the inspiration behind 'Grace', he flung himself into two relationships. One, which he always claimed was 'cuddles-only', was with a 21-year-old male musician. The other was with the punk-edged-style folk singer, Brenda Kahn whose first album, *Goldfish Don't Talk Back*, had been released in 1990 to a fanfare of critical acclaim. At the time of meeting Jeff, she had just released her equally revered *Epiphany in Brooklyn*, which saw *People* magazine comparing her with Patti Smith. After Jeff's death, she would record a spoken-word acoustic album, *Hunger*, which she would dedicate to his memory.

Meanwhile, Jeff's 'acting' experiences led to him being approached by Gap, to appear on one of their poster advertising campaigns – a strange request, for with his fondness for second-hand clothes and grungy appearance, he was hardly what one would have called fashion conscious. He turned the offer down, along with the huge fee which accompanied it, declaring that he was not interested in promoting his body – just his voice. This pleased Steve Berkowitz. His protégé had been invited to perform at Columbia's annual June convention, in Florida, and Berkowitz wanted everyone at the label and its parent company, Sony, to be impressed with Jeff's musical abilities, not some pretty face on a poster.

'This next important chapter in the musical odyssey of Jeff Buckley, which could well become an important chapter in American popular music,' was how Sony's newsletter heralded Jeff's appearance at the convention. His 15-minute set went down inordinately well. One of the items he chose, to demonstrate his unique ability of switching from one end of the musical spectrum to the other within the space of a song, was Leonard Cohen's hymnal, 'Hallelujah' – a future Buckley standard which like most others he covered would soon become a 'property' song. Jeff's version of 'Hallelujah' was longer than the Cohen original that had featured on his *Various Positions* album – he chose the one with extra verses from ex-Velvet Underground member John Cale's *I'm Your Fan*. The Sony people had already heard some of Jeff's rough-edged studio work, but like the artists he promoted – chiefly Piaf and Judy – none of these tracks even remotely compared with the way that he sounded live. It was therefore decided that, while he was working on his album, two of his café-concert performances would be recorded and released on a 4-track EP. The first session was set for 19 July.

Columbia's first mistake was in recording Jeff at Sin-É during the afternoon – at a time when there was little ambience, and when his voice was at its least malleable. The company also arranged for the event to be filmed, not that this affected Jeff's dress sense – he turned up in a crumpled T-shirt and ragamuffin Army pants. Neither was the event strictly legal. Sin-É's policy of allowing performers to solicit tips from the customers was perfectly in order – using the establishment for commercial gain, however, and with someone else (Sony) paying the artist's fee was against the law if the proprietor had not obtained a local authority permit. Not that anyone considered taking any action: the official responsible for checking up on such things was an avid Jeff Buckley fan!

If Steve Berkowitz was contented with Jeff's matinee performance at Sin-É, Jeff himself hated it to such an extent that it threw him into a state of depressive fatigue, something which had never happened before. Merri Cyr recalled how, immediately after it, Jeff draped himself across a row of chairs, placed his head on her lap, and promptly passed out.

Jeff had been acutely aware of the recording engineers, he said, and felt that he had strived too hard to give a contrived performance that he could not possibly allow into the public domain. At a cost of $12,000, which included Jeff's repeat fee, Columbia organised a second session at Sin-É for 17 August, and this went much better. The company now had around 50 songs and monologues on tape, from which they selected four for the EP: 'Mojo Pin', 'Eternal Life', Van Morrison's 'The Way Young Lovers Do' and Edith Piaf's 1939 million-seller, 'Je n'en Connais pas la Fin'. Written by Marguerite Monnot and Raymond Asso, Harold Rome (not credited on Jeff's recording) had adapted it into English in 1950 as 'My Lost Melody', and it had become Piaf's theme song in America. It is this lyric that Jeff always sang, but for some reason he believed that having a French title in his repertoire would make him appear more sophisticated, though the English lyric tells a completely different story from the French original. In 'Je n'en connais pas la fin', the subject of the song is another song that the narrator cannot get out of her head, save that she does not know how it ends. In the adaptation, the subject is a local fair the narrator recalls from her youth.

Grace, Jeff's debut album, finally went into production in September 1993, a year after he signed the Columbia contract. Steve Berkowitz chose Andy Wallace to produce: he had worked with Ozzy Osborne, Henry Rollins and more importantly Kurt Cobain on Nirvana's *Nevermind* album, whose initial pressing of 50,000 copies had sold out in 48 hours. Berkowitz was convinced that with the right promotion behind him, Jeff would fare equally well.

Jeff had originally wanted to provide all the backing instrumentals for the album: guitars, piano, organ, harmonium and woodwind. Now, exercising his contractual rights, he changed his mind and demanded a band. George Stein tried to talk him out of this: his café-concert performances had been that much more special *because* he had been a one-man operation. When it became clear that he was not going to change his mind, Jeff was begged to consider hiring musicians with proven track records – at the very least to offer the work to some of his colleagues from the Musicians Institute. He refused to capitulate, and Columbia were too afraid of losing him *not* to allow him to have his own way. Jeff announced that *he* would choose his own musicians, not necessarily by way of merit, but by intuition. The executives at Columbia would regret not making him toe the line, as happened with most of their other artists, for from now on, Jeff would cause them nothing but anguish. The *Grace* album would be an almighty headache for them, from start to finish.

Chapter Fourteen

One With a Travelling Heart

First to join the Jeff Buckley Band was Mick Grondahl, a 25-year-old Danish man for whom music had been a swift volte-face, having majored in sculpture at Skidmore College. He and Jeff had met at a Daniel Harnett and Glim show at the Postcrypt Café on New York's Columbia campus, and had gone on to jam at Fez. Later he would say of Jeff's unorthodox working and recording methods, 'He was a person who just wanted to fall into the abyss and trust that he'd land on his two feet, much like a cat.' Next, Jeff hired 22-year-old Texan drummer-construction worker Matt Johnson, a friend of Rebecca Moore's who would later play for Buckley worshipper Rufus Wainwright. Neither had had much on-stage experience.

Grace was taped at the Bearsville Studios in Woodstock, New York, over a five-week period. It was said to have been a consummate joy for Jeff and his musicians – and an unbridled nightmare for everyone else. With his Yma Sumac-style vocal embellishments, Jeff never knew how he was going to approach a song until he began singing it, and he would sometimes rocket an entire octave or more without warning – or launch into a double-trill from Sumac's 'Chuncho', or an ear-splitting *qawwali* wail and expect the band to follow his lead.

Grondahl and Johnson quickly adapted to this unorthodoxy, but for the session men it was all they could do to keep up with him – in full throttle, he became so involved in the song that it was impossible to halt the proceedings until he had finished. Jeff had instructed Andy Wallace to organise *two* different recording set-ups within the same studio, each with its own drum kit and microphone system – one for loud takes, the other for the lighter stuff. Additionally, like Jacques Brel and many of the European *chansonniers*, Jeff asked for a stage to be set up in the studio for the more intimate musical interludes.

Of the 20 or so songs from which 10 would be selected for the album, there were no single takes. This had nothing to do with lack of professionalism, or cock-ups: quite simply, whatever Jeff did, no matter how superb it sounded to everyone else, *he* always believed that he could do better. Benjamin Britten's 'Corpus Christi Carol', which he performs in a mixture of mezzo-vocalese and schoolboy treble, was wrapped up in just four attempts. There were 10 takes of 'Grace' (for which Jeff welcomed Gary Lucas into the fold, the least he could do seeing that Lucas had co-written it), 19 for 'Last Goodbye', and 23 for 'Hallelujah'. This effectively resulted in Jeff's most requested song, in its commercial version, being a complete fake – its seven minutes comprising a dozen fragments recorded over a month-long period and spliced together by the engineer.

The *Grace* sessions were not helped by Columbia's insistence that, like the Sin-É performances, Jeff's every moment at Woodstock be captured on celluloid. It was as if someone had had a terrible premonition that, four years from now, these clips would be broadcast as part of their new star's obituary tributes.

There was a brief reunion with Rebecca Moore, when her father died. Otherwise, Jeff had moved on, allegedly afraid of making long-term commitments because he had been let down so many times in the past by those he had cared about. Indeed, such was his determination to leave this part of his life behind that, towards the end of his stay at Woodstock, he wrote a song, 'Forget Her', which expressed exactly how he felt about his ex-girlfriend. This one was recorded in a single take – Jeff made it very clear that there would only *be* one take – and afterwards he would neither sing it again nor listen to it. 'She was heartache from the moment you met her,' he tells himself before reverting to the first person and opining, 'My heart is frozen still as I try to find the will to forget her . . . Her love was a joke from the day that we met.' Jeff left Woodstock on 30 October 1993, though the album was not finished, and immediately hit the East Village café circuit. It was as if he was desperate to return to reality, as he knew it. On 16 November he celebrated his 27th birthday at Fez: Ellen Cavolina was holidaying in the Far East, but had left instructions for the staff to present Jeff with a huge cake, which only reduced him to tears.

Three weeks later, the *Live at Sin-É* EP was released, with Jeff loathing the title. He had wanted to call it *Café Days: Live at Sin-É*, and intended it to be the first in a series – following in the tradition of Columbia's *Edith Piaf à l'Olympia* and Marlene Dietrich's *Café Istanbul* radio shows, their theory being that, despite mega stardom, regularly returning to their recital roots prevented them from becoming complacent. Columbia disagreed in Jeff's case. An East Village greasy spoon with no foreseeable future and where the acts collected tips in a beer jug, they declared, was a far cry from the most prestigious music hall in Europe, or even ABC Radio's fictitious setting for the legendary Dietrich broadcasts.

Neither did Columbia approve of Jeff's choice of sleeve. Snapped by Merri Cyr from up in the rafters at Sin-É it depicts Jeff, between songs, tuning his guitar in front of a group of clearly uninterested patrons. All sit with their backs to him, and one man is reading his newspaper, seemingly oblivious to what is going on. Jeff defended himself by saying that the photograph represented, 'A regular dude, doing his own thing like every other dude in the room.' In retrospect, of course (albeit wrongly) some regarded this as Jeff adopting Nick Drake's existentialist 'Fruit Tree' theory of being ignored while alive, fêted when dead.

The EP did not chart, *because* it was an EP and not eligible for the singles charts, but it sold well in the United States – even better in Britain and France. Here, it was released to coincide with the 30th anniversary of Edith Piaf's death. While dozens of home-grown entertainers were releasing tributes of their own, mostly inferior, in a country where the public and the media frowned upon just about everyone emulating their biggest ever entertainer, for some reason only those by Mireille Mathieu and Jeff were played extensively on the radio. On account of 'Je n'en connais pas la fin', the EP sold 15,000 copies in France in less than a month.

Between 15 January and 5 March 1994, still with no album to promote, Jeff embarked on his first North American tour. Columbia wanted him to work the college campuses and smaller theatres as a support act, but he refused to even consider the idea. His aim, he said, was to combine being a headliner with the old music-hall tradition of working his way up the ranks – from flea pits to pinnacle venues – but *only* as a one-man show! He therefore picked out for himself the kind of establishments Columbia least wanted him to perform in: small backstreet clubs, lounge bars, coffee houses, and even music stores whose audiences, he declared, might be sparse but at least they would appreciate him.

The tour would routinely be interrupted for visits to studios in New York, New Jersey and Los Angeles – whichever was nearest – to add finishing touches to a project which Columbia was starting to think might never see the light of day. Jeff was having problems with 'Dream Brother'. Three sets of lyrics had been written, the latest centring on an episode in the life of his friend, Chris Dowd, who Jeff learned was thinking of dumping his pregnant girlfriend. Jeff drew comparison with Tim Buckley's harsh treatment of Mary Guibert. 'Don't be like the one who made me old,' he warns the buddy from his *Babylon Dungeon* days. 'Don't belie the one who left behind his name!'

Another last-minute addition to *Grace* was *So Real*, which Jeff wrote with 21-year-old Michael Tighe, another of Rebecca Moore's musician friends with whom he had been acquainted these past two years. Tighe had acted in several New York Downtown Theater productions. After Jeff's death he would play with several bands, including Black Beetle, and return to acting – appearing in television's *The Shield*, and having a bit-part in the movie, *Pirates of the Caribbean*. Tighe was summoned to New York's Montana Studios, initially as a session guitarist, but found himself invited to augment the Jeff Buckley Band after his first jamming session with Jeff, Mick Grondahl and Matt Johnson.

Columbia was up in arms. Whereas Grondahl and Johnson knew Jeff's songs but could still be thrown by his unexpected key and octave changes, Tighe was forced to learn everything from scratch – a process which would take time the company could now ill afford, with production costs soaring on a daily basis. Their apprehension over Tighe, however, was nothing compared with their concern over Jeff questioning the competence of Karl Berger, brought in at his own request to orchestrate sections of *Grace* which he wanted augmenting with a string quartet. Berger (b. 1935) had founded the Creative Music Studio, in Woodstock, with Ornette Coleman. As a jazz pianist-vibraphonist he had won the Downbeat critics poll every year between 1969 and 1975. Equally importantly, if not more so, he was principal conductor with the Frankfurt Symphony Orchestra, and when meeting Jeff for the first time – wearing his 'street-wise' charity-shop garb, nail varnish, and with his hair looking like it had been dragged through the proverbial hedge – Berger is believed to have mistaken him for the studio janitor! Berger very nearly walked off the project when Jeff grabbed one of his manuscripts and proceeded to vet and rewrite his string section arrangements – until he realised that Jeff was an ex-student of the Musicians Institute, and clearly knew what he was doing. Berger is said to have been amused upon reading his credits in the liner notes, along with Jeff's quip, 'Here's to Shostakovich and King Buzzo!'

Dave Lory, who shared the frequently frustrating responsibility of managing Jeff with George Stein, allegorised these snap decisions that Jeff always got away with, as Jeff falling off a cliff with a parachute made out of dirty Kleenex. 'And knowing Jeff, it'd open up,' he observed in Merri Cyr's *A Wished For Song*. 'He was like a freight-train out of control, he just kept getting better and better and better.'

By now, producer Andy Wallace had moved on to another commission, and Jeff was more or less spearheading the project himself – and protesting loudly against Columbia's plans to put out 'Forget Her' as the first single from the album. The song, he declared, was an error of judgement composed when he had been at his lowest ebb – during the split from Rebecca Moore. Not only did he *despise* the song, he flatly refused to have it on the album and vowed never to sing it as long as he lived, a promise he adhered to. Columbia elected not to argue, and asked him to choose an alternative track for the single. He plumped for 'So Real' – then, once the paperwork had been signed, dropped the bombshell that he and new boy Michael Tighe had not finished writing it!

So Real, which some fans find fascinating, while others denounce it as downright boring – on account of the sheer number of times Jeff repeats the phrase – sees him speaking of the various losses in his life, platonic and otherwise. There is Rebecca Moore again (also the subject of 'Lover, You Should Have Come Over'), the cuddles-only lover ('I love you, but I'm *afraid* to love you!'), and Mary Guibert ('I never stepped on the cracks 'cause I thought I'd hurt my mother'). The Columbia executives hated the song as much as Jeff had detested *their* choice, but when they threatened to pull rank and Jeff shrugged his shoulders and vowed *only* to promote the album on the New York café-concert circuit, they gave in.

On 8 March, the Jeff Buckley band hit Europe – Jeff's first trip overseas. The Sin-É EP had been released here on the Big Cat label, and the promoters had, at Jeff's personal request, fixed him up with 10 café-concert appearances – he had stipulated that none of the venues should be above 300-capacity. His British debut took place at Gleneagles, in Scotland, on 11 March where he was photographed 'doing a Joan Crawford in *Queen Bee*' – wearing a second-hand faux-fur coat, one of the sleeves of which had been ripped off and re-attached with safety pins!

Before Jeff's show, there was an altercation with Sony's chairman, Tommy Mottola, an all-powerful executive who had been instrumental to the recording careers of Hall & Oates, Barbra Streisand, Bruce Springsteen and Maria Carey who he had subsequently married. Jeff may have only been joking when he marched up to him and asked if he had had plastic surgery to make him look less Japanese. Mottola was Bronx-born, of Jewish-Italian extraction, and did not see the funny side. Neither did Jeff let the matter rest when he went on stage. Halfway through his set, he started clowning around and slipped in one of his cutting monologues – 'Tommy Mottola, sleeps in a room with his face in a jar by the door' – which he mimicked to the tune of the Beatles' 'Eleanor Rigby'.

This did not go down well at all. The previous November, at Sin-É before singing Bob Dylan's 'Just Like a Woman', Jeff had launched into a deadpan impersonation of the singer's overtly nasal delivery, unaware that one of Dylan's entourage had been sitting in the audience. A few days later, Columbia had received a letter of complaint, and Jeff had ended up on the mat – not that this had prevented him from mocking Dylan again. Lampooning the Sony chairman, however, was another matter and very nearly resulted in the cancellation of Jeff's remaining tour dates. From Scotland, the band flew to Amsterdam, then back to Dublin – where Jeff was again warned about upsetting his peers, though no details of what he said, or did, have emerged. In London, on 15 March, the band played Borderline. Two evenings later they played a live set on GLR, the BBC's local station on Marylebone (where I was working in an adjacent studio), and followed this with a show at Upstairs at the Garage. Here, the celebrity guests included tennis legend John McEnroe, and The Pretenders' Chrissie Hynde.

Jeff may not have known that Hynde had once had a 'thing' for his father. As a freelance journalist back in 1974, she had reviewed a Tim Buckley album for the *NME* and concluded, 'Still feeling dizzy at just meeting the guy whose singing sends me into raptures. I'm even tempted to ask his stud fee!' Now, she asked Jeff if he would play with The Pretenders, that same night – bringing the response that he would be delighted to, so long as he did not have to hump his heavy amplifier (which he hated *anyone* touching) down the Garage's rickety stairs to the taxi waiting out in the street. The task was assigned to McEnroe, but only after he had pronounced his infamous catchphrase, 'You can't be *serious*!'

The next evening, the Jeff Buckley Band played Bunjie's, in Covent Garden. This engagement had been advertised on GLR, and when Jeff learned that it was virtually the same size as his beloved Sin-É, he sent out for 60 white roses – one for each member of the audience. 'I'm pretending to be Morrissey,' he piped, before singing 'I Know It's Over!' Among the small crowd was the manager of Andy's Forge, a nightclub in Charing Cross Road. Jeff was asked if he might perform there that same night, and willingly agreed. As the venue was but a few minutes walk it was decided to carry the band's equipment.

There was no shortage of helpers – all six patrons from Bunjie's!

Returning home on 23 March, Jeff became embroiled in another row with Columbia – over the artwork for the *Grace* sleeve. Contractually, the record company had no say in this, providing he kept within their 'decency boundary' ruling. They strongly objected to a photograph of this supposed 'ladies' man' which, in their opinion, made Jeff look 'undeniably gay'.

The shoot had been undertaken by Merri Cyr in a Brooklyn studio, with no outside influence. Jeff had turned up with a bag of second-hand clothes from the nearest Oxfam shop – Army pullovers and baggy pants, T-shirts with holes in them, and a woman's gold lurex jacket similar to the ones Judy Garland had worn on stage. Cyr had snapped him wearing this in a variety of poses – impersonating a lounge singer, acting the fool, eating a banana – but it was the 'Judy look' which ended up on the sleeve of *Grace*, Jeff clutching a replica of the microphone which Judy and Piaf had used for their legendary Carnegie Hall concerts. Jeff later said that he had chosen the study because he had not wanted to look like 'just another pretty pop singer'. In fact, this is *exactly* how he looks, albeit nicely macho with his studious expression and designer stubble. Merri Cyr took some exceptionally fine photographs of Jeff Buckley, but this one was the most striking so far.

With the album *still* being worked on, Columbia ignored Jeff's request to put out *So Real* on a single. Instead, they issued a second promotional EP, the curiously titled *Peyote Radio Theater* – peyote being the Mexican cactus whose tops had been used to make the hallucinogenics favoured by The Flying Burrito Brothers. Columbia then set Jeff up with a series of media interviews, hitting another snag when he issued them with a list of Dos and Don'ts. Firstly, he should not under any circumstances be referred to as 'Tim Buckley's son' – indeed, his father's name was forbidden in any interview, unless he himself broached the subject, which was unlikely. Secondly, he should not be questioned about his mother, and discussing his love life was also strictly out of bounds. He cast doubts on his sexuality when one reporter asked him if he was straight or gay and he responded, 'I'm not telling. Now please fuck off!' Nick Drake had inadvertently nurtured his own mystique be refraining from speaking to the press, who had respected his wishes by leaving him alone. By being purposely belligerent, Jeff would only wind them up and end up being ignored by leading music journalists who could have helped further his career.

Promoting Jeff was not as straightforward as Columbia had first anticipated. With songs as vastly different as 'Eternal Life' and 'Lilac Wine', not to mention

'Corpus Christi Carol', he was impossible to categorise. The *Grace* album would be sold in record stores' 'rock and pop' departments, yet truthfully he belonged to neither. As for airplay, in Britain this would be simple: he would be plugged more or less equally on Radios One and Two, while most of the major European stations were legally obliged to play all styles of music, including ethnic and classical. In the United States there were so many commercial stations devoted entirely to one style – garage, jazz, rap, fusion, hip-hop, country, heavy metal – that Columbia did not know where to begin. The *Peyote Radio Theater* EP contained 'Mojo Pin', the 'Nag Champa' mix (so named after Jeff's favourite joss-sticks!) of 'Eternal Brother', and a gruelling to listen to cover version of underground rock outfit Big Star's 'Kanga-Roo'.

The latter was Jeff's latest fad – a near-tuneless concert closer, 14 minutes on the EP, but which would only get longer. The EP was dispatched to college stations, while a promotional single of 'Grace' went to everyone else. This led to confusion for Jeff's growing fan-base. Few of the independent stations wanted to air 'Kanga-Roo', not just because of its length, but because Big Star were better known to their listeners than Jeff Buckley. Also, the word *peyote* bothered them – they did not wish to be accused of promoting drugs. Similarly, anyone wanting to buy 'Grace' would be disappointed to learn that, to get it, they would have to wait for the album! The 60-date 'Peyote Radio Theater' tour kicked off on 1 June 1994. Accompanied by two road managers (Gene Bowen and Reggie Smith) and with Merri Cyr tagging along with her camera, the first stop was Ashbury Park, New Jersey, famed for its Bruce Springsteen concerts. Columbia had hired the Stone Pony Club for two days of rehearsals that Jeff promptly ignored. Having fun, jamming into the early hours, and getting to know everyone was to him more important than the military-style rota drawn up by Steve Berkowitz. Neither did the Columbia executives approve of Jeff's on-stage presentation, first seen at Rochester, New York. Instead of the regular set-up with the frontman centre-stage, Jeff favoured the Continental approach, standing stage-right a few feet from the wings – initially confusing audiences who had heard but not seen him until now, for they assumed the vocalist was Matt Johnson, sitting centre-stage behind the drum kit!

These early audiences were sparse. But few of them owned a Jeff Buckley record, and the one he was promoting was unavailable! Matters improved by 17 June when the band played New York. By now, irked by the missing album, the promoter had re-baptised the tour 'The Kiss Me Goodbye Concerts' – freeing Jeff from the dilemma of promoting anything but himself. As the tour progressed, covering much of the United States and Canada, the band's confidence grew, as did the size of the audiences. In Iowa City on 9 July they headlined at Gabe's, supported by two rock outfits: the Memphis-based Grifters, and alternative band, The Dambuilders. For The Dambuilder's 24-year-old violinist, Joan Wasser, it was love at first sight – even though she later confessed that, until being assigned the date, she had never even heard of Jeff Buckley! Formerly with the Boston Symphony Orchestra, Wasser would later found the aforementioned Black Beetle with Michael Tighe, and after Jeff's death work with Elton John, Lou Reed and Rufus Wainwright.

Jeff had wanted the North American leg of his tour to round off at his old stomping ground, Sin-É, but this was no longer practical. For starters, the band's equipment would never fit into the tiny auditorium. The show for 16 August was therefore reconvened to the roomier Wetlands Club. The entire concert was taped, but to date only the odd song has been released, mostly on bootlegs.

Two days later, Jeff flew to London alone in advance of the British/European leg of his tour, now renamed the 'Grace' tour. This opened in Dublin on 23 August, the day the album was released in America. Here, the band had been winding up each set with 'Kanga-Roo', riding on the crest of the wave of Big Star's popularity. In England it was another matter. By the time of Jeff's show at The Garage on 1 September the song had been extended to an extremely raucous 25 minutes. This led to him being reprimanded by Sony's British representative, who accused him of demoting his talent, and warned that if this continued he would succeed only in sending audiences rushing for the nearest exit.

Jeff flatly refused to remove the number from his set, but trimmed it to six minutes. By the time the Jeff Buckley Band reached Oslo for the start of their Scandinavian tour, however, it was back to 21 minutes. This time he received a personal call from Sony chief Tommy Mottola, ordering him to drop 'Kanga-Roo', or else. No one had ever taken this tone of voice with Jeff before, and he took it to heart. Not only did he sink into what for him an unusually black depression, his resistance slumped to the extent that he caught a chill during the boat journey to Copenhagen, and when this developed into bronchitis, the next few shows had to be cancelled. Jeff had recovered by 13 September for a concert at Hamburg's Knust Club, a showcase event for which Sony/Columbia executives were flown in from around the world. He mocked one of these in a monologue – though not well enough this time for the executive to recognise himself – then announced that his next song was to have been 'Kanga-Roo', which 'the men in suits' had prohibited him from singing. Then, he launched into the noisiest 'Eternal Life' ever – pointing accusingly while belting out the line, 'While all these ugly gentlemen play out their foolish games!' Fifteen minutes later, he had them shuffling in their seats with embarrassment with his 'Going to the Bathroom' monologue: 'You always see men washing their hands after they pee, and it's so stupid. My penis is cool, unless I'm totally sweaty. But little boys are taught that it's dirty not to, so you must wash up!' The concert had been recorded for possible commercial release, an idea which was subsequently aborted. Once more, Jeff was read the riot act.

Grace, in the meantime, had finally reached the public domain, some two years since Jeff had signed the Columbia contract – an eponymous epic of crashing guitars and subtle rhythms, musical mood-swings, classical gems and anthems. It provided the listener with a spot-on mirror reflection of Jeff Buckley's personality: complex, unpredictable, exciting, brash and beautiful, multi-faceted, unique. He rocks with the best of them, wails in the finest *quawwali* tradition, climbs into the skin of the *chanson* and is unafraid of going way over the top with gushing sentimentality, *à la* Garland, breaking lines and sometimes even words in torchy moments to catch his breath. 'As each song unravels, it fills you with a desperation that sucks at the heart and puts sparks in the eyes,' enthused the usually acerbic Caitlan Moran, in *B-Side*. 'It moves through the blood and makes the veins glow. It crackles across the skin and leaves scratch marks.'

The European tour had ended on 22 September, with a concert at the Passage du Nord-Ouest, in Paris. Jeff had audaciously given the promoters a list of music halls associated with Edith Piaf – the Olympia, Bobino, Bouffes du Nord – with an instruction that if they could not make arrangements for his French debut to take place where she had sung, then he would do so himself, even if it meant paying the hire fee out of his own pocket. Piaf had managed the cabaret at the 300-seater Passage du Nord-Ouest immediately after World War II, where she had introduced her latest discovery and lover, Yves Montand. As a tribute to her, Jeff had closed the show with a Piaf medley which included the English adaptation of 'Les Amants d'Un Jour', the song which tells of the young lovers who, unable to cope with the pressure from their families, book into a tawdry hotel room for one last night before ending it all.

From Paris, Jeff and the band had flown home, arriving in New York with just hours to spare before playing the CMJ Convention at the Supper Club. *Grace* was not selling particularly well – so far it had moved just 5,000 copies in the United States – so Columbia hyped Jeff up a little for the next leg of the tour, which ran from 19 October to 18 December. Gone was the old 12-seater minibus from the last tour – replaced with a state-of-the-arts tour mobile with lounge, bedrooms, a bathroom and a kitchen with all mod-cons. Also introduced to the Buckley package were programmes, laminated passes and matching T-shirts.

The ruse worked. Lots of screaming, hysterical young men emulating his dreadful dress sense flocked to Jeff's concerts and learned by heart the words to even the most obscure Buckley cover – only the *qawwali* songs out-foxed them. Thrown into the mix were teenybopper girls, ageing converted heavy metal freaks, and grunge enthusiasts who copied Jeff's latest fad of shoddy charity-shop plaid shirts.

Jeff began opening the show *without* the band, a solitary figure warming up with a snatch of *qawwali* – more often than not Nusrat Fateh Ali Khan's 'Yeh Jo Halka Halka Saroor Hal'. Then, with Grondahl, Tighe and Johnson clustered to one side, he would work through the *Grace* numbers, and throw in some 'oddity' – though the band were not always informed beforehand that it had been included in the set. And he *always* included 'Kanga-Roo'.

As an artist, Jeff had matured. Though reasonably quiet and unassuming off the stage – unless being harassed by 'enemy executives' – in full throttle on stage he began casting caution to the wind. He had witnessed Morrissey shedding his shirt and completing his show *torse-nu*, flexing his not inconsiderable pecs and driving the fans wild. Jeff tried this just the once in France. Forty pounds lighter and almost half a foot shorter than Morrissey, he was whistled – a sign of derision on the Continent – and someone standing in the wings had shouted for him to put his shirt back *on*! Now, he began stripping down to his vest, and looked good with his ribs covered up – so good, in fact, that women began flinging their underwear at him. His name was included among that year's *People* magazine's 'Fifty Most Beautiful People in the World'. Receiving 42 per cent of the votes, he was listed at Number 35 – ahead of supermodels Elle Macpherson and Claudia Schiffer.

Any other man might have been flattered, but Jeff only regarded the accolade as the supreme insult. He *loathed* pretty-boy pop stars, and had rejected the Gap campaign precisely for this reason. He wanted people to show interest in him for his work, not for how he looked – one of the reasons, no doubt, why he sometimes went out of his way to make himself look *un*attractive. In February 1994 he had told *Interview*'s Ray Rogers, who had complimented him on his good looks, 'I still think I look really geeky. The way you look doesn't mean shit if you can't sing, or if you're mean to people. It doesn't mean shit if you're not truthful with yourself. I have very different ideas about beauty than the rest of the world.'

Now, as if to prove a point, Jeff hit the grunge trail with a vengeance. He, who had denounced smoking as dirty and anti-social, was rarely seen in public without a cigarette dangling from the corner of his mouth. Though still obsessed with personal hygiene and showering twice every day, he refrained from washing and brushing his hair if he had to be anywhere or meet anyone of importance.

Jeff believed that an artist had sunk to their lowest level to even *consider* being seen on MTV, and did not hold back when asked for his opinion of the station during an interview – throwing in more than his usual share of expletives and causing MTV to seriously consider suing him for defamation. There was another irate call from Tommy Mottola – put through to Jeff's dressing room at Chicago's Green Mill Theater on 8 November, 30 minutes before he was due to go on stage. This time he gave Mottola a piece of his mind – then cooled off by downing a bottle of tequila.

The audience that evening was witness to the usual exemplary performance – even when drunk, Jeff was able to hold it together, save that an excess of liquor loosened his tongue. Green Mill was also one of his favourite venues – he had played here before, telling Kylie Buddin of *You Could Not Do Worse Zine*, 'It used to be owned by Al Capone. There's still a bootleg basement. And you wouldn't believe the decor in this place. I mean, Martin Scorcese would get a tremendous erection over this place!' There were the usual monologues, but this time the more deprecating comments were levelled at himself, particularly when he pronounced, 'Take a good look – you're looking at a fucking loser!' The banner headline for the concert's review in the *Chicago Tribune* read, 'Buckley's Show Sobering For All But Its Vocalist!'

According to one source (David Browne: *Dream Brother*), there was also an incident in Denver, Colorado, when a group of Tim Buckley fans touched a nerve by heckling for him to sing some of his father's songs. Under duress he gave them 'Once I Was', telling the audience, 'This is to show all the hippies how good I can do this song so they can all go masturbate naked to their copy of *Hello Goodbye* and leave the rest of us normal people alone. Now shut the fuck up for the rest of the night!' He was no less feisty when asked to appear on a New Year's Eve *Late Night With David Letterman* special. Having been told that Letterman was only really interested in chatting about *Tim* Buckley, Jeff told the producer, 'No dice. I only spend New Year with people I care about!' He then gave an impromptu acoustic recital at Sin-É.

The Sony executives were furious, though Jeff's on-the-road exploits were tame compared with those of some of his rock contemporaries. There were no backstage revelries, no wrecked hotel rooms, no incidents with groupies, no drugs save for the occasional joint – just the most vituperative insults aimed at anyone in authority who tried to convince Jeff that their 'fatherly advice' was ostensibly for his own good. He submitted to Columbia's demands for the promotional video, albeit begrudgingly so, and never let his peers forget for one moment that he was doing it against his will. The company were releasing 'Last Goodbye' as a single, but Jeff had the last say over who should direct it: his friend, John Jesurun, assisted by Merri Cyr. He also insisted upon a Morrissey-style scenario – in other words, as had happened with British director Tim Broad's mini-epics (*Girlfriend in a Coma, November Spawned a Monster*, etc) each would have absolutely nothing in common with the song being promoted, other than who was singing it. Then he fixed the shoot for 23 January 1995, a day he knew he would be in Paris rehearsing for his forthcoming French tour – hoping that this might propel Columbia into cancelling the shoot altogether.

At the beginning of January, Jeff and the band embarked on a gruelling five-week tour which would see them performing in Britain, France, Belgium, Italy, Holland, Germany and Japan. As before, this was set to begin in Dublin, with Jeff joking that he would not be singing a note until he had downed his first pint of Guinness. Then a Columbia executive tossed a spanner into the works, calling him in the middle of the night and announcing that, on account of an unforeseen press conference, and 'at considerable expense', his departure had been brought forward by two days. Totally unprepared to leave – claiming that he was working on a last-minute arrangement for a new song which he wanted to introduce to his British fans – Jeff refused to fly out with the band. Then, once they had left, he informed Columbia that the song was finished, and demanded to be put on to the next Concorde to London. This was Jeff at his most contrary, and there were raised eyebrows when, after being warned to be on his best behaviour, he stomped into the executive lounge at Heathrow – wearing Caterpillar boots, trousers two sizes too big for him, and the 'Joan Crawford' fur coat held together with safety pins. He spent the night in London and flew to Dublin the next morning – wearing the same clothes, which he told reporters he had slept in because his record company had been too tight-fisted to pay for him to have a room with heating!

The Dublin concert was a huge success. Jeff was in good spirits, spurred on by a plentiful supply of his favourite Guinness. When somebody called out

Tim's name he shot back, 'Actually, I'm the son of *Mary Guibert*!' When he arrived at the warehouse on the outskirts of Paris for the video shoot, however, he was in a malevolent mood. He was all sweetness and light towards the French cameraman and technicians – genuinely so, for in this country he was revered and never stepped out of line, no matter how provoked. On the other hand, he was downright belligerent towards the Sony representative, an American, who wanted to know why he had neither shaved nor washed his hair – then informed him that he would be *miming* the words to 'Last Goodbye'.

Jeff yelled at the man, 'Go fuck yourself!', then raved on about how he had never mimed in his life and that he had no intention of doing so now. He lost this particular fight when Tommy Mottola attempted to put him in his place: Jeff would do as he was told, or Sony would sue him for the cost of the shoot, an estimated $80,000. Jeff however would have the last laugh. The video was classed as artwork, which meant that he had final say over the editing. As he was unable to leave France because he was preparing for a concert at the Ba-ta-clan on 11 February, the rough-cuts for 'Last Goodbye' had to be transmitted 19 times between Paris and New York until he and Columbia had agreed on the one which would be used. By this time the tab would have risen to a staggering $200,000.

The subsequent *Grace* videos were less problematic, not that Jeff enjoyed making them. The one for 'Grace' itself was shot in monochrome: it alternates between Jeff performing the song with long, straggly hair and a buzz-cut. 'Eternal Life' was filmed on stage in Chicago. In 'Forget Her', which Jeff still refused to perform live, he is seen taking a night-time trip around Paris and, very briefly, singing something else at the Ba-ta-clan. And in the city which he declared to be the most romantic in the world he ungallantly emphasises the thing he hated most about his break-up with Rebecca Moore – namely, 'The smell of the bed when I knew what she'd done.'

The 'Last Goodbye' video was premiered on MTV. It is resplendent with homoerotic imagery. We see Jeff nuzzling the throat of one of his musicians – a shot too extreme in close-up to reveal which one, though when he pronounces, 'It's over', he turns around and appears to glare at all three. Jeff also hosted MTV's alternative rock magazine, *120 Minutes*. Though the video did nothing to sell the single, it introduced Jeff to a wider audience and helped propel *Grace* into the *Billboard* chart – albeit at Number 174 – bringing the total sales to 8,000. This was no great shakes, but better than it might have done.

Jeff's brief French tour opened on 8 February at the 800-seater Le Bikini, at

Ramonville, near Toulouse. Jeff blew a fuse when he learned that he was to be the *vedette-americaine* (the act which traditionally comes on immediately before the interval) throughout the tour for Dutch rockers Bettie Serveert. How he managed to get the theatre manager to swap things around so that *they* came on before the interval, enabling *him* to top the bill is not known – suffice to say, Bettie Serveert's manager strongly disapproved, and pulled them from the rest of the tour. Extraordinarily, not one of their fans asked for their money back once they had listened to Jeff, whose 30-minute set had been extended to an hour. 'Somebody in the crowd shouted "Get your soul out!", and that's exactly what he did,' observed Philippe Perret, who had been commissioned to cover the tour for *L'Indic*. 'He *unveiled* his soul, not by way of exhibitionism, but because he needed to share his every emotion with us.'

There was a minor incident after the show when, minus his shirt and rubbing his hair with a towel, Jeff walked into his dressing room to find two half-naked women waiting for him. According to one eyewitness, with no security man around, Jeff was left to fight off their advances, and did so in 'the most gentlemanly manner', telling them, 'Sorry girls, but I'm shattered right now. Come round to my hotel first thing tomorrow morning and I'll fuck you both before breakfast!' The women were so taken aback that they put their tops back on and fled!

Next stop on the road was the Victoire 2, a 700-seater venue on the outskirts of Montpellier which many French acts avoided because of it oppressive atmosphere. Most of the crowd had been expecting Bettie Serveert, and during his opening song, 'Mojo Pin', some of those closest to the stage started booing. Later in the show, when someone called out for a Tim Buckley song, he yelled back, 'You're at the wrong concert, baby!' and this helped to relieve the tension. There were however no curtain calls. Halfway through his closing number, 'Kanga-Roo', he shouted, 'Good night, folks. Sweet dreams!' and walked off the stage.

Things were much better the next afternoon, when Jeff and the musicians arrived in Lyons. Fifty or so fans and a handful of reporters mobbed him outside his hotel, and he invited them all inside – to the manager's horror – for an impromptu mini press conference. He was asked if a person called Grace was the inspiration behind the song, and was asked if the name was actually an anagram of *garce*, a French term for a prostitute! 'It's about *grace*,' he enlightened the gathering. 'It's neither mystical nor religious. Just ordinary grace, the thing that renders people divine!' Then, smiling at Mick Grondahl, he added, 'It's the quality I most appreciate in a person, especially in a man because it's *so* rare!'

Had Jeff said such a thing in America, or England, journalists might have put two and two together and come up with five. Curiosity about one's sexuality, however, has never really interested the French. The next 15 minutes were spent talking about Jeff's influences (his pantheon of inspiration now included Joni Mitchell, MC5 and Siouxie and the Banshees!), the difference between American and European critics, and the structure of his songs. Despite Jeff's fondness for what the French called *une chanson à trois temps* (three verses, three refrains as favoured by Piaf and her contemporaries), Jeff said that he had always striven towards a more liberal approach when it came to writing his material, citing Bob Dylan and Morrissey as his principal influences. 'These are people I can't praise enough,' he said. 'People who are more interested in getting the message across rather than making the verses equal length and the lines rhyme. That's what *real* song writing is about!' Jeff's show that evening was at B-52, a small venue where, during his first song, one of the amplifier cables became disconnected – no worry for Jeff, who while his road manager was rectifying the problem, sang the next few songs a cappella, sitting on the edge of the stage.

The Ba-ta-clan concert, the next evening, was a trial of sorts. Jeff was being considered for a concert at the Paris Olympia later in the summer, and tonight was to allow the French promoter and the Olympia's director, Patricia Coquatrix, to work out if he could face the prospect of facing one of the most critical audiences in the world. The Ba-ta-clan, an imposing architectural sepulchre on boulevard Voltaire, belonged to the century-old tradition of the Casino and the Folies Bergère: *all* the great French music-hall stars had trod its boards, but only after reaching the peak of their profession. More crucially rock and pop stars were taboo!

The manager of the Ba-ta-clan had heard a tape of Jeff singing 'La Vie en Rose' in French, and went against tradition by agreeing to take him on – providing he perform a Piaf melody. Jeff chose 'Je n'en connais pas la fin', naturally – but instead of 'La Vie en Rose', he chose 'Hymne à l'Amour', which he was forbidden to sing in anything but English.

Edith Piaf had written the French lyrics to one of her biggest hits in memory of her lover, Marcel Cerdan, the world heavyweight boxing champion who had perished in an air crash in 1949 while their love affair had been at its zenith. As such, the French words to this were still considered Piaf's personal property, and therefore sacred. Jeff used Piaf's own arrangement, paying meticulous attention to detail. Each note was exactly the same length, every syllable and nuance delivered exactly the same way she had done. Far from offending the audience, which the promoters had feared, Jeff brought the house down. The tragedy of the evening was, though the whole 90-minutes performance was taped and relayed on France Inter radio, only the Piaf songs and three others were released commercially, and then only on a promotional EP.

Jeff blew a fuse upon hearing that a female reporter from the *New Musical Express* was in Paris and hoping to talk to him, declaring that he would never breathe the same air as 'a hack' from the publication which had attempted to sabotage Morrissey's career. In August 1992, the *NME* had virulently attacked the singer after his performance at Finsbury Park, where he had appeared on stage wrapped in a Union Jack, in front of a skinhead backdrop – regarded by some as fascist imagery. Since then, Morrissey had been falsely accused of racism, and I had published my defence, *Morrissey: Landscapes of the Mind*, which had earned me a 'Bastard of the Year' award from the music press. Tickled by this, Jeff told *Les Inrockuptibles*' Jean-Daniel Beauvallet, 'Thank fuck for David Bret!' Whether this *NME* reporter was the Amy Raphael who had tried to interview Jeff in Toulouse ('Tell her to politely fuck off,' he had told the theatre manager, though he had relented and agreed to give her the benefit of the doubt) is not known, though Jeff certainly gave her a hard time. When asked *why* the French had taken to him in such a big way, he snarled, 'I don't know. Ask a French person!' And as the young woman walked away from him, he made a vulgar gesture behind her back.

After a few more European concerts, notably at Nighttown in Rotterdam (taped, part of this was released on another promotional EP), Jeff and the band flew home. Between April and June, sales of *Grace* were boosted considerably by a media-hyped joint tour of North America with Juliana Hadfield – a period which saw Jeff's 'super-grunge' image hitting its peak. At Roseland on 2 June, the closing venue, he wore the gold lurex jacket from the *Grace* sleeve, grinned sheepishly as the wolf whistles and catcalls rained down on him, but removed the jacket before posing for pictures with Paul and Linda McCartney – to whom he quipped, 'But for the grace of God, you could have ended up being my stepmom!'

Several of the North American 'Mystery White Boy' tour concerts had been filmed, but it was the one of 13 May at Chicago's Cabaret Metro which would be selected for commercial release, though not until after Jeff's death. Following his last visit to the Windy City, when he had gone on stage drunk at the Green Mill Theater, he had been warned to stay off the bottle, but most of all to refrain from swearing because there were children in the audience. By this stage of his career, Jeff had become a law unto himself. He had obviously had a few drinks before curtain-up, and begins by dedicating the show to *People* magazine and Cuervo tequila – saying of the publication which had *dared* to call him beautiful, and of his favourite tipple, 'Both induce failure and delusion.' He curses a lot between songs, spends far too much time messing about with his hair and tuning his guitars, though vocally he is mesmerising. He also mimics Morrissey, having denounced every musical decade as 'bullshit', save for the one which had produced The Smiths: 'Everyday is like Halloween . . . All the apples have razor-blades . . . But nobody cares any more, especially policemen,' he sings, to the tune of 'Everyday is Like Sunday'.

A few days after the Roseland show, Jeff was approached by a representative of Tristar Pictures, currently casting the supporting roles in Barbra Streisand's latest movie, *The Mirror Has Two Faces*, which she was producing and directing. This told the story of an unattractive woman who tries to woo back her adulterous husband by having plastic surgery. Jeff was offered the small but important part of the student, and initially was very enthusiastic. He was a huge Streisand fan, and also an admirer of Lauren Bacall, playing her mother in the film. He eventually rejected the role – and the $60,000 fee – when told that Streisand wanted him to begin shooting his scenes at once. By public demand, an 'emergency' European tour had just been arranged.

Chapter Fifteen

Remember Me, Forget My Fate

In June 1995, Jeff flew to Edinburgh, leaving a scandal behind him that he could well have done without. According to press reports, his love life was inordinately busy – besides Joan Wasser and M_, the 'cuddles-only' lover (who he described to a Belgian reporter as 'my boyfriend'), he had become involved with the horrendously controversial Courtney Love, widow of troubled Nirvana frontman, Kurt Cobain, who had blown his brains out the previous year.

Love apparently contacted Jeff while he and the band were in the studio recording 'Eternal Life', and audaciously asked *him* out on a date. It would appear that the two had known each other for a while – Jeff is thought to have sent her his condolences after Cobain's suicide – and she took him to the latest Broadway production of *Hamlet*. Jeff later said that he had anticipated just an ordinary evening out with 'an old buddy', but that matters had got out of control when they had been pursued by the paparazzi, giving way to some rather unsavoury tabloid headlines. Matters were not helped by a 'posthumous' statement from Kristin Pfaff, a member of Love's band, Hole, who had died of a drugs overdose the previous year. According to one of Pfaff's friends, Pfaff had once watched Love giving an inebriated Jeff a blow-job – that he had refused to make love with her in the conventional way because, he claimed, he had not considered himself worthy of inserting his penis 'where Kurt's holy rod had been'.

For Jeff, then, Europe provided a welcome escape from the pressures back home. On 13 April, against some very fierce competition, he had been awarded the Grand Prix du Disque, presented annually by the Académie Charles Gros. Previous recipients included Edith Piaf, Barbara, Jacques Brel, Georges Brassens and Leonard Cohen. The so-called *société honorable* deplored the academy's decision to reward what they regarded as a pop singer with the French music industry's most coveted award. Truthfully, Jeff had earned it and the French media's respect for the sensitive way he had handled 'Je n'en connais pas la fin', now his theme song here, and the other Piaf material.

The 'Mystery White Boy' tour would see Jeff playing to his largest audiences ever – over 80,000 at the Belgium and Roskilde festivals. He was special guest at the South Bank's annual Meltdown Festival, hosted each year by a different rock icon – on this occasion, Elvis Costello. His greatest triumphs, however – indeed, arguably the most *distinguished* performances of his career – took place at the Paris Olympia.

The Olympia, on the Boulevard des Capucines, had been re-opened by Bruno Coquatrix in 1954, to rapidly become *the* pinnacle of European entertainment. In France, absolutely no entertainer is worthy of their salt unless they have played the Olympia. Its audiences are unbelievably, if not cruelly, discerning and hypercritical. The great stadiums such as the 18,000-seater at Bercy are easier to fill than the 2,300-seater Olympia, yet to sell out at the Olympia and receive curtain calls after one's performance is considered the greatest achievement an artist may have in France. Frank Sinatra appeared here just once (halfway through a sell-out Barbara season), and boasted, 'If this French broad can sell out here for a month, filling the joint for one night will be like taking a piss!' Ticket sales had been so poor that the audience had been asked to move forwards and a screen erected behind them so that Sinatra believed he was singing to a full house. Since 1990, non-French entertainers have usually been engaged for a one-off performance, almost always on a Monday evening when traditionally most French theatres close. When tickets for Jeff sold out within days, director Patricia Coquatrix (Bruno's daughter) decided to book him for another show, with the proviso that this be filmed and recorded for posterity – another Olympia tradition. Even so, a *générale* (dress rehearsal) was deemed necessary to iron out any last-minute hitches. This took place on 4 July at the Festival de Fourvière, in Lyons.

Jeff told Jean-Daniel Beauvallet of *Les Inrockuptibles*, 'I only discovered Paris last year, and already I'm playing the Olympia, an honour which I find both tremendous and terrifying. How do *I* follow Piaf? I really can't understand why the French have taken to me. Maybe it's because they like underdogs, and with somebody like me there's always a story to tell!'

Two evenings later, the famous big red curtains swung open on a scenario Jeff had never witnessed before, nor would again – those fans clustered in front of the stage, who minutes before had chanted 'Je n'en connais pas la fin', sinking to their *knees*. Moved almost to tears, he told them, 'Remember me, forget my fate' – words which would prove portentously prophetic less than two years down the line.

Jeff sang 20 songs, opening with 'Mojo Pin', and closing with 'Hallelujah', which he dedicated to Nina Simone and Leonard Cohen. The film footage of this is heartbreaking. All about him is pitch black: we see only his face in extreme close-up, tears streaming down his cheeks. Halfway through the second refrain, emotion gets the better of him and he misses his cue as hundreds of fans flick on their cigarette lighters. Before this, a new arrangement of 'Grace', with its Yma Sumac embellishments, has to be heard, to be believed. There is also an hilarious monologue which sees him impersonating a Led Zeppelin record being played at the wrong speed. Not surprisingly, 'Je n'en connais pas la fin' and Jeff's little between-songs speeches in French bring the wildest applause. On the recording of the concert, he inserts a monologue where he imitates Piaf – clasping his hands in mock supplication he sings, 'Mangez le Fromage' – heavy on the vibrato, though if the audience of mostly young people accepted this, the Olympia's management did not, and decided that this would not be included in the filmed performance. 'Some things are sacred here, Monsieur Buckley,' he was told, after the show, and Edith Piaf was one of them. The next evening, Jeff sang the song again, and 'Hymne à l'Amour', minus the monologue, and this was inserted in the Olympia film. 'I feel so *humble*,' Jeff mutters into the microphone, 'but also so very grateful. Thank you very much.'

Hot on the heels of his Olympia triumph, Jeff headlined at *the* event in the French live music calendar: *Les Eurockeenes*, at Belfort. Then he travelled to Saint-Florent-le-Vieil, near Nantes, where unusually he had been asked to participate in the town's annual sacred music festival. Jeff told a reporter, jokingly, that he was dreading the event because he would be singing in a monastery, and therefore prohibited from saying 'fuck' for a whole evening! The real source of anguish, however, owed much to the fact that he would be sharing the stage with iconic Azerbaijani *mugham* (the classical music of the Caucasus and Turkish-speaking nations of Central Asia) singer, Alim Qasimov. He was so het up prior to their set that he actually had to be counselled into performing, though he was worrying over nothing. The concert was another tremendous success, its highlight being Jeff and Qasimov's duet of 'What Will You Say?'.

The Jeff Buckley Band returned home. Sales of *Grace* had now passed the half-million mark, most of them in Britain and France where he was more appreciated and much less often compared with his father. In America, during his absence, 'Last Goodbye' had peaked at Number 19 on *Billboard*'s Modern Rock Chart. Columbia wanted to follow this with the single of 'Hallelujah' (instead of the already promised 'Eternal Life' road version) in time for the Christmas market. Jeff felt exasperated. In Europe he had been fêted, there had been no tantrums because the 'interfering fuck-faces' had kept their distance and left him to his own devices. Now, the way he saw it, they were bullying again. An uneasy compromise was reached. Columbia agreed to release 'Hallelujah' in the December, while Jeff's next single would be *So Real*. What *actually* happened was another matter. 'Hallelujah', taken from the Ba-ta-clan tape, appeared around the world on various promotional-only EPs, while 'So Real' was only commercially released in Australasia.

Jeff later said that he had had tremendous fun shooting the *So Real* video, whose scenario, like that of its predecessors, had absolutely nothing to do with the song. In it, Jeff combines the 'ordinariness' of The Smiths' 'Stop Me If You've Heard This One Before' video with the Dali-esque absurdity of some of the later Queen videos. Whereas Morrissey had cycled around a dreary Manchester suburb, trailed by a bevvy of lookalikes, Jeff does so around his own neighbourhood – wearing a crumpled ill-fitting suit and tie that make him resemble an overgrown schoolboy. He enters a diner and is shocked to be the centre of attention – one man films him, while another gives him the eye. Responding to neither, he rushes outside and observes three 'apes' stealing his bike. Stripping to the waist, he chases them along the street, but they get way. And interacting with this hugely enjoyable nonsense for no particular reason, Jeff and the band are seen on stage with paper bags over their heads – Jeff wearing a ghastly red-checked suit, while one of the musicians struts around in a replica of Edith Piaf's famous black dress!

With this video in the can, Jeff and the band flew to Australia for a six-date tour that opened on 28 August. The 'road version' of 'Eternal Life' had just entered the lower reaches of the charts. However, a combination of long flights and the intense heat soon took its toll. After his show at Sydney's Phoenician Theatre, Jeff informed George Stein that, after more than 200 live appearances – not to mention the media frenzy in between – that he had 'had a gutful' of *Grace*. The 50 or so concerts and personal appearances scheduled for North America between now and the end of the year were cancelled. Columbia might have been more understanding, had Jeff taken the time off to recuperate but instead, he went back to performing on the New York café-concert circuit, and on New Year's Eve eschewed yet another guest slot on a top rating television show for an impromptu concert at Sin-É.

It was now over a year since *Grace*'s release, and Columbia were pressing Jeff for a follow-up. Truthfully, the way he had sometimes behaved, he was lucky that they were still interested in recording him. Even so, he rocked the boat again, informing them that the lengthy delay between albums was their fault entirely: they had kept him on the road for so long, he had not any time to write new material. 'I've become just another commodity for them,' he had told *Les Inrockuptibles*. 'They made me feel cheap and used, but I'm not going to give in to their whims. I belong in front of an audience, and if that's what I do, singing the same Jeff Buckley songs, who cares? There are plenty of other things in my repertoire to stop audiences getting bored!'

In an attempt to meet Columbia halfway, Jeff, Michael Tighe and Mick Grondahl temporarily relocated to a house owned by Grondahl's family at Sag Harbor, Long Island. As had happened at Bearsville, the trio spent most of their time jamming and having fun. Without Columbia's knowledge, but using their funds, Jeff hired a new drummer, Eric Eidel, a friend of Grondahl's. For some time, Matt Johnson had been threatening to leave the band. Suffering from tinnitus on account of the noise blasting back from the speakers as the music had become progressively louder, Johnson was also beginning to tire of Jeff's off-stage shenanigans – 'the drinking, smoking pot, but most of all the mood swings'.

Additionally, Matt Johnson disliked Jeff referring to him as 'Jesus' on account of his long hair and sanguine features, and Johnson did not get along with Mick Grondahl. Rumour had it that Grondahl was Jeff's favourite because they may have been amorously involved – a rumour exacerbated by Jeff's boasting that his band would soon be changing their name to the Two Ninas. David Browne (*Dream Brother*) quotes the inspiration for the name as having come from a comment made by someone who had seen a photograph of Jeff and Grondahl (subsequently published in Merri Cyr's *A Wished For Song*) looking so feminine, they 'resembled a couple of Ninas'. There is no proof that the two were more than just friends, however, and Grondahl was *not* the M_ with whom Jeff had enjoyed a 'cuddles-only' relationship these past four years. As for the new name, this idea was thankfully short lived, though the 'feminine' jibe may well have been one of the contributory factors to Jeff announcing that his new album would be 'butcher, heavier, and above all *louder*' than his last – which must have worried Matt Johnson, with his hearing problem.

In the meantime, Jeff accepted an offer to work with former punk priestess-poet, Patti Smith, currently recording *Gone Again*, her first album in a decade at New York's Electric Lady. Smith had announced this as 'a celebration of grief' and in it would pay tribute to those she had loved and lost in her life: Kurt Cobain, the photographer Robert Mapplethorpe, Jerry Garcia and, most recently, her husband Fred 'Sonic' Smith and her brother. Jeff provided mezzo-soprano backing on 'Southern Cross' and played *essrage* on another track, 'Fireflies'. He had bought one of these curious bowed instruments, with its unique wobbly sound, after hearing legendary Egyptian singer Oum Kalthoum (1904–75) on the radio. Not only had he learned how to play this by simply listening to her records, he had learned one of her very original songs, 'Ya Laylet El-Id Insitina', by heart. Jeff had sung it once, on stage in France, though sadly he never got around to recording it. 'I like Oum Kalthoum. *You* ever heard of her?' an aggravated Jeff would ask *Double Take*'s supposed music expert, Josh Farrar, in Melbourne in February 1996. 'Amazing woman! All those 45-minute songs, 60-minute songs. There'd be a line of strings, and a line of drums, and a man on a plucked dulcimer. I like ornateness!'

Also guesting on Smith's album was Tom Verlaine, the 45-year-old guitarist with New York rock outfit, Television, who once had come close to joining Morrissey's band. The fact that Verlaine, a legendary musician, but one who had enjoyed little commercial success, confessed to never having heard any of Jeff's material did not deter Jeff. What really mattered was that, born plain Tom Miller, he had chosen his stage name in honour of Jeff's favourite poet and Jeff wanted him to produce his new album.

Promising Columbia – but most of all himself – that he would at least try to compose new songs, Jeff and the band, along with Joan Wasser, flew to Auckland in February 1996 for a 15-date tour of Australia and New Zealand. Anticipating problems as before, and unsure of Matt Johnson's reliability – Johnson had agreed to hang on a little longer to see how the land lay – he baptised this one the 'Hard Luck' tour.

There were sell-out concerts at Melbourne's Palais Theatre, where Jeff introduced his and Michael Tighe's 'Moodswing Whiskey' – the mood swing referring to himself and the *e* in whiskey denoting his paternal grandfather's Irish ancestry. Supporting were The Grifters. There was a new arrangement of Edith Piaf's 'La Vie en Rose', along with another rarely performed Piaf song, 'Un Jeune Homme Chantait', which she sung in America as 'On the Highway'. There was also an emotionally charged rendition of Billie Holiday's classic, 'Strange Fruit'. As for Matt Johnson, he threw in the towel towards the end of the tour, walking off the stage during Jeff's show at Selina's, in Sydney.

Back in New York, Steve Berkowitz and the Sony executives tried to talk Jeff out of hiring Tom Verlaine to produce the new, still largely unwritten album. They had taken the liberty of drawing up a shortlist of replacements, headed by Steve Lillywhite – who two years previously had produced Morrissey's chart-topping *Vauxhall and I*. Despite his reverence for Morrissey, Jeff would not be swayed. His contract stipulated that he had *complete* artistic control of his recordings, and he was sticking to his guns. Tom Verlaine joined the Buckley camp, and immediately rattled a few cages by refusing to meet with George Stein to discuss the project. Like Jeff, Verlaine was suspicious of officialdom and interested only on getting on with the job in hand. Columbia reciprocated by releasing sufficient funds to tape just four songs, which they said would be released on an EP.

On 15 June, Jeff and the band entered New York's Sorcerer Studios. The sessions were reportedly far from relaxed. Tom Verlaine obviously had not done his homework otherwise he would have been aware of his unorthodox working methods – rehashing, adding to and rehearsing half-written songs in a costly studio environment was not what this producer had had in mind. Additionally, there were problems with drummer Eric Eidel who, besides having a personality clash with Mick Grondahl, was finding it hard getting used to the studio's geography – the fact that the drum kit was not in the same room where Jeff and the other musicians were working.

Under considerable duress, the four songs were taped. 'The Sky is a Landfill' had already been earmarked as the opening track for the album, which Jeff was calling 'My Sweetheart the Drunk'. 'Vancouver', 'Morning Theft' and 'You & I' had been premiered in Australia and well received by fans. All four were tinged with cynical bitterness and said to be targeted at Rebecca Moore. Clearly, Jeff had a fixation for this young woman.

Columbia were satisfied with the rough takes. Jeff was not. He regarded everything he did in the studio as a work in progress, and believed that in this instance record company penny-pinching had forced him to work too quickly. The band had reservations about working with Tom Verlaine, claiming that he was abrupt and pushy, but that was hardly surprising, considering the restricted budget and the pressure he was under.

Drained and frustrated, Jeff tried to unwind by hitting the road with Joan Wasser. The pair teamed up with a friend, Nathan Larson, the singer-guitarist with Shudder To Think, and called themselves Mind Science of the Mind. There were other collaborations. Despite his apparent ill feeling towards some of his former girlfriends, Jeff guested on Rebecca Moore's *Admiral Charcoal's Song* album, on Brenda Kahn's *Destination Anywhere* and on Inger Lorre's, the eccentric Nymphs' frontwoman, on *Kerouac Kicks Joy Darkness*.

There was also the so-called 'Phantom Solo' tour, an act of sheer folly that very nearly resulted in Columbia terminating Jeff's contract. His appearances at Sin-É they could just about tolerate, but to have Jeff wasting invaluable promotional time – and losing money – by turning up unannounced at minuscule venues up and down the country was too much, particularly when he was alternatively billed as Father Demo, Smackrobiotic, Topless America, The Crackrobots, A Puppet-Show Named Julio, and Martha & the Nicotines! In no uncertain terms, Jeff was told to sort himself out. And of course, ordering him around only made matters worse.

Jeff was guzzling a bottle of beer in the back of Inger Lorre's car – against the law in New York – when they were pulled over by the police. The cop recognised Jeff and might have overlooked the offence, had it not been for the plastic bag of cannabis sticking out of his jacket pocket. At the subsequent hearing, the judge let him off with a good behaviour bond, but this, coupled with news that Columbia had changed its mind and would not now be releasing the EP of his new songs, sent him into a black depression.

Jeff did what he usually did when feeling low – rather than foist his bad moods on everyone he cared about, he hit the road on a brief acoustic tour, just himself and his guitar, with Joan Wasser and Merri Cyr tagging along for moral support. When he returned to base, realising that there were still problems with Eric Eidel and not having the heart to fire him, Jeff simply informed him that he was not good enough, and Eidel left the band of his own accord.

Wishing for a change of scenery – New York, he said, was starting to get him down – Jeff made arrangements for *My Sweetheart the Drunk* to be completed at the Easley Studios, in Memphis. The suggestion came from The Grifters' Dave Shouse. In the meantime, Jeff rounded off his city diary. On 4 February 1997, there was a reunion with Gary Lucas when they played the Knitting Factory. Five evenings later, Jeff and the band aired much of *My Sweetheart the Drunk* at the Arlene Grocery, a new establishment owned by Brendan Doyle – Sin-É had closed the previous November. Here, Jeff's behaviour reached its most bizarre. With three Piaf songs in his set-list, along with the monologue from the Paris Olympia, he walked on to the stage with his hair more ruffled than usual – and wearing a black dress!

On 11 February, Jeff spent much of the day at Sorcerer Sound with Deborah

Harry, Marianne Faithfull, beat-poet Allen Ginsberg and actor Christopher Walken recording his most unusual project – a spoken recital of Edgar Allan Poe's most famous works (Jeff read 'Ulalume') for the double compilation CD, *Closed on Account of Rabies*. Released in 1997, this would be dedicated to Jeff and Ginsberg, who would die of hepatitis-aggravated liver cancer one month before Jeff.

Three days later Jeff, his musicians and Tom Verlaine flew to Memphis. Initially, all stayed at the Claridge House Apartments, in a run-down quarter of the city. Columbia had booked the Easley Studios for just two weeks to put down the sketches for the new album, but Jeff felt so instantly at home – reunited with his Grifters friends, and imbibing the aura left behind by Elvis Presley and his jazz-blues idols – that he rented a small bungalow at 91 North Rembert Street so that he could spend the summer here, a rash decision which would ultimately cost him his life.

Jeff's new base was within walking distance of what would become his latest fad – Memphis Zoo, which he visited every day for a week. After his death, fans would pay to have two brass memorial plaques erected here, near the tigers' enclosure. Blissfully content for the first time in months, he began living the ultimate bohemian existence. The kind of man who made friends at the drop of a hat, there was no shortage of helpers when he moved in – friends who turned up with second-hand furniture, pots, pans, cutlery and household furnishings which ordinarily would have ended up in their dustbins. One gave him a large square of packing-foam that he folded in two to make a mattress!

Sometimes Jeff ate out at greasy spoons, but most of the time he cycled to the nearest Chinese takeaway – not just to pick up his own order, but those of his near neighbours who he conned into believing that he was a delivery boy! If such a thing was possible, North Rembert Street's newest resident became more eccentric than ever. Jeff had cut down on his smoking and stopped dyeing his hair and parting it down the middle, but he had begun painting his toe and fingernails vivid green, and his dress sense had deteriorated even further. Jeff was still clothed by the charity-shop and is thought to have owned just two items of apparel which were new – his black felt hat, and the horrendous green suit he had bought to match his nails. On warm days, he would don this to 'sunbathe' on his lawn – a wilderness of foot-high grass from which he would shout to passers-by who, on account of his camouflage, would wonder where the voice was coming from! He achieved a similar effect within the bungalow, reclining on the same-colour sofa given to him by Dave Shouse of The Grifters. Green, he declared, had always been his favourite colour, and as an aficionado of Continental music he never heeded the *chansonnier*'s age-old superstition that this was a colour to be avoided at *all costs*.

The studio pressures in Memphis were no less severe than they had been in New York. According to Jeff, Columbia still wanted their pound of flesh, and having been told of Tom Verlaine's alleged bullying tactics were rather hoping that Jeff might drop him once the sketches had been put down, and record the actual album with Andy Wallace. Most of the songs premiered in Australia and at the Arlene Grocery were taped. Lyrically, compared to the songs on *Grace*, they are quite heavy – having found his Verlaine, it was as if Jeff had reinvented himself as Rimbaud with his odes to darkness, homoeroticism, suicide and death.

There is no doubting that at this stage of his life, Jeff had entered a latent period of homosexuality. In 'Opened Once', the object of his affection is another man, but if there is to be no shame in this – 'We fly right over the minds of so many in pain' – he cannot help concluding derisively of himself, 'I am a railroad track abandoned, with the sunset forgetting I ever happened.' In 'Nightmares by the Sea', he issues the warning, 'Beware the bottled thoughts of angry young men', before going on about bones scratching windows and nightmares that blind the mind's eye. 'I've loved so many times and drowned them all,' he portentously proclaims, before offering the invitation which, for obvious reasons, would send shivers down fans' spines, 'Stay with me under these waves tonight.' Sad but dramatic stuff.

'The Sky is a Landfill' is a vicious, witty, acerbic and not so very veiled attack on the Clinton administration, with the line, 'Don't suck the milk of flaccid Bill K.'s empty promise', juxtaposing the Monica Lewinsky scandal with presidential inefficiency and callousness. One wonders, if he attacked Clinton in such a way for his international policies, how Jeff would have dealt with George Bush!

The song is also the first of several on the album to feature what appears to be an obsession with ejaculation. 'My belly released the stars and tears between the scars,' he pronounces in 'Vancouver'. In 'Jewel Box', he starts off speaking to a woman, but he is referring to a male partner when he pronounces, with a shrug of the shoulder after they have obviously not practised safe sex, 'Oh, you left some stars in my belly.' And in the ode to oral sex that is 'Your Flesh is So Nice', he tells the friend of the one he has the hots for (who may be male or female, given the predilection of some gay men to address each other as *she*), 'She's ass-slapping pretty . . . wanna let her lick me, stick the thick of my pussy . . . Come on, let me give you that "O"!'

'Yard of Blonde Girls' is thought to be Jeff's tribute to the movie that had set Marlene Dietrich on the pathway towards international stardom. 'The streets where Lola played,' he sings, referring to her character in *The Blue Angel* and parodying her song, 'Blonde Women': 'It's in your heart, it's in your art, your beauty . . . Very sexy! Okay, okay!' And in 'Everybody Here Wants You', Jeff belatedly celebrates the birthday he regarded as his most important thus far – his 29th, the one that had seen him achieving something his father had not. Some years later, Mary Guibert would recall in a BBC radio interview how proud her son had been of 'getting one over' on Tim Buckley by living longer than him.

Following the sessions at the Easley Studios, Jeff worked on the tapes in a makeshift studio at his bungalow, which he was now thinking of buying. Every other week, Joan Wasser visited him, and Steve Berkowitz dropped in regularly for a progress check. Jeff informed him that he was dissatisfied with most of the work he had done with Tom Verlaine, confessed that he had made a big mistake hiring him, and asked Berkowitz to get him Andy Wallace or Steve Lillywhite. A date was set for cutting the album: 23 June. To keep himself occupied until then, Jeff began performing as a solo act again.

During their first week in Memphis, The Jeff Buckley Band had played Barrister's, a small downtown club that had reminded him of Sin-É. At the end of March, Jeff accepted a regular Monday evening spot here. With no pressure from his peers, and no musicians to worry about, the fact that he was only earning $100 a show did not bother him unduly. In his own words, he 'started clearing the shit from his head'. He had also posted an announcement on his website, to the effect that he preferred the relative safety of these type of shows because he was apprehensive, if not actually afraid, of hitting the big time, with its attendant problems, anxieties, complexities and expectations:

> *There was a time in my life not too long ago when I could show up in a café and simply do what I do – make music, learn from performing my music, explore what it means to me, have fun while I irritate and/or entertain an audience who don't know me or what I'm about. In this situation I have had that precious and irreplaceable luxury of failure, of risk, of surrender. I worked very hard to get this kind of thing together, this work forum. I loved it then and I missed it when it disappeared. All I'm doing is reclaiming it now.*

Chapter Sixteen
Early Evening Theft

Much has been discussed about the last 10 days of Jeff Buckley's woefully all-too-short life. So many people claim to have been witness to episodes of so-called 'odd behaviour' – *so* many people claimed he had called them, particularly towards the end, spending hours on the telephone, with Jeff closing the conversation with some cryptic little message suggesting that he was aware that he was going to die. As such it has become almost impossible to separate truth from hearsay. 'They were all glad to hear from him but also distressed,' observed David Browne in his biography, *Dream Brother*. 'Was he lonely? Upset? Feeling a desire to reach out? And why now? What was *happening in Memphis*?'

Nothing, of course, was happening in Memphis, and with each passing year these 'confessions' grow more contrived, less credible, suggesting little more than wishful thinking and attention seeking by most of these confidants, who were known to the outside world *solely* on account of Jeff Buckley and whose tragedy permitted them their requisite 15 minutes of fame.

Jeff is believed to have seen Joan Wasser for the last time on 19 May, when he travelled by Greyhound bus to see her perform in Atlanta, Georgia. Though they were an item – exactly how serious had never been determined – they had never shared a home and, like her predecessors, Wasser had always been compelled to take second place to Jeff's career. One may also be sure that, given his track record, this relationship would have eventually gone the same acrimonious way as the others, and doubtless led to some very cutting lyrics.

Three days after leaving Atlanta, Jeff called his band in New York and informed them of his plans for *My Sweetheart the Drunk*. He needed a clear head, he said, for rehearsing, so arrangements were made for them to join him in Memphis on 29 May. On Monday, 26 May, Jeff sang for the last time in his life at Barrister's, closing the show, as was usual now, with 'Hallelujah'. Two days later his road manager, Gene Bowen, drove the band's equipment down to

Memphis. With him was 24-year-old Keith Foti, a mutual musician friend, described by Jeff as 'groovy' – because he dressed even more garishly than himself, and had spiky blue hair! Jeff insisted on Bowen and Foti – the band, too – staying at his bungalow when they arrived, even though there was nothing to sleep on but his horrible green sofa, and the hard floor.

Bowen and Foti politely declined the offer, though they did arrange for a local shop to deliver mattresses for the band. According to various reports, Jeff was going through a cross-dressing phase, parading around the bungalow wearing his black felt hat and a short skirt that he claimed belonged to his girlfriend, and which he was wearing *only* because doing so enabled him not to miss her so much. This may also explain the reported brief spells of clinical depression whenever he and Joan Wasser were apart – exactly the same thing had happened a few years earlier with Rebecca Moore.

Additionally, the same tabloids that had made a meal of his 'affair' with Courtney Love seem to have cottoned on to Jeff's friendship with the aforementioned musician and put two and two together: 'Jeff and this guitarist guy shared a hotel room in New York, and another in Paris,' a *People* reporter told me in December 2002. 'When I asked them if anything was going on between them, he said, "Not yet. We're waiting until after we're married!" But Jeff *did* have a guilty expression his face – and the room *did* only have the one bed.' The 'wedding' comment was, of course, a classic example of Jeff's offbeat sense of humour and, the *People* reporter added, one way of his hoping that the snippet would not end up in the tabloids. *Had* it made it to the press, however, one doubts it would have had any effect at all on Jeff's career. The fans loved him so much, they would have accepted anything.

During the afternoon of 29 May, according to Gene Bowen, the two of them had gone shopping in downtown Memphis – where Jeff had attempted to buy a wheel-less car at a service station, and opened an account with a supermarket bank! Then, at around 8pm, leaving Bowen to collect the band from Memphis airport, Jeff and Keith Foti had set off for the rehearsal room on Young Avenue, a destination they never reached.

We only have Foti's account of events, a curious interview given by Mary Guibert (repeated by Jean-Daniel Beauvallet of *Les Inrockuptibles* in April 2001), and the Memphis police's report to determine what happened next.

Jeff had changed out of his skirt and put on jeans, a long-sleeved Rolling Stones T-shirt and heavy ankle boots. En route to Young Avenue, with Keith Foti driving the rental truck used to transport the band's gear to Memphis, and with Jeff navigating, they had become lost – ending up in the vicinity of the Wolf River, near its intersection with the Mississippi.

The river at this spot was known to be particularly deceptive and dangerous, its undercurrents exacerbated by passing tugboats and barges. Bathing was strictly prohibited, though there were no signs (then) informing the public of this – according to local lore, these were unnecessary because everyone *knew* how bad the river could be. Being new to Memphis, Jeff almost certainly would not have known, and neither did his friend on that muggy evening.

According to Foti's statement to the police, he and Jeff had come here to jam; also, he had swum in the same spot several times before – which, of course, more than suggests that Jeff had *not* got them lost with his bad navigation, and that ending up here *had* been his intention. Furthermore, he had insisted on jamming not on the promenade, but on the actual shore, which had been a mess of weeds, sharp rocks and rubbish.

At around 9pm, Jeff had positioned the ghetto blaster on a flat rock, close to the water's edge. According to Mary Guibert (speaking to Jean-Daniel Beauvallet via telephone in April 1998), Jeff had told Foti that he wanted to offer him a gift to prove how much their friendship meant to him. Foti's response to this had been, 'Jeff, I don't want a present. Just let me kiss you!' The two men had kissed, after which Jeff had inserted a cassette of Led Zeppelin's 'Whole Lotta Love' into the ghetto blaster and, as Foti had begun plucking his guitar, Jeff had suddenly waded backwards into the river and begun backstroking—something he had apparently done several times before, fully clothed, in Australia.

Foti later said how Jeff had ignored his pleas not to swim out of his depth, but continued singing along to the tape while making his way towards the bank on the other side. A passing boat had narrowly missed him, but the combination of the swell caused by this and the barge which followed, along with the weight of Jeff's clothes and boots, sucked him under. At just 30, one of the brightest lights of the international music scene had been snuffed out.

Ironically, it was Corpus Christi Day.

So, what *really* happened? Sadly, we may never know. As with any young, good-looking talent – one instinctively thinks of James Dean, Elvis Presley, Marilyn Monroe, Claude Francois – there are those who believed then, their senses and better judgement stupefied by grief, and who will go on believing that, like these other icons, Jeff Buckley's death cannot have been as straightforward as was eventually made out; that someone, somewhere, must have had an ulterior agenda for him to be taken away so dramatically and unexpectedly. For all those that he had blinded with his charm and innate charisma, there had been others that Jeff had wound up the wrong way with his cutting remarks, monologues and cynicism. One may be certain that his passing was not mourned by some of the record company executives he had upset and had he lived, Columbia would most likely have found a way of disassociating themselves from a young man who, though phenomenally talented, had been bad news much of the time with his attitude towards authority.

What is astonishing is that, if Jeff had been playing a ghetto blaster as Keith Foti said in his statement, why were there no other witnesses? Is it possible that Jeff had decided, on the spur of the moment, to 'toss a coin', so to speak; that his swimming *backwards* across a busy, hazardous river was his allegorical way of deciding upon the direction that his life should take – to either get to the other side safely, or to be brought down by whatever obstacles were thrown into his path. Not exactly suicide, but a form of Russian roulette, combined with the giddy bravado so typical of Jeff, but which this time went tragically wrong? A bizarre 'accidental suicide', in other words? Any suspicion that Jeff may have taken his own life was added to by Joan Wasser's words, for she has often spoken of Jeff's confession the day before he disappeared, that he had recently been diagnosed with bipolar disorder, and that this was the reason for his mood swings of late.

In a panic, Keith Foti rushed to the Welcome Center, a nearby tourist information bureau. The place was closed, but the night watchman called the police. Within the hour, the area was swarming with patrol cars and a full search was under way: scuba divers, horse and foot-patrol officers combing the area, and the man handling the search, Lieutenant Willie Lemons, informing the press that, even so soon, such was the unpredictability of the Mississippi in this spot that his team did not expect to find Jeff alive.

Gene Bowen and Jeff's band, fresh in from New York, visited the scene and, unable to help, returned to North Rembert Street to deal with calls from anguished friends and colleagues. They were not allowed in. Because the police were yet to rule out foul play, the bungalow had been designated a crime scene and the place was still being searched – though no one was sure what they were looking for. An hour before the police's arrival, Jeff's 'team' had conducted a search of their own, removing anything relating to the album he had been working on – tapes, documents, notebooks – for safe keeping.

The next day Joan Wasser, George Stein and Steve Berkowitz flew into

Memphis, as did Mary Guibert and Dave Lory. It was probably he who put the call through to an unnamed friend in New York, asking them to pick up the Sorcerer Sound Studio tapes to prevent them from falling into 'disreputable' hands. Simultaneously, the Memphis Chief of Police had allegedly received word from Taylor Buckley – Tim's son and Jeff's stepbrother. According to Taylor, Jeff had fallen out with his mother, since which time he had recognised *him* as his next of kin. Mary, therefore, took the appropriate action to ensure that none of her son's effects ended up Taylor's possession.

Columbia, who for a while believed Jeff may have merely pulled a stunt and gone walkabout to evade the pressure he had accused them of putting him under before heading for Memphis, waited until 2 June before issuing a statement to the press that he had almost certainly drowned. Prior to this, Mary Guibert issued a statement of her own:

> *It has become apparent to me that my son will not be walking out of the river. It is now time to make plans to celebrate a life that was golden. I ask people who cared about Jeff to please be honorable and faithful to his memory, to send their best wishes to Jeff and all of us who are mourning his passing.*

Many of Jeff's fans and friends accused his mother of insensitivity for 'jumping the gun' – particularly as Mary also announced that she was planning Jeff's memorial service, without *really* knowing if he was alive or dead.

At 4.40 on the afternoon of Wednesday 4 June, six days after he had disappeared, Jeff's body was spotted by passengers aboard the *American Queen* riverboat, close to the mouth of the Mississippi, near Beale Street. Hundreds of fans who had been keeping vigil were gathered on the river bank, along with dozens of photographers hoping for an exclusive – a shot of the corpse of a singer many of them had never heard of until now. The police prevented this, though the operation was filmed from a helicopter hovering above the scene, and later relayed on the late evening news. There was nothing distasteful about this: rather than use one of Jeff's songs for the report, the editor chose him singing The Smiths' 'I Know It's Over'.

Mary Guibert is said to have been too distressed to see Jeff's body until he had been prepared and embalmed. The grim task of identifying the bloated corpse was left to Gene Bowen, who recognised him only by his naval stud and his wristwatch that, incredibly, was still ticking. That same night, outside the former

Sin-É, Jeff's New York friends held a vigil. Another took place at George Stein's apartment. One week later, part of the city's Tibetan Freedom Festival was dedicated to his memory: REM, Patti Smith and Bono all paid tribute.

On 11 June, Mary Guibert further alienated herself from many fans by heading for St Mark's Church, in New York's East Village, where a memorial service was in progress – then refusing to enter the building. Despite having wanted to arrange a similar service *before* Jeff's body had been found, she now claimed that it was too soon after his death to be holding such an event. Her own two-part eulogy – one private, the other public – concluded on 1 August with a funerary recital at St Anne's, in Brooklyn, where Jeff's career had effectively begun. Among the contributors were Michael Tighe, Elvis Costello, Marianne Faithful, girlfriends past and present, including Rebecca Moore and Joan Wasser, and Jeff's musician lover.

Jeff's sudden death had left his loved ones in a state of trauma. Mick Grondahl is reported to have entered rehab. M_ suffered a nervous breakdown. Later he told *Les Inrockuptibles* Jean-Daniel Beauvallet, 'Losing him was an immense shock. I felt anger and frustration. Part of myself had died with him. But slowly, life returned to normal, more intense and more beautiful through having known him.'

The inquest recorded a verdict of death by accidental drowning. No drugs were found in Jeff's system – no one had expected there to be any, for he had spent his entire adult life trying *not* to follow his father's example – and shortly before taking the final swim, he had consumed just one small bottle of beer. The coroner observed that though he had been a fairly strong swimmer, the weight of his boots and clothes had contributed to his death. Also attached to his belt had been a metal ring containing some 50 keys – mementoes collected on his travels.

Even so, the suicide theory would persist, so much so that even several years after Jeff's death, Mary Guibert felt obliged to put 'certain journalists' in order by issuing a statement via her son's official website:

> *Jeff Buckley's death was not 'mysterious', related to drugs, alcohol, or suicide. We have a police report, a medical examiner's report, and an eyewitness to prove that it was an accidental drowning, and that Mr Buckley was in a good frame of mind prior to the accident.*

There were some who chose to believe this statement, some who would not. Jeff's death was in fact *very* mysterious, and while it is true that there were neither drugs nor excessive alcohol in his system, cynics might say that even medical reports have been known to be wrong where celebrities are concerned, that eyewitnesses can make mistakes, and that whether through distress or confusion, Keith Foti's story was full of holes. And the fact that Jeff had been in good spirits would have borne little credence if this really had been a happy suicide. Before allowing his body to be cremated, and his ashes 'interred on the estate', whatever this is supposed to have meant, Jeff's mother asked for DNA samples to be taken, and a toxicology report – in the event of future paternity suits. This his friends accepted. What most of those professionally associated with him could not condone, was his mother's insistence that she had known her son better than they had, during his last months, or her 'interference' in his legacy.

Though Mary *did* have every right to have her say, being Jeff's only legal heir, his band were initially against her because, at the time of his death, Jeff and his mother had not been on speaking terms. Moreover, these musicians who had stuck by him had been compelled to listen to Jeff, in moments of black depression, berating Mary for 'trying to ruin' his life. The reason for the bust up between mother and son was because the previous year, Mary had replied to questions on the Internet concerning Jeff's sex life, notably his involvement with Courtney Love and Elizabeth Fraser of the Cocteau Twins. Jeff and Fraser had had a fling in London in 1994, when they had written and recorded 'All Flowers in Time'.

Jeff's management were so incensed that they challenged Mary's custodianship of his estate, but though she soon apologised for the Internet gaffe, she fervently denied there had been any rift between Jeff and herself. 'It's a horrible, heinous lie,' she told music journalist Toby Manning. 'I spoke to him for two-and-half hours before his death. If it hadn't been for that conversation, I would have felt totally lost.' True or not, an open letter posted on the Jeff Buckley website, criticising Mary for her alleged mishandling of his posthumous affairs, was countersigned by hundreds of fans.

No one cared about the $50,000 lying in Jeff's bank account. The real cause for concern was his *musical* legacy. Jeff's band championed this, claiming that he had been so fickle – proof provided by the sheer length of time it had taken to complete *Grace* – that, had he lived, he would have had the Tom Verlaine tapes vaulted and started the *My Sweetheart the Drunk* project from scratch, taking his time with the new material as he had with *Grace*. The musicians' argument was supported by the fact that, as part of his team, they had known him more intimately than anyone during the last few years – not just Jeff the man, but the workings of his complex musical brain. In their opinion, therefore, Mary Guibert was not *qualified* to handle his work.

Joan Wasser, perhaps closer than anyone to Jeff when he died – but not legally entitled to have any say in his affairs – was also against continuing with the album. Sony/Columbia, for their part, had invested a lot of money in Jeff Buckley and were eager to release *something*, for two reasons. Firstly, tribute albums were almost invariably guaranteed little earners. Secondly, Jeff had been tipped for a posthumous Grammy (for 'Everybody Here Wants You', which subsequently lost out to a song by Lenny Kravitz).

Initially, Jeff's band were not involved in the collation of his new album, though Mick Grondahl and Michael Tighe had co-written some of the songs. Mary had elected to call it *Sketches For My Sweetheart the Drunk* – exactly what it would contain, for not one of the 30 songs worked on by Jeff in Memphis, and short-listed for release, had been completed. Tighe even commented that he found the whole concept repellent, though he would approve of the finished result once Andy Wallace had worked his magic. Jeff's mother, however, disapproved, and brought in Jeff's friends Michael Clouse, and Soundgarden's Chris Cornell, whom he had met in London in 1994.

Clouse and Cornell shared Mary's opinion that, so far as was possible, the songs should remain exactly as Jeff had left them, with no overdubbing. Neither was Mary interested in rushing out an album solely for monetary gain. She, like everyone else associated with Jeff, she declared, needed a decent period of mourning to hopefully come to terms with losing him.

Jeff's band may have regarded this as a somewhat hypocritical stance to take, particularly after the way Mary seems to have treated them following his death. However, in January 1998 they would be brought in to offer their input on the project, and rightly so. In the meantime, the final selection was made. Instead of a single album, it was decided to release a double-CD. One would contain the Verlaine sessions, the other the four-track tapes which Jeff had laid down at the bungalow on North Rembert Street. All but one of the tracks, 'You & I' (mixed by Tom Verlaine), had been mixed by Andy Wallace, which caused more dissension between Mary and Jeff's band, as she explained to Kim Hughes of *Now* magazine:

> *The bone of contention was that the songs on the first disc were mixed without involvement from me or the band. The band resented that and felt I should go to battle with Sony and wipe out the Wallace mixes. That was something I just couldn't do . . . especially knowing that Andy and Jeff were so simpatico.*

Sketches For My Sweetheart the Drunk was released in Europe and Australasia on 12 May 1998, in time for the first anniversary of Jeff's death, a week earlier than in the United States – a nice gesture considering he had been more appreciated here than on his home turf. It sold 150,000 copies in its first year, going platinum in France and Australia. Also, one of the tracks – 'Gunshot Glitter' – was not permitted on the US release, on account of the title and its reference to a 'paranoid politician diva'.

As had happened with Nick Drake's *Pink Moon*, critics and fans trawled through the lyrics in search of portentous references to impending death and doom. As already explained, these were of course there. The coral graves in 'Nightmares by the Sea' and the invitation to 'Stay with me under the waves, tonight'. The funeral references, the 'calm below that poisoned river wild', of 'You & I' and the 'graveyard bell' of 'Murder Suicide Meteor Slave'. If the fans – and more than a few of Jeff's friends – believed that there were *too* many references in the album to drowning for it not to have been a well-planned, 'happy suicide' and that the lyrics were Jeff's way of leaving a suicide note, then his mother appeared to still be keeping an open mind, one year down the track, when discussing the 'creepiness' of his lyrics in the same *Now* interview with Kim Hughes:

> *You mean lyrics like, 'I've had so many loves and drowned them all'. Or from* 'So Real', *'The nightmare that pulled me in and sucked me under'. Or, 'I lost myself on a cool damp night' from* 'Lilac Wine'. *Yeah. Well, if the boy knew he was going to die by drowning, he couldn't have given folks more stuff to chat about, could he?*

Then, Mary had offered, as if by way of a palpable excuse, 'He was into very metaphysical symbols, and I'm as much to blame for that as anybody. A focus on the soul and spirit really shaped his lyrics.'

The last part of Mary's statement rang true. What the wishful thinkers and cynics were forgetting was that, like Nick Drake, and to a certain extent Gram Parsons, Jeff had been first and foremost a realist poet-interpreter for whom the topics of death and despair were accepted as the norm. *This* was why the French had taken him to their hearts and awarded him the Grand Prix du Disque.

What must also be taken into account is that the finished album is *not* how it would have ended up, had Jeff lived. Because he was dead, others had added to the portent by including phrases, even entire songs, which he might have ditched. Even his mother, the orchestrator of these 'messages', confesses in the liner notes of the album, 'If Jeff had lived and chosen to erase these *Sketches*, it would have been a relatively minor loss. He could have written hundreds of songs and made dozens of albums in their place.'

Mary Guibert's decision to personalise the package by including extracts from Jeff's diaries, reproduced in his own handwriting, outraged his friends. These intrusions into his privacy included comments he had made about his father, and part of a letter he had written to Bob Dylan. Some felt so intensely angry; they subsequently refused to acknowledge having had anything to do with the project. On the other hand, a nice touch was someone's decision to dedicate the album to Nusrat Fateh Ali Khan: 'You are the sound within the sound, the voice within the voice. Insha'Allah.' These were Jeff's words, which he would have wanted there.

Two months after the album's release, George Stein forwarded Mary an invoice for $3,000 – the amount he claimed he had spent, wrapping up Jeff's affairs, paying off the rent for the bungalow, and expenses he had incurred after his death. He then served her with a writ for breach of contract, declaring that as Jeff's manager he was legally entitled to 15 per cent of his earnings, past and present and future, for any material produced, written or recorded while Jeff had been his client. Mary countersued, claiming that any such arrangement with Jeff had ended with his death. This bickering would continue for another two years, until lawyers for both parties reached an amicable agreement.

By the spring of 1999, as tempers cooled, Mary had in her possession 100 live recordings of Jeff, dating back to his Sin-É days. The best ones, she believed, were his 1995–6 shows in Australia and France. In June 2000, nine of these along with three songs performed in Hamburg, Seattle and San Francisco, were released on *Mystery White Boy*. In the liner notes, Mary more than made up for any alleged former culpabilities, going out of her way to praise Jeff's musicians – Michael Tighe in particular – describing the Jeff Buckley Band as, 'One instrument with forty fingers, four heartbeats and a singularly magnificent voice.'

Jeff's greatest ever performance, the July 1995 Paris Olympia recital – or at least 10 of the 20 songs – was released in June 2001. In the liner notes, Jeff's mother was gracious in confessing how the French had been instrumental in recognising his talent. *Live at Sin-É*, released in 2003, was of tremendous historical importance because far too many of the songs he had been performing back then had been overlooked since *Grace*. Sadly, many regular numbers never made it to the double-CD: Edith Piaf's 'La Vie en Rose' and 'Un Jeune Homme Chantait', Elvis Costello's 'So Like Candy', Bob Dylan's 'The Times They Are

A-Changing', Mahalia Jackson's 'Nobody But You Lord' and Alain Toussaint's 'From a Whisper to a Scream' are but a few classics offered the unique Buckley treatment, which one hopes might be released in the future. Still, we must be grateful for small mercies, for what we do have here stretches *way* beyond the merely splendid. Among the gems it contains are Billie Holiday's 'Strange Fruit', Nina Simone's 'If You Knew' (knowing that this is what Jeff would have wanted, the release is dedicated to her), and a lengthy bravado rendition of a Nusrat Fateh Ali Khan set piece. There was also the added bonus of a short DVD that enables us to see what Sin-É looked like.

In 2004 came the ultimate tribute: *Grace: The Legacy Edition*, a double-CD which contains the original album, plus numerous out-takes from the Bearsville sessions *and* a DVD containing the *Grace* videos. Many believed that at 14 minutes, the ever-so-repetitive 'Kanga-Roo' should have been left off to make way for rarer, more important material. Even so, there are definitive versions of Hank William's 'Lost Highway', Lieber and Stoller's 'Alligator Wine', Bob Dylan's 'You've Been On My Mind' (which Jeff had dedicated to his mother), and a superb reading of Bukka White's anti-racist standard, 'Parchman Farm Blues' – the song which links Jeff with Gram Parsons and Nick Drake. Comparisons with the two had already been made, a few days after Jeff's death by the *Sydney Morning Herald*'s Richard Jinman, who had observed in his moving obituary,

> *Jeff Buckley had more in common with Drake, Parsons, and his father than fragile good looks and a tendency to wear his heart on his sleeve. If he does become a cult figure, it will be due primarily to his extraordinary voice and a songwriter talent, which was beginning to rival his ability to interpret other people's work.*

If anyone had ever had doubts concerning Mary Guibert's sincerity and distress over the loss of her beloved son, they only had to listen to *Mystery White Boy*, the intensely loving tribute commissioned by the BBC at around this time and broadcast on Radio Two. Yet despite her grief, still there six years on, Mary transformed the proceedings not into a lament for Jeff, but into a celebration of his life – the golden life she had spoken about while scuba divers had still been searching for his body.

Narrated by Chrissie Hynde, the programme included Jeff's musicians, biographer David Browne, producer Andy Wallace, and MC5's Wayne Kramer, whose 'Kick Out the Jams' had been a Buckley concert set piece. Comparing Jeff with Tim Buckley, whom he had also known, Kramer observed, 'The apple doesn't fall far from the tree.' Matt Johnson spoke of Jeff's unconventional approach to his concerts – how he had never practised his scales or warmed up before going on stage, as if he had *wanted* to leave himself vulnerable to error. Not inadvertently, Johnson's departure from the band was discussed while Jeff was crooning *The Man That Got Away*. And were we *really* supposed to believe that Michael Tighe had turned towards drummer Parker Kindred, upon observing the blackening clouds through the plane window as it had descended on Memphis on that fateful Corpus Christi Day, and pronounced, '*That* reminds me of what I imagine death to be like'?

In *Mystery White Boy*, a list of the acts Jeff had influenced from beyond the grave was reeled off: the likes of Coldplay, Badly Drawn Boy, P. J. Harvey – names which almost certainly will have been forgotten long, long before his. Only one original and very individual artist has emerged who with equal certainty will stand the test of time and five-minute-wonderdom, a precocious talent which brings full circle the three lodestar forces within this book.

Rufus Wainwright, born in New York in 1973 and the product of another famous broken marriage – folk singers Loudon Wainwright and Kate McGarrigle – combines Gram Parsons' beauty and plaintive delivery with Nick Drake's fragility and poetic sensibility, and Jeff Buckley's diversity of repertoire and vocal pyrotechnics. Unlike this trio, he travels with no excess baggage – openly gay and proud of his sexuality, he readily confesses to having lived through the catalogue of joys, sorrows and hedonism that enrich his work. Like Nick and Jeff, he has been heavily influenced by Edith Piaf. Elton John defines him as 'the best songwriter on the planet', and cites his 2004 *Want One* album as the best since Jeff's *Grace*.

It would seem almost certain that Jeff and Rufus Wainwright dated at some time, and though there is no way of knowing if their relationship progressed beyond the platonic, there seems little doubt that Wainright at least wanted it to. In 2004, Rufus released his million-selling *Want Two* album, which includes arguably the best tribute to Jeff to date. 'Memphis Skyline' contains the line, 'Turn back the wheels of time under the Memphis skyline', after which Rufus pronounces, 'Always hated him for the way he looked in the gaslight of the morning, Then came hallelujah sounding like Ophelia.' The former line, some believe, is Rufus describing Jeff in post-coital mood, whereas the Ophelia is his way of questioning whether Jeff's death was an accident, or suicide, as happens in *Hamlet*. Then, as the song closes, Rufus laments, 'So kiss me, my darling, stay with me till morning.'

And yet Rufus openly confesses that, initially, he disliked Jeff and was jealous of him – for no other reason than, while Jeff had been the much-loved muse of

Sin-É, proprietor Brendan Doyle had turned *him* down three times. 'I equated that and blamed Jeff, who was a star there,' he told the *Sun* in February 2005. 'Then years later I was playing a show and he was in the audience. We hung out that night and had a wonderful time. I think I harboured a secret crush on him.'

Jeff's greatest triumph occurred inadvertently at the end of 2008, 11 years after his death and as the result of one of those glitzy television talent contest which most artists of great standing only frown upon. When it was announced that the winner of Independent Television's *The X-Factor* would be performing and releasing a cover-version of 'Hallelujah', a group of Buckley fans – headed by the show-business editor of the *Sun* newspaper, campaigned for Jeff's fans to download his version from the Internet. What is interesting is that almost everyone who wrote about the song, not just in the *Sun* but also in other newspapers, referred to 'Hallelujah' as a Jeff Buckley song – this was how much he had made it his own. The subsequent winner of the competition, Alexander Burke – who did not sing all the verses – took the song to the top of the British charts, but such was the devotion of Jeff's fans that his version shot to Number Two. Earlier in the year, the soprano Katherine Jenkins had performed a similarly trimmed version of the song on her album, *Sacred Arias*.

How would Jeff have reacted to this posthumous adulation? His former girlfriend, Inger Lorre, told Merri Cyr, 'Jeff was nobody's martyr, and I don't think he would like people turning him into the tragic young beautiful thing. He would hate that. He was very humble.' This, however, is *exactly* what the fans and media have done, for this is precisely how he will be remembered – the fun-loving, mega-talented, self-labelled little punk who turned the music of his own generation on to its head by juxtaposing new with retro, weaving a multi-coloured, multifaceted tapestry of styles like no other, before or since.

Jeff Buckley inadvertently eulogised himself twice during his brief career. At the close of the *Making of Grace* documentary, he posed the question *and* gave the answer: 'What do I want people to get from my music? Anything they want!' And in 'Satisfied Mind', the closing number on *Sketches For My Sweetheart the Drunk*, and a song *not* written by him, he proclaims,

When my life is over and my time has run out,
My friends and my loved ones, I'll leave them no doubt...
I'll leave this old world with a satisfied mind.

For we thousands of fans, he left it a sad place indeed.

Jeff Buckley Discography

Attempting to assemble a Jeff Buckley discography is complicated, to say the least. He completed just one album, *Grace*, during his lifetime. Such was his perfectionism and disdain with almost everything he did, however, that there are literally hundreds of out-takes of the 40 or so songs he worked on in the studio. Added to these are the taped performances – some professionally recorded but never released, not just on account of his wayward antics, but because of his antagonism and sometimes downright belligerence towards record-company executives. Then there are dozens of bootlegs of his café-concert performances in New York, London and Paris, far too many to mention here. *Additionally* there are the tour tapes: Jeff in America, Europe, Australasia and the Far East, besides many home-made recordings and countless backstage jamming sessions! The following represents as many commercial Jeff Buckley releases as can be listed without becoming too repetitive, and is therefore by no means exhaustive. Similarly, guest appearances on other artists' recordings are not included.

Live at Sin-É (November 1993)
Mojo Pin/ Eternal Life/ Je n'en Connais pas la Fin/ The Way Young Lovers Do
(EP) BIGCAT ABB 61xCD

Peyote Radio Theater (July 1994)
Mojo Pin/ Dream Brother (Nag Champa Mix)*; Kanga-Roo*
(EP) COLUMBIA SAMPCD 2290. Promo only

***Grace* (album version)** (July 1994)
(Single) COLUMBIA CD CSK 6453. Promo only
(Single) COLUMBIA SAMPCD 24031 (edit) Promo, Europe only

Grace (August 1994)
Mojo Pin/ Last Goodbye/ Lilac Wine/ So Real/ Hallelujah/ Lover, You Should Have Come Over/ Corpus Christi Carol/ Eternal Life/ Dream Brother
(Album) COLUMBIA 475928-1
Later issued (COLUMBIA 475928-2) as a package which included a bonus shrink-wrapped promo, *Live From Nighttown*

The Grace EP (January 1995)
Grace (edit)*/ Tongue/ Kanga-Roo/ Grace*
(EP) COLUMBIA 661107-2

Last Goodbye (January 1995)
Last Goodbye (album edit)/ *Mojo Pin* (Chocolate version, Wetlands)/ *Kanga-Roo/ Lost Highway*
(EP) COLUMBIA SRCS 7592. Japan only

Live at Nighttown (May 1995)
So Real/ Grace/ Dream Brother
Recorded live, 25 February 1995, at Nighttown, Rotterdam.
(EP) COLUMBIA SAMPCD 2776. Promo, Holland only

Last Goodbye (May 1995)
Last Goodbye (edit)/ *Lover, You Should Have Come Over* (live in Japan)/ *Tongue* (live)
(10" vinyl, picture sleeve, limited edition 5,000 copies) COLUMBIA 662042-1

Last Goodbye (May 1995)
Last Goodbye (full version)/ *Dream Brother* (live in Hamburg)/ *So Real* (live in Japan)
(EP) COLUMBIA 662042-5

Last Goodbye (edit)/ *Last Goodbye* (full version) (May 1995)
(Single) COLUMBIA CSK 6844. Promo only
(Single) COLUMBIA 662042-2. Digipak

Eternal Life (September 1995)
Eternal Life (album version)/ *Eternal Life* (road version)/ *Last Goodbye* (live in Japan)/ *Lover, You Should Have Come Over*
(EP) COLUMBIA CD 6622382. Australia only
(EP) COLUMBIA CD 6621912. Austria only, tracks in different order

Live From the Ba-ta-clan (October 1995)
Dream Brother/ The Way Young Lovers Do/ Je n'en Connais pas la Fin/ Hymne à l'Amour/ Hallelujah
Recorded live at the Ba-ta-clan, Paris, 11 February 1995
(EP) COLUMBIA SAMP CD2746. Promo, France only

Grace/Live From the Ba-ta-clan (November 1995)
The *Grace* album, plus the *Ba-ta-clan* EP, released as a package
(Albums) COLUMBIA 662155-2. France and Austria only

Grace: Special Edition One (November 1995)
The *Grace* album, plus bonus CD: *Jeff Buckley Live*: *So Real* (live in Japan)/ *Dream Brother/ Grace/ Mojo Pin* (live at Wetlands)
(Albums) COLUMBIA 481061-2. Australia only

Grace: Special Edition Two (November 1995)
The *Grace* album, plus bonus CD: *Eternal Life* (album version)/ *Last Goodbye* (live in Japan) / *Lover, You Should Have Come Over* (live in Japan)
(Albums) SONY 662543-2. Australia only

Eternal Life (road version)/ *Eternal Life* (album version) (December 1995)
(Single) COLUMBIA SAMPCD 2802. Promo only

Everybody Here Wants You (February 1996)
Everybody Here Wants You/ Thousand Fold/ Eternal Life (road version)/ *Hallelujah* (live at Ba-ta-clan)/ *Last Goodbye* (live in Sydney)
(EP) COLUMBIA 665848-2. Australia only.

So Real/ Tongue/ Lost Highway (February 1996)
(Single) COLUMBIA662543-2. Australia only

Grace (February 1996)
Grace (album edit)/ *Grace* (live)/ *Mojo Pin* (live)/ *Hallelujah* (live)
(EP) COLUMBIA 663085-2. Australia only

So Real/ So Real (live in Japan)/ *Last Goodbye* (live in Japan)
(Single) COLUMBIA CSK 7197. Promo only

Sketches For My Sweetheart the Drunk (April 1998)
Everybody Here Wants You/ The Sky is a Landfill/ Morning Theft/ Vancouver/ You & I
(EP) COLUMBIA XPCD 992-5-5

Everybody Here Wants You (April 1998)
(1-track single) COLUMBIA XPCD 983

Three Songs For My Sweetheart the Drunk (April 1998)
Everybody Here Wants You, The Sky is A Landfill/ Haven't You Heard
(EP) COLUMBIA CSK 3285-3. US only.

Vancouver (April 1998)
(1-track single) COLUMBIA SAMPCS 5362. France only. Given away free with *Les Inrockuptibles* magazine

Everybody Here Wants You (May 1998)
Everybody Here Wants You/ Thousand Fold/ Eternal Life (road version)/ *Hallelujah* (Ba-ta-clan)
(EP) COLUMBIA 665791-2

Everybody Here Wants You/ Lover, You Should Have Come Over (live in Japan)/ *Tongue* (May 1998)
(Single) COLUMBIA 665791-5

Sketches For My Sweetheart the Drunk (May 1998)
The Sky is a Landfill/ Everybody Here Wants You/ Opened Once/ Nightmares By the Sea (1)/ Yard of Blonde Girls/ Witches' Rave/ New Year's Prayer (1)/ Morning Theft/ Vancouver/ You & I/ Nightmares by the Sea (2)/ New Year's Prayer (2)/ Haven't You Heard/ I Know We Could Have Been So Happy/ Baby/ Murder Suicide Meteor Slave/ Back in NYC/ Gunshot Glitter/ Demon John/ Your Flesh is Nice/ Jewel Box/ Satisfied Mind
Note:The above tracks represent the non-US international release. *Gunshot Glitter* does not appear on the US release. The Japanese release contains an extra track: *Thousand Fold*
(3 LPs) COLUMBIA 3C 67228
(2 CDs) COLUMBIA 488661-6

Jeff Buckley: Live in Chicago (May 2000)
Filmed at the Cabaret Metro, Chicago, 13 May 1995
Dream Brother/ Lover, You Should Have Come Over/ Mojo Pin/ So Real/ Last Goodbye/ Eternal Life/ Kick Out the Jams/ Lilac Wine/ What Will You Say/ Grace/ Vancouver/ Kanga-Roo/ Hallelujah
Bonuses: *Electronic Press Kit/ So Real* (acoustic)/ *Last Goodbye* (acoustic)
(DVD) SONY 50216-9

Mystery White Boy: Live 95-96 (June 2000)
*Dream Brother */ I Woke Up in a Strange Place **/ Mojo Pin ***/ Lilac Wine **/ What Will You Say ***/ Last Goodbye ****/ Eternal Life **/ Grace **/ Moodswing Whiskey**/ The Man That Got Away *****/ Kanga-Roo ******/ Hallelujah/I Know It's Over ********
* Hamburg 22 February 1995, ** Melbourne 28 February 1996, *** Lyon 4 July 1995, **** Paris 7 July 1995, ***** San Francisco 4 May 1995, ****** Sydney 6 September 1995, ******* Seattle 7 May 1995
(LP) COLUMBIA 4979721
(CD) COLUMBIA 4979722

Live à l'Olympia (June 2001)
*Lover, You Should Have Come Over/ Dream Brother/ Eternal Life/ Kick Out the Jams/ Lilac Wine/ Grace/ That's All I Ask/ Kashmir/ Je n'en Connais pas la Fin/ Hallelujah/ What Will You Say **
Recorded at the Paris, Olympia 6 July 1995
* with Alim Qasimov, recorded at Le Festival Saint-Florent-le-Vieil, 18 July 1995
(Album) COLUMBIA 503204-2. France only.
COLUMBIA 503204-9. Rest of world.

The Grace EPs (November 2002)
Peyote Radio Theater/ So Real/ Live From the Ba-ta-clan/ Grace/ Last Goodbye
Commemorative re-issue of previously released commercial/promotional EPs
(5 EPs) COLUMBIA 5011782

Songs to No One (November 2002)
An album of rehearsal tapes, studio tapes and live performances with Gary Lucas and various session musicians and members of Gods and Monsters: (Jared Nickerson, Tony Lewis, Tony Maimone, Anton Fier, Bill Frisell, Steven Bernstein, Briggan Krauss, Tony Sherr, Kenny Wollensen, Brian Mitchell).
Hymne à l'Amour (with Lucas at his home, February 1992)/ *How Long Will it Take* (with Lucas, CBGB's, New York, April 1992)/ *Mojo Pin* (with Lukas, Knitting Factory, New York, April 1992)/ *Song to No One* (with Lucas at his home, October 1991)/ *Grace* (band, Krypton Studios, New York, August 1991)/ *Satisfied Mind* (solo, Knitting Factory, March 1992)/ *Cruel* (band, Knitting Factory, March 1992)/ *She is Free* (with Lucas at his home, January 1992)/ *Harem Man* (with Lucas at his home, January 1992)/ *Malign Fiesta* (No Soul) (band, Knitting Factory, March 1992); *Grace* (with Lucas, Club Roulette, New York, April 1992)
(Album) CIRCUS FYL 014

Live at Sin-É (Legacy Edition) (September 2003)
Disc One: *Be Your Husband/ Lover, You Should Have Come Over/ Mojo Pin/ Grace/ Strange Fruit/ Night Flight/ If You Knew/ Last Goodbye/ Twelfth of Never/ Eternal Life/ Just Like A Woman/ Calling You*
Disc Two: *Yeh Jo Halka Halka Saroor Hal/ If You See Her, Say Hello/ Dink's Song/ Drown In My Own Tears/ The Way Young Lovers Do/ Je n'en Connais pas la Fin/ I Shall Be Released/ Sweet Thing/ Hallelujah*
DVD: *Interview/ The Way Young Lovers Do/ Kick Out the Jams/ New Year's Prayer*
Recorded live at Sin-É, with monologues, July to August 1993
(2 CDs + DVD) COLUMBIA 512257-3

Grace (Legacy Edition) (August 2004)
Package containing the original *Grace* album, various out-takes from the *Grace* sessions, plus an expanded version of *The Making of Grace* documentary, filmed at the Bearsville Studios.
Disc One: *Mojo Pin/ Grace/ Last Goodbye/ Lilac Wine/ So Real/ Hallelujah/ Lover, You Should Have Come Over/ Corpus Christi Carol/ Eternal Life*
Disc Two: *Forget Her/ Dream Brother* (alternative take)*/ Lost Highway/ Alligator Wine/ Mama, You've Been On My Mind/ Parchman Farm Blues/ The Other Woman/ Kanga-Roo/ I Want Someone Badly* (with Shudder To Think)*/ Eternal Life* (road version)*; Kick Out the Jams* (live on Columbia Radio Hour)*/ Dream Brother* (Nag Champa Mix)
DVD: includes *The Grace Videos: Grace/ Last Goodbye/ So Real/ Eternal Life/ Forget Her*
(2 CDs + DVD) COLUMBIA 517460-3

So Real: Songs from Jeff Buckley (May 1997)
An album of classics and rarities released to commemorate the 10th anniversary of Jeff's death
*Last Goodbye/ Lover, You Should Have Come Over/ Forget Her/ Eternal Life (*road version*)/ Dream Brother (*alternative take*)/ The Sky is a Landfill/ Everybody Here Wants You/ So Real (*live/acoustic in Japan*)/ Mojo Pin (live at Sin-É)/ Vancouver/ Je n'en Connais pas la Fin (*live at Sin-É*)/ Grace/ Hallelujah/ I Know It's Over (*recorded at Sony Studios, New York, April 1995*)*
(CD) COLUMBIA 88697035702

Bibliography

Alley, Jonathan,'A Few Thoughts on the Passing of Jeff Buckley', RRR Radio, Melbourne, August 1995
Barrera, Paul, *Nick Drake: No Reply*, Agenda, 1997
Barrera, Paul, *Tim Buckley: Once he Was*, Agenda, 1997
BBC2 documentary, *A Stranger Among Us: Searching for Nick Drake*, 1998
BBC Radio One interview, 'Jeff Buckley', March 1995
BBC Radio Two, 'The Jeff Buckley Story', 2004
BBC documentary, *Mystery White Boy: The Jeff Buckley Story*, 2003
Beauvallet, J.D., 'Dream Mother: Mary Guibert, mère de Jeff Buckley', May 1998
Beauvallet, J.D., 'Jeff Buckley: The Last Goodbye', *Les Inrockuptibles*, June 1997
Beauvallet, J.D., 'Jeff Buckley: L'empire des sens', *Les Inrockuptibles*, June 1995
Beauvallet, J.D., 'Sur la déroute de Memphis', *Les Inrockuptibles*, April 2000
Berkowitz, Steve, Bill Flanagan, Mary Guibert, *Grace Legacy Edition*: liner notes, 2004
Berkvens, Jeroen, *A Skin Too Few*, independent film, Holland, 2000
Bidault, Michel, author interviews, 2003–6
Brazier, Chris, *Way To Blue*, amateur film, *c*.1985
Bret, David, author interviews: J. D. Beauvallet; *People* magazine; 'Cuddles'; Equipes de l'Olympia and Ba-ta-clan 2002–2
Bret, David, *Doris Day, Reluctant Star*, JR Books, 2008
Bret, David, *Morrissey: Landscapes of the Mind*, Robson Books, 1994
Bret, David, *Morrissey: Scandal & Passion*, Robson Books, 2004
Bret, David, *The Piaf Legend*, Robson Books, 1988
Browne, David, *Dream Brother*, Fourth Estate, 2001
Buckley, Jeff, press conferences: Ba-ta-clan, Olympia, Lyons, Toulouse, 1995

Buddin, Kylie, 'Jeff Buckley, *You Could Do Worse #3*' (fanzine) c.1995
Cohen, Mitchell, Mary Guibert and Steve Berkowitz, *Live At Sin-É*: liner notes, 2003
Conley, Jim, 'Chatter Patter, Nick Drake', *Abilene Reporter*, June 1972
Cooper, Mark, 'Eternal Lost Boy, The', *Word*, June 2004
Cox, Tom, 'One Great Overlookd Genius', *Guardian*, January 1999
Creswell, Toby, 'Grace Under Fire', *Juice*, February 1996
Cyr, Merri, *Jeff Buckley: A Wished For Song*, Hal Leonard, 2002
Diehl, Matt, 'The Son Also Rises', *Rolling Stone*, October 1994
Farrar, Josh, 'Jeff Buckley', *Doubletake*, February 1996
Flanagan, Bill, 'The Arrival of Jeff Buckley', *Musician*, February 1994
Fong-Torres, Ben: *Hickory Wind: The Life & Times of Gram Parsons*, Pocket Books
Frederick, Robin, on Nick Drake, www3.sympatico.com, 1997
Gilbert, Jerry, 'Something Else For Nick?', *Sounds*, March 1971
Gram Parsons Project (Internet site, various)
Griffin, Sid: *Gram Parsons: A Music Biography*, Sierra, 1985
Guibert, Mary and J.D. Beauvallet, *Jeff Buckley à l'Olympia*: liner notes, July 1995 and April 1991
Guibert, Mary, *Sketches For My Sweetheart the Drunk*: liner notes, 1998
Hughes, Kim, 'Mother Preserving Jeff Buckley's Legacy', *Now*, May 1998
Humphries, Patrick, *Nick Drake*, Bloomsbury, 1997
Johnson, Matt, Michael Tighe, Mick Grondhal, *The Grace EP*: liner notes, 2002
Katz, Gary, *Death By Rock & Roll*, Robson Books, 1995
Kaufman, Phil and White, Colin, *Road Mangler Deluxe*, White-Boucke, 2005
Keep, Chas, 'Nick Drake Profile', *Record Collector*, February 1992
Kirk, Kris, author interview, 1990
Kirk, Kris, 'The Leave Taking', interview with Gabrielle Drake, *Melody Maker*, July 1987
Kirby, Robert, Swedish interview, undated c.1990
Lipscomb, Marjorie, *BBC Audition Report*, October 1969
Mojo, '100 Most Miserable Songs', June 2004
Moran, Caitlan, 'Orgasm Addict', *B-Side*, August 1984
Norot, Anne-Claire, 'L'état de Grace', *Les Inrockuptibles*, June 2005
Parsons, Gram: Interview with *Fusion*, November 1968
Parsons, Gram: Interview with Chuck Casell, *Chemical Imbalance*, 1972

Parsons, Gram: Interview with Jan Donkers, 1972
Parsons, Gram: Interview with Judith Sims, *Rolling Stone*, March 1973
Pynk Moon Fanzine: Nos 1-18, edited by Jason Creed, 1994–9
Record Collector, 'Jeff Buckley', March 2003
Record Collector, 'Nick Drake Tape Find', November 1998; *Mojo*, December 1998
Richards, Keith: Interview, contactmusic.com June 2006
Richards, Keith: Interview with *Rolling Stone*, April 2005
Rogan, Johnny: *The Byrds: Timeless Flight Revisited*, Rogan House, 1998
Rogers, Ray, 'Jeff Buckley: Heir Apparent', *Interview*, February 1994
Rotondi, James, 'The Power of Grace', *Guitar Player*, April 1995
Sandison, David, 'Heaven is a Wild Flower', *ZigZag*, January 1975
Soave, Daniela, 'Lone Star', Sky International, July 1995
Sun, 'A Rough Guide to Rufus Wainwright', March 2005
Sutherland, Steve, 'Nick Drake: Could It Be Tragic', *NME*, May 2004
Tanworth Tapes, The, 1967–8
Tignor, Steve, 'A Live Thing', *Puncture*, spring 1994
Vaziri, Aidin, 'Jeff Buckley', *Raygun*, August 1994
Walker, Jason: *Gram Parsons: God's Own Singer*, Helter Skelter, 2002
Wagner, Vit, 'That Car Ad', *Toronto Star*, August 2000
www3.sympatico.com 'Nature's Son', 1997
Yates, Amy Beth 'Painting With Words', *B-Side*, October 1994
Young, Paul, 'Talking Music: Confessing To Strangers', *Buzz*, September 1994

Index